INNOVATIONS IN
PARENT AND FAMILY INVOLVEMENT

By
J. William Rioux
and
Nancy Berla

EYE ON EDUCATION
P.O. BOX 388
PRINCETON JUNCTION, NEW JERSEY 08550

For
Steven, Moira, Jennifer
J.W.R.

For
My husband, children, and grandchildren
N.B.

Library of Congress Catalog Number: 93-071523

ISBN 1-883001-03-X

Printed in the United States of America

Printing 9 8 7 6 5 4 3 2 1

ABOUT THE AUTHORS

J. William Rioux was most recently Executive Director and cofounder of the National Committee for Citizens in Education, a national organization of parents and citizens in a broad array of public school improvement efforts. He is the author of several books including *You Can Improve Your Child's School*, and co-author with Stuart Sandow of *Children, Parents and School Records*.

Nancy Berla has served on the staff of the National Committee for Citizens in Education as Director of the Clearinghouse of Education Information for Parents. She has co-authored several publications, including *The Middle School Years: A Parents Handbook*, with Anne Henderson and William Kerewsky, and *Beyond the Open Door: A Citizens Guide to Increasing Public Access to Local School Boards*, with Susan Hlesciak Hall.

Table of Contents

FOREWORD

The enterprise of public education is inexorably coming to understand that careful, continuous collaboration between schools and the families of the children they serve really pays off. Not only do the conventional standards of student achievement such as grades, test scores and graduation rates tend to improve, but so do teacher morale and job satisfaction, community confidence in the quality of schools, and taxpayer support for school finance measures.

If children arriving at school find teachers and staff who look, talk and dress differently from their families, who expect and reward different behaviors, and who subject them to standards they don't understand or accept, they will have difficulty connecting to school. The reverse is true, too. If teachers are confronted with students who don't appear to be prepared or receptive, they will expect little of them—and may even suspect that their families are not providing proper support. These difficulties tend to clear up if the school makes an effort to build a trusting respectful relationship betweeen staff and families. Both learn that the others want the same thing for the children— for them to become happy, successful and productive.

This is an unusual book. While the authors acknowledge the changes in social and family structure that make it ever more challenging for schools to work together with families, they nevertheless firmly reject the contention that it is not possible to involve parents in their children's education. Here you will find successful programs that embrace Native Americans on reservations, Southern families in rural isolation, Hispanic immigrants newly arrived to California, and African American families in urban public housing projects. This diversity is fully addressed in the sweep and scope of the programs that attempt to serve them.

Much of what we hear about public education is not encouraging. Daunting problems of quality, equity and financial support must be faced and resolved. Yet many good things are taking place that receive little attention, and that could yield important lessons for future policies. Here you will find testimony to the creativity, determination, and dedication of public school staff and families who entrust their children to them every day.

The most well-known programs work with very young children and parents. As a social investment, preschool and early childhood programs bear impressive returns, for both the short and long term. But it is refreshing also to learn of programs that engage families of middle and high school students, who benefit tremendously from such support at a time of great change in their lives. In addition, there are valuable examples of community-wide programs, where local organizations also make important contributions. Increasingly, local leadership is coming to realize that building a network of support for children through and around the public schools is central to the well-being of the entire community.

In a New Yorker profile, The Rev. Jesse Jackson spoke about his upbringing in Greenville, South Carolina, where he was surrounded by what he called "a love triangle". "Mother, grandmother here, teacher over here, and preacher over here. Within that love triangle, I was protected, got a sense of security and worth. Even mean ole segregation couldn't break in on me and steal my soul. It protected me long enough until I was able to break out and survive on my own. When it's working, that't what that thing really does." (2/10/92)

Their own extensive work in the field of family-school

partnerships uniquely qualifies the authors for the task of identifying and analyzing some of the most innovative programs. Bill Rioux and Nancy Berla provide a rare opportunity to learn from the creative efforts of unrecognized leaders in public education. This book should receive the careful attention of all those concerned with the future of public education who are looking for allies in the struggle to improve the quality of our schools and the life prospects of our children.

Anne T. Henderson
Senior Consultant
National Committee for Citizens in Education
Washington, D.C.

Acknowledgements

Special thanks are due our colleague Mindy Golden who served as our research assistant. Her information gathering skills, enthusiasm, and incisive questions contributed in important ways to meeting the standards we had set. We are grateful to Marion Hoffman for editing skills that improved the overall manuscript. We also express appreciation to Chrissie Bamber, our long-time colleague, for her willingness to take time from a busy schedule to read and comment on key sections of the book. As always she helped us identify areas that needed to be strengthened.

We received valuable advice, suggestions, and questions from a focus/advisory group formed soon after the book was proposed and outlined. Three of the six members are in "firing line" positions as school principals, two work in national organizations dedicated to increasing parent involvement in schools, and one is the leader of an important local parent group in Washington, DC. From this mix we hoped for, and received, a reflection of the everyday problems faced by children, families, and schools, and we are indebted to them for straight talk that served to guide us.

The members of the group are:

Glynn Bates, Principal
West Springfield High School
Springfield, VA

Gioia Forman, Principal
Dranesville Elementary School
Herndon, VA

Anne T. Henderson
National Committee for Citizens
  in Education
Washington, DC

Oliver Moles
Office of Educational Research
  and Improvement
U.S. Department of Education
Washington, DC

Andrea Robinson, Principal
Garrison Elementary School
Washington, DC

Delabian Rice Thurston
Executive Director
Parents United
Washington, DC

Friends and Colleagues who made Important Suggestions
for Innovative Projects to Consider

Becky Burns
Appalachian Educational
  Laboratory
Charleston, WV

Sherry Castle
National Education Association
Washington, DC

Annie Ching
ARC Associates
Oakland, CA

Janet Chrispeels
San Diego County Office of
  Education
San Diego, CA

Dr. Reginald Clark
California State University
Fullerton, CA

Dr. Terry Clark
Educational Resources Group
New York, NY

Ernest Cortes
Texas Interfaith Education Fund
Austin, TX

Christopher Cross
Business Roundtable
Washington, DC

Diane D'Angelo
RMC Research Corporation
Hampton, NH

Dr. Don Davies
Institute for Responsive
  Education
Boston, MA

Dr. Joyce Epstein
Center for Families,
 Communities, Schools and
 Children's Learning
Baltimore, MD

Arnold Fege
National PTA
Washington, DC

Ted Fiske
Green Farms, CT

Johnnie Follins
Educational Testing Service
Atlanta, GA

Norman Fruchter
Academy for Educational
 Development
New York, NY

Herbert Green
Public Education Institute
New Brunswick, NJ

Catherine Greenburg
HIPPY USA
New York, NY

Grace Pung Guthrie
Far West Educational
 Laboratory
San Francisco, CA

Patsy Jones
Bureau of Indian Affairs
Washington, DC

Marcia Klenbort
Southern Regional Council
Atlanta, GA

Judy McBroom
Citizens Education Center
Seattle, WA

Edward Meade
Montclair, NJ

William Mehojah
Bureau of Indian Affairs
Washington, DC

Paula Mintzes
Rockville, MD

M. Hayes Mizell
Edna McConnell Clark
 Foundation
New York, NY

Evelyn K. Moore
National Black Child
 Development Institute
Washington, DC

Dr. Frank Nardine
University of Wisconsin
Milwaukee, WI

Dr. Joe Nathan
Center for School Change
Minneapolis, MN

Siobhan Nicolau
Hispanic Development
  Policy Project
New York, NY

Theodora Oooms
Family Impact Seminar
Washington, DC

Douglas Powell
Child Development and
  Family Studies
Purdue University
W. Lafayette, IN

Dorothy Rich
Home and School Institute
Washington, DC

Dr. Daniel Safran
Center for the Study of
  Parent Involvement
Orinda, CA

Edna Suarez-Colombo
Office of Parent Involvement
New York City Public Schools
Brooklyn, NY

Edna Vega-Garcia
New York State Department of
  Education
New York, NY

Izona Warner
Director, QEP Programs
Indianapolis, IN

John Wedemeyer
June Burnett Institute
San Diego, CA

Dr. Howard Weiss
Ackerman Institute
New York, NY

Lynne White
Public Education Fund Network
Washington, DC

Karen Reed Wikelund
Northwest Regional Educational
  Laboratory
Portland, OR

David Williams
Southwest Education
  Development Laboratory
Austin, TX

Bob Witherspoon
RaSaun & Associates, Inc.
Herndon, VA

Arlene Zilke
National PTA
Chicago, IL

Chapter 1

Introduction

Parent-family involvement in public schools has now reached a new level of acceptance as one of the many factors considered to improve the quality of schools. However, acceptance does not translate into implementation, commitment, or creativity. It is certainly true that designing ways to involve parents and families in their children's education and in the schools their children attend is not a science. It is decidedly an art form, allowing for innovation, adaptation, revision, and invention.

We live in very different times from those of a decade or two ago. Adding "family" to parent in referring to the area of parent involvement in schools is an explicit reflection of the changes which confront us. Some children do not live with both parents or a single parent but with extended family members. Others are cared for by nonfamily adults. All arrangements of contributing, nurturing adults respond to our definition of parent-family.

If we have come to a time when parent-family involvement in schools is at a high point of general acceptance as an important factor in the achievement of children and the operation of schools, why is there not more widespread implementation of such programs? Two reasons loom large. The professionals in schools, except in rare instances, have not been trained to work with families. They worry that increased parent involvement will mean adding to an already busy, demanding workday. In addition, they worry about whether movement in the direction of closer relationships with parents and families means giving up power and dimensions of professional decision making.

Parents, on the other hand, are often not informed and are unsure of themselves. What are my rights? How far can I go in asking questions, making suggestions, and pressing for change? If I "rock the boat" at school, will my child be punished for my actions by a teacher or a principal who is annoyed or feels threatened?

So the two groups of most importance to children in how well they succeed in school are largely uncertain about the actions that might be taken. It is the purpose of this book to display a broad range of carefully investigated operational parent-family involvement programs. For the professionals who have not been trained and for busy parents who are motivated but uncertain, it is our goal to say:

- Look at this; here is a possibility. Have you ever thought of parent-family involvement as looking like this?

- Here is what other schools and school systems and the parents and families in other parts of the country have created and supported in a way that caused the programs to grow and become a part of school operation.

- Would this work in your neighborhood school? If it wouldn't work in exactly this form, would a modified form interest other parents and school officials?

- If you have not seen exactly what might work in your schools, have you seen elements of various programs that help you reach conclusions about a parent-family involvement program that would have the best chance for succeeding in your community?

In presenting this material, we do not mean to imply that parent-family involvement in the education of their children by itself will radically improve schools. The problems facing public schools are complex. Our position is that parent-family involvement is a dimension of enormous potential that has too long been ignored and has not received the attention and respect it deserves. It seems fashionable to be cynical about school improvement efforts by implying that the advocates of particular efforts view it as a "silver bullet" that will alone transform schools. At the onset we emphasize that we view parent-family involvement in schools as a powerful factor in a range of efforts that need to be made simultaneously to improve public schools. Our position is simple and straightforward: parents and families are important to children—children need role models, encouragement, and indications from influential adults that school is important, worthy of attention, and viewed as a vital part of life.

In preparing this book we spent long hours searching for innovative and effective operating programs, gathering information about program operation, and talking with parents and others about the day-to-day realities of how these programs operate. We requested recommendations of innovative and successful programs from a group of educators and activists whose judgment we respect. Extensive efforts were made to find a broad range of program examples and settings in order to increase the chances that you would find one similar to your own community and school. Our earlier experiences in parent-family involvement, and the experience of writing this book, convinced us that creating successful parent-family involvement programs will, in many instances, require that community resources be made an important part of programs.

We present these programs as worthy of your careful consideration. We do not consider them as flawless models. We present them as exciting, often different, possibilities to help you think beyond the ordinary ways that parent-family involvement is considered or approached. We do believe that we are at a threshold in which parent-family involvement efforts could, with good information and encouragement, expand dramatically and contribute to the overall effort to improve public schools.

One final point. In the past, many leaders in parent-family involvement have acknowledged that their efforts are often hampered by the lack of any respectable "hard evidence" that these efforts result in either important gains for children and/or in changes in the ways schools operate. However, things are changing. We believe the evidence is accumulating in ways that deserve attention and respect. We have, in each of the programs selected, attempted to inform you of whatever evaluation and research information exists for that program. We have, in addition, devoted two chapters to the best research and evaluation of programs and practices currently available about the contribution of parent-family involvement efforts to children and education. We recognize, however, that those who run programs must devote most of their energies to service and program development, and that structured research, when conducted, will be done by outside individuals and organizations whose major concern and expertise is research and evaluation.

We hope what you find here will interest you, excite you, and move you to a new consideration of parent-family involvement in the scheme of efforts that should be made on behalf of children in public schools.

DEFINITIONS

What We Mean By "Parent-Family Involvement"

For us, from the parent-family side, this is the range of possibilities: from new and different arrangements at home to see that homework is completed and that family members know what is going on in the school life of the child, to involvement at the local school in school councils that set policy and regularly review the effectiveness of school operation. The following list suggests a number of activities which fall along this continuum:

- Home based learning activities guided by parents.

- Regular visits to school (far beyond Education Week).

- Becoming familiar with the content of student records.

- Regular contacts with a child's teacher—when things appear to be going well, and when there appear to be signs of problems.

- Requesting copies of written school and school district policies.

- Attending school board meetings.

- Participating in (or organizing) parent-family organizations. Groups of parents will always achieve more and be attended to more seriously than one parent working alone.

- Appealing local school or school system decisions that you question or do not understand.

- Getting involved in curriculum activities.

- Influencing school policies.

- Running for school board.

- Seeking membership on school-based improvement-local school councils where parents have equal status with professionals and representatives of the community.

Principals, teachers and other school personnel also have skills and creativity to bring to the expansion of the parent-family involvement process. For instance:

- Make all families feel they are valued and valuable.

- Welcome parents in the school at all times. Establish a Parent Center. Encourage parents to visit the classroom.

- Communicate with parents through written newsletters and notices, telephone calls (with positive news as well as negative), computer-based response to parent calls on a wide variety of questions, and home visits.

- Make sure all written communications are translated for parents with limited English; remember to have translators available for parent/teacher conferences and other school meetings.

- Conduct a survey of parents/families to assess their skills, interests, and needs. Use the results to establish a volunteer program and plan other activities.

- Sponsor workshops geared toward expressed needs of families in the community (*e.g.*, topics on parenting, curriculum, discipline, homework, drug awareness, adolescence).

- Prepare a parent/student handbook (in consultation with and assistance from parents) with information on the school schedule, school policies on discipline and absenteeism, curriculum, grading, testing, and other educational issues. An increasing number of schools are creating audio-video tapes to communicate such information quickly and accurately.

- Be sensitive and flexible to accommodate the diverse needs of families of the '90s: single parents, working parents, families without transportation, immigrant families, families without telephones, migrant worker families.

- Enlist help from families of different racial and ethnic backgrounds to assist in cultural awareness activities.

What We Mean By "Program"

In our view, a program has

- A vision and stated mission.

- Broad goals, short-term and long-term objectives.

- Discrete elements that can be duplicated.

- A clear operating plan, which includes designation of persons responsible for the day-to-day running of the program.

- Continuity – a program that has been in operation for 2–3 years and is intended to be ongoing.

- A developed process for bringing about changes in people's attitudes and practices.

- Flexibility and the capability of assessing strengths and weaknesses and revising the elements of the program accordingly.

- A method of evaluating the impact and outcomes of the program.

What We Mean By "Innovations"

In general, we have included

- Programs and projects that engaged parents, families, and professionals in different ways.

- Different combinations and collaborations between and among the key persons of influence on children: parents, their family members, professionals, and community members.

- Programs and people who are pushing at boundaries and designing efforts that have a fresh view of how to bring people together, how resources in the community can be used to bolster the efforts, and how to support people to bring out the best they have to give.

- Programs that clearly take into account the way the world really is in the 1990s for parents and families caught up in the harsh realities of work and time constraints.

- Programs that recognize the hectic and demanding life of school professionals who have been asked to take on complexities and challenges in providing a good education that are far beyond what their predecessors were asked to accommodate.

- Programs that come to grips with, and rise above, budget constraints.

- Programs that optimistically and realistically are designed to meet the special needs of the thousands of families who migrated to this country in recent years, with attention to the language and cultural traditions that deserve attention and respect.

We know that the response of others to the definition of innovation might very well be different. What has been said here is our meaning.

What We Mean By "Successful"

We certainly place improvements in student achievement high on a list of "markers" of success in parent-family involvement programs. *However,* it is important that we be understood as having a broader view of benchmarks in determining success. In addition to improvements in student achievement, we give importance to the following in our definition or meaning of successful.

- Increased parent-family participation in school activities.

- Changes in the "climate" of the school—friendlier, more accessible.

- Increases in student attendance.

- Decreases in dropout rates.

- Increases in equal partnership efforts between school personnel and parents-families.

- Improvements in social and interpersonal relationships of students.

- Reductions of in-school violence.

- Greater acceptance and understanding of students and parents from other cultures.

- Education and empowerment of parents.

- Changes in attitudes of parents and leaders toward each other.

- Greater family/community support of schools.

The list, of course, could be very long. The important point is to take the larger view of "successful" and compile your own priority list for your local situation. Then measure the outcome of your efforts against that thoughtful and important set of goals.

Chapter 2

Preschool Programs

One of the most successful and enduring legacies of the War on Poverty is Head Start. In a dramatic fashion, national in scope, it fixed in the minds of millions that it was important to nurture and provide for the growth and development of the very young. It established, in a way that early childhood specialists had advocated with only modest success for many years, that infancy to age 5 represented a never to be repeated opportunity to have a marked influence on the development of children.

In the nearly thirty years since Head Start's beginnings, the unparalleled establishment and expansion of new programs for very young children underscores how much it has become fixed in the public mind that young children—*all* young children—must have the services and support they need if they are to develop fully. This understanding and acceptance appears to run deepest for those very young children from low-income and minority families. Without discounting the importance of preschool programs for children from middle-

and upper-income families, there is support for the extra efforts that need to be made to reach low-income, minority children.

The programs described in this section not only testify to the validity of the basic principles of Head Start and other early childhood programs, but they reveal, in dramatic terms, how serious and fundamental are the problems in the families attempting to provide their children with the basics that will afford at least a fighting chance for success in the years ahead. It is still the case that most Americans have not been exposed to the consequences of poverty, discrimination, isolation, and a sense of hopelessness in their own lives or in the lives of the poor whose paths cross theirs infrequently. It is also the case that, whether we are personally aware or not, we all pay the bill for unattended needs—particularly in young children for whom there is the opportunity to make a large impression and a large difference.

These programs also give a substantial sense of hope and optimism that with dedicated staff, reasonable financial support, and opportunities to be flexible, families who struggle to do the very best for the very young will receive the kind of effective programs they and their children deserve. Thirty years after Head Start began, we still reach less than one-half of the children who should be receiving early childhood services. We will continue to pay a large price for the unproductive and undeveloped potential of the other half. We should keep up the pressure to involve more and more young children in high-quality preschool programs typified by the descriptions in this section.

PRESCHOOL PARENT INVOLVEMENT PROGRAMS

Blackfeet Reservation, Browning, Montana

     Head Start and Family Service Center

Ferguson-Florissant School District, Florissant, Missouri

     Parents as Teachers

Poudre School District R-1, Ft. Collins, Colorado

     Even Start Program

Takini School, Howes, South Dakota

    Family Education Program

Warrensville Heights City School District, Warrensville Hts., Ohio

    Warrensville HIPPY—Home Instruction Program for Preschool Youngsters

SUMMARY OF PROGRAM CHARACTERISTICS
Preschool Programs

Name of Program	Population Served	Major Components	Beginnings	Special Features
Blackfeet Reservation Browning, MT Head Start Program Family Service Center	310 children in program 100% Native Amer. 90% low-income	Head Start Family Service Ctr. Parent volunteers Parent participation in decisionmaking Home visits	Federally sponsored; Head Start began in 1966; Family Service Center opened 1991	Personnel files for parent volunteers Parent empowerment Bilingual curriculum
Ferguson-Florissant School District Florissant, MO Parents as Teachers Early Education Programs	Birth–5 and their families 70% White 30% African-Amer. 20% Low-income	Home visits Group meetings Educational Checkups Literacy Services Boxes for Babes Saturday School	Parents as Teachers program required in all school districts by 1984 Missouri legislation	Contact with teenage parents Testing for preschoolers Linking parents to social services
Poudre School Dist. R-1 Fort Collins, CO Even Start	Birth–5 and their families 50% Latino 50% White 95% Low-income Residents of two mobile home parks	Home visits Parent classes Tutoring program Family enrichment activities Preschool children's group	Grant from federal Even Start program	Parent Center in Mobile Home Park Empowerment

Takini School Cheyenne River Reservation Howes, SD Family Education	59 families 76 adults 115 children 99% Native Amer. 100% low-income	Early Childhood Education Adult Education Parent Time Parent and Child Time Home visits	Began as pilot program in 1990. Sponsored by Bureau of Indian Affairs	Holistic Education The Learning Wheel
Warrensville Heights City Schools Warrensville Hts., OH Warrensville HIPPY	75 families served 99% African-Amer. 75% low-income	Home visits Group meetings Field trips	Program started in Israel 1969, U.S. in 1984; sponsored by National Council of Jewish Women	Parents-Aides Referral to Community Services Self-Sufficiency Empowerment

HEAD START PROGRAM AND FAMILY SERVICE CENTER
Blackfeet Reservation
Browning, MT

Major Components:
>Head Start
>Family Service Center
>Parent volunteers
>Parent participation in decision making
>Home visits

Special Features:
>Personnel files for parent volunteers
>Parent empowerment
>Bilingual curriculum in Head Start program

Profile of Reservation and Head Start Families:

Population of Blackfeet Reservation	14,000
Percentage of families who are low-income	90%
Unemployment rate on reservation	80%
Number of children in Head Start Program	310
% American	100%
Number of families served by Family Service Center	300

The goals of the **Head Start Program** are:

- To provide comprehensive educational services for preschool-age children and their families;
- To prepare the children for entry into kindergarten;
- To improve the health and well being of the children and to help them develop socially; and
- To refer the families to community agencies and the Indian Health Service to receive medical, mental health, dental, and nutritional assistance.

The goal of the **Family Service Center** is:

- To work with families on employability, parenting, literacy, substance abuse, and other issues related to education and quality of life.

BACKGROUND

Browning is a small town, located on the Blackfeet Reservation in the northwestern part of Montana. The Reservation occupies 14,650 square miles and has a population of 14,000.

Two public school districts serve the Blackfeet Reservation: the district centered in Browning includes six schools (one school each for K-2, grades 3-4, grades 5-6, grades 7-8, and grades 9-12, and one school serving all grades, K-12).

The Head Start Program has been in operation on the Blackfeet reservation for 27 years. In addition to providing preschool educational services for 3- and 4-year olds, the Head Start program is intended to be a referral service for parents, to assist them in health, nutrition, housing, education, employment, and social services. The Parent-Child Center, sponsored by Head Start, serves children birth to 3 years of age and provides their parents with prenatal and preventive health education, parenting, and early childhood development information. The Blackfeet Head Start staff realized that there were no services available to which they could refer the parents. Their federal funding only covered the Head Start classrooms, so they were unable to hire additional staff to provide the needed services.

In 1990, Head Start conducted a needs assessment to gather information to be included in a grant proposal to the federal Head Start office, requesting funds to establish a Family Service Center which could provide some of the services needed by the area's population. The funds were approved in 1990 and the Family Service Center opened as a pilot project. It is a 3-year demonstration project; its future depends in part on whether funding for the Head Start program will continue on a permanent basis.

DESCRIPTION OF THE PROGRAM

The Head Start Program and the Family Service Center are operated by a Parent Policy Board formed and directed by the Blackfeet Tribe. The goals of the Head Start Program are to provide comprehensive educational services for preschool-age children and their families and to improve the nutrition and physical and mental health of the children and their families.

The Family Service Center works with families on employability, parenting, literacy, substance abuse, and other issues related to education and quality of life. Its services are targeted at the parents of children enrolled in Head Start, in order to enhance the activities of the Head Start Program. However, it does not exclude others in the reservation with children in the public schools who can benefit from the services available.

Components of the Program

Head Start

The Blackfeet Head Start program is housed in 16 classrooms in a central site in Browning and four outlying centers in other parts of the reservation, 40–70 miles away from the central office in Browning. A total of 310 children attend the Head Start classes: 210 in Browning and 100 in the four other locations. Approximately 20 children are enrolled in each class. The program has a waiting list of 20–30 children, and could fill another one or two classrooms. All of the children in the program are Native American, from the Blackfeet tribe, and 90% are from low-income families.

Head Start also sponsors a Parent Child Center serving 60 children between birth and 3-years of age.

The Head Start program has a staff of 96 persons, including two teachers for each of the 16 classrooms, a center coordinator for each of the four outlying centers, five component coordinators for each of the five components of the program (education, health, nutrition, parent involvement, and social service), maintenance staff, cooks, and three additional administrative staff.

The Head Start classes are offered every day, from 9:30 a.m. until 1:45 p.m. The teachers plan their own curriculum; in addition to activities to promote the developmental and educational growth of the children, the teachers are introducing Blackfeet language and multicultural education. The teachers and staff who are not fluent in the Blackfeet language are learning it, and in turn are helping all of the children learn their native language along with English.

Family Service Center

The Family Service Center is located in Browning. It serves about 300 families, assisting them with health, economic, educational, social service, housing, and nutritional needs. Seven staff members operate the Family Service Center. Home visits are made to families, where the services of the Center are explained and parents are informed about opportunities for classes, jobs, and further education.

Parent Volunteers

The Head Start program requires a major focus on parent involvement in the preschool classrooms. Many parents in the Blackfeet program feel they are not qualified to help because of their own limited educational background. This program has developed an approach to parent volunteers in the classroom and elsewhere in the program which serves to provide the parents with greater self-confidence and with experience which is useable in the future to obtain regular employment.

In order to accomplish this, a job description is written for the volunteer position and a personnel file is established for the parent filling the position. The position is handled as a regular job; records are kept of the number of hours worked, and regular evaluations of the volunteer's performance are completed. When regular jobs open up in the Head Start program, the Family Service Center, or other public agencies, the parent volunteer can document his/her background, experience, and skills through the use of the personnel file. This system has increased parent involvement in the Head Start program by 55%, since many parents see the potential value of their volunteer efforts.

Parent Participation in Decision Making and Governance

There are many advisory committees and policy boards associated with the Head Start program and the Family Service

Center. The Parent Policy Board for Head Start has responsibility for policymaking and budget decisions, and is comprised of six parents and four community leaders. Each of the four outlying Head Start centers selects a parent to represent them on the Policy Board, along with a Parent-Child Center representative. An Advisory Committee is formed to address each of the five components of Head Start.

Home Visits

Three staff members from the Family Service Center are assigned to make home visits to identify family needs. The needs are identified through a Family Needs Assessment process: identification, goal setting, identification of family strengths, and locating community resources available to achieve these. The home visitors inform the parents of educational opportunities, GED classes, health services, and social services, and encourage the parents to take advantage of them. The staff members also act as advocates if needed.

Family Activities

Initially, classes and workshops were scheduled for parents on such topics as employability and parenting. The staff learned that this initial approach was unproductive; the parents did not attend, because the content and the format were inappropriate for their situation. Since there are so few jobs and many parents lack confidence that they have any skills to contribute to a job, the class on employability did not attract any interest. A formal workshop on parenting was unpopular because the parents felt it would be critical of them, and, therefore, they were not inclined to attend.

The Family Activities series now consists of three 6-week sessions, publicized as the opportunity for parents to come together as a support group to discuss topics of common interest. The topics which are introduced in these sessions are similar to those which were to have been included in the employability class or the parenting workshop, but the material is not given in a lecture-type format. The leaders provide information, lead a group discussion, introduce a hands-on activity, and choose a topic for the next meeting from interests expressed by the attending parents. The approach is casual and informal; the groups resemble support groups more than they do classes or workshops, and this seems to be the key factor to the success of the Family Activities.

The staff has learned that it is more effective to schedule several Family Activities sessions during the same time period, keeping the groups small. They meet at different times, to fit into the schedules of the participants—mornings, afternoons, or nights.

GED Classes

There is much interest among parents in completing their high school studies through obtaining the GED. During the 1991–1992 school year, a total of 13 parents participated in the GED course. This number more than doubled, to 29 parents, enrolled in the course in 1992–1993.

Parent Involvement in Planning, Operating, and Monitoring

Parents have the opportunity to participate in the planning and monitoring of the Head Start program through the Advisory Committees, the Center Committees, and the Policy Board. They also are involved as volunteers in the classroom.

Strengths and Weaknesses

As indicated earlier, the organized sessions concerning "Parenting" and "Employability" were not successful in attracting parent attendance. When the staff realized the shortcomings of this approach and shifted to "Family Activities," parents began to attend the meetings. A major factor is flexibility, in terms of subject matter, scheduling, and format. The Family Activities meetings are small, they take place at many different times of the day and evening, and the parents attending suggest the topics to be covered in the discussions.

Two major barriers hinder parent involvement in Head

Start classes, the schools, and the activities sponsored by the Family Service Center. The first barrier is lack of adequate transportation. The reservation covers a large area and most families do not have transportation available. The home visitors are paid hourly, plus mileage, to pick up parents to attend various activities, and there are four small vans available for transportation. A 40-passenger bus has recently been purchased, which should assist with some of the transportation needs.

The second barrier relates to the lack of facilities for both the Head Start Program and the Family Service Center. They are housed at two different sites in Browning, plus six trailers located near one of the main buildings. All of the offices, classrooms, and activity rooms are crowded. The Blackfeet Tribe has donated a building and site area in Browning for the new Comprehensive Early Childhood Center, being planned for Head Start. New classrooms, a multipurpose room, offices, Parent Learning Center, and playground are being planned. The building will be renovated and enlarged in order to house all of the necessary facilities, and should be completed by 1995.

Outcomes and Evaluation

The Head Start program is reviewed on-site every 3 years by representatives from the federal government. The public schools track the Head Start students, up to Grade 3, to determine whether the gains made in Head Start continue through the early elementary grades. The parents of Head Start students have been empowered as a result of their participation in Head Start, and are more prepared to be advocates for their children when they enter the public schools. Parent involvement is not a strong component in the public schools on the reservation.

Budget and Funding

Both the Head Start program and the Family Service Center are funded by federal Head Start monies.

For Further Information Contact

Susan Carlson, Family Service Center
Judy White, Head Start Program
Blackfeet Head Start Program and Family Service
    Center
P.O. Box 537
Browning, MT 59417
(406) 338–7411

PARENTS AS TEACHERS
Early Education Program
Ferguson-Florissant School District
Florissant, MO

Major Components:
- Home visits
- Group meetings
- Educational checkups
- Literacy services
- Boxes for Babes
- Saturday School

Special Features:
- Contact with teenage parents
- Testing for high risk preschool-age children
- Linking parents to social services

Profile of School District:

Population of Florissant	51,206
Population of Ferguson	25,000
Number of school-aged children in district	10,900
Number of schools in school district	21
Elementary Schools	15
Middle Schools	3
High Schools	3
Number of families in Parents as Teachers Program in Ferguson-Florissant School District	1,250
% African-American	30%
% White	70%
% Low-income	20%

The **goals** of the Parents as Teachers (PAT) program are:

- To provide parent education and support;
- To provide information to parents about child growth and development;
- To link parents with community resources and aid families with particular problems; and
- To build interaction skills between parent and child.

BACKGROUND

In 1981, the Missouri Department of Elementary and Secondary Education invited organizations and school districts to submit proposals for a grant program which would implement parent-child education from birth to age 3 years. The Ferguson-Florissant School District submitted a proposal and was one of four schools selected to receive a 3-year grant to implement a pilot project. Dr. Burton White, noted expert in early childhood development, served as a consultant to the program, trained staff from the four projects, and worked with them to develop the Parents as Teachers (PAT) model.

Under the Early Childhood Development Act, passed by the Missouri state legislature in 1984, each of the state's 543 school districts are required to provide parent education from birth to kindergarten entry. Parents as Teachers now reaches 37% of the population with children under age 3, and has broadened to include many parenting issues in addition to child development. Each school district is required to offer a program; parents may choose to participate. Special efforts are made to enroll first-time parents and at-risk families.

The Parents as Teachers model is now operating at more than 1,000 sites in 41 states, the District of Columbia, Australia, England, and New Zealand. About 60,000 families are served in the state of Missouri annually. A comparable number of families with 3–5 year olds also participate in parent education. The stated goal of the governor of Missouri and the State Board of Education is to provide adequate funding for this program by the year 2000, to serve all families wishing to participate. More than 4,500 parent educators have been trained by the National Center in the PAT model.

DESCRIPTION OF THE PROGRAM

The Parents as Teachers (PAT) program works with parents of infants from birth to 3 years of age. A total of 23 part-time staff work to implement the components of this program.

The program has worked to establish a cooperative relationship with the local schools, and encourages a number of activities to keep the teachers and administrators aware of the

PAT program. The Parent Educator will invite a principal to a home visit in the neighborhood where the school is located. The schools keep a computer printout on families with preschool-age children. The Parent Educators may meet with the kindergarten teachers or the school counselors concerning PAT children.

The Ferguson-Florissant School District also offers programs for children ages 3–4 and their parents. These programs stress parent involvement and provide a continuous program until the child's entrance into kindergarten.

Components of the Program

Home Visits

A certified Parent Educator makes regular home visits, every 4–6 weeks, to parents in the program. The Parent Educator provides parents with information on child development and assists parents in developing observational skills for watching their babies grow and develop.

Group Meetings

Meetings with other parents provide a time to share experiences, discuss topics related to infants, observe development, and share learning activities with parents and children. Issues include: discipline, toilet training, dealing with tantrums and fears, and lowering the stress level of parenting.

Regular Educational Checkups

Periodic checkups assess the child's development in understanding and expressing language, use of small and large muscles, self-help, and social skills. Hearing and vision testing are also provided for early detection of disabilities.

Other Components of the Early Education Program

In addition to the PAT program, the Ferguson-Florissant School District provides additional programs and services.

Literacy Services

Basic education classes are provided for parents who need assistance with literacy.

Boxes for Babes

This activity, which was started in 1991, is based on the work of Gerald Mahoney. The purpose is to assist parents of infants from 10–16 months old learn how to interact with their children through the use of toys. The Parent Educator demonstrates specific activities so parents will learn how to use various toys to play with their children and for educational purposes. During the first year of the program, 25 parents participated; the number of parents doubled to 50 in the second year of the Boxes for Babes program.

Teen Parents

The PAT program works with about 200 teen parents in the schools to teach them how to interact with their children and become more successful parents.

Testing for 3's and 4's

An educational checkup is offered to families with preschool age children to detect any problem that could affect a child's learning. Any child indicating a need receives special instruction during the school year.

Saturday School

This program is open to all 4-year olds in the school district. About 625 children are enrolled. The children receive a weekly home teaching visit for 1 hour, and attend a 3-hour session in school on Saturdays. A weekly *Home Activity Guide* provides ideas for activities for parents and their children to do at home throughout the week. The parents assist as teachers in Saturday School on a regular basis.

The Link Program

This program serves as a connecting LINK between parents and community resources. Group activities for parents and young children are offered at two resource centers.

Child Development Centers

Three centers provide an educational program for children ages 2, 3, and 4, whose parents are in need of child care. High school students enrolled in the course in Child Development offer assistance.

Parent Involvement in Planning, Operating, and Monitoring

The Parent Educators meet with parents in the program on a regular basis, and use that opportunity to learn about parents' concerns, needs, and attitudes. A primary aspect of the program is that it takes place on the parents' "home turf." The Parent Educators are aware that parents know more about their own child than anyone else. The purpose of the home visits is to be supportive of the parents, at the same time as parents are developing observation skills and techniques for interacting with their children.

At the group meetings, staff have another opportunity to communicate with parents and learn about their problems.

The PAT program schedules staff meetings weekly, where the Parent Educators can share their experiences from the home visits. A psychologist attends meetings with the staff twice a month, and often works with staff in small groups on particular problems. The psychologist is also available to meet with the families if the Parent Educator thinks that is advisable and appropriate.

The PAT program has a parent advisory committee which meets several times a year. The parents have input on planning group meetings and may raise problems with the program which need attention. Before the program was well known, the parent advisory committee put much effort into publicizing the program. The advisory committee meetings have not been as successful as the staff would like, but they do provide another opportunity for parent participation.

Strengths and Weaknesses

The home visits are the key to the PAT program; the relationship between the Parent Educator and the parent is crucial to the success of the program. The Parent Educators are continually improving and strengthening their skills in observation and assessment of young children—and they pass these skills on to the parents during the home visits.

One weakness of the program is the lack of sufficient funding to enable PAT to reach all of the infants and children who are eligible. The level of funding results in services to only 30% of the families who might benefit from the program. The Ferguson-Florissant School District would like to schedule more home visits for those in the program, but that, too, is constrained by budget limitations. They are making every effort, however, to target those families with the greatest need.

In 1981, at the beginning of the pilot program, much effort was needed to find families who wished to participate in the PAT program. First-time parents did not identify with the school and some were unaware of the importance of educational activities with infants and young children. Now there is no difficulty in locating enough parents; referrals come from doctors' offices, churches, schools, and social service agencies.

Outcomes and Evaluation

Both parents and staff are asked to fill out a formal evaluation at the end of the school year. The staff has indicated that they benefit most from the inservice training offered to prepare them for the program. They observe that parents who are heavily involved in this program tend to be those most active in the schools.

The National Parents as Teachers Center has sponsored a number of evaluations and assessments of the program. An independent evaluation of the pilot program in 1985 showed that children who participated in PAT were significantly advanced over their peers in language, social development, problem solving, and other intellectual abilities. A follow-up study of the pilot program, completed in 1989, showed that PAT children scored significantly higher on standardized measures of reading and math achievement in the first grade. In all areas evaluated by teachers, PAT children were rated higher than comparison children. A significantly higher proportion of PAT parents initiated contacts with teachers and took an active role in their child's schooling.

Results of the 1991 Second Wave evaluation of the PAT Program's impact on 400 randomly selected families enrolled in 37 diverse school districts across the state, indicate that both children and parents continue to benefit from PAT. PAT children performed significantly higher than national norms on measures of intellectual and language abilities, despite the fact that the Second Wave sample was overrepresented on all traditional characteristics of risk. As measured after 3 years' participation in the program, parent knowledge of child development and parenting practices significantly increased for all types of families.

Budget and Funding

The cost of the PAT program is estimated at $240 per family per year. The major component of the cost is the staff. Funding for the PAT program and the other early childhood educational initiatives comes from many sources, including the state, the local school district, the Roblee Foundation, the City Corporation, the Danforth Foundation, and the Institute for Responsive Education.

For Further Information Contact

Marion Wilson, Director of Early Childhood Education
Parents as Teachers
Early Education Program
Ferguson-Florissant School District
1005 Waterford Dr.
Florissant, MO 63033
(314) 831–8809

For information on the National Parents as Teachers Program, contact:

Mildred M. Winter
Executive Director
Parents as Teachers National Center, Inc.
9374 Olive Blvd.
St. Louis, MO 63132
(314) 432–4330

EVEN START
Poudre School District R-1
Fort Collins, CO

Components:
 Instructional home visits
 Learning Center classes
 Tutoring program
 Family enrichment activities
 Preschool children's group

Special Features:
 Located in mobile home parks
 Empowerment

Profile of School District:

Population of Fort Collins	90,000
Enrollment in public schools	20,000
Number of schools in district	37
Elementary Schools	26
Junior High Schools	7
High Schools	3
Alternative High School	1
Demographics of school district	
% Latino	8%
% Asian	2%
% White	89%
Number of families in mobile home parks	400–450
Percentage eligible for free/reduced lunch	95%

The **goals** of the Even Start program are:

- To help get children ready for school;
- To assist parents in becoming the first teachers of their children; and
- To promote family literacy.

Guiding the project is the belief that educational empowerment of all persons is beneficial to society.

BACKGROUND

The proposal to the U.S. Department of Education for an Even Start grant to Poudre School District was submitted and approved in 1989. It was prepared as a collaborative effort, with school district officials, community leaders, and Colorado State University's School of Occupational and Educational Studies.

The hiring of staff began in January 1990, and the program became operational in April 1990. The grant covers a 4-year period; after that time, application for further funding may be made to the Colorado Department of Education.

DESCRIPTION OF THE PROGRAM

The goal of the Even Start program is involvement of the whole family in the education of young children (birth to 7 years). The program emphasizes that parents are their children's first teachers; one Even Start objective is to teach parents to be teachers of their children, so that the children are ready for school. Another aspect of the program is to promote adult and family literacy by providing educational opportunities for the parents in the family.

The Even Start program at Poudre R-1 School District is designed to comply with federal guidelines which apply to all programs throughout the country. Those designing the proposal drew from their work with low-income, minority, and at-risk youth, and from the literature on dropout prevention and special education. The diverse language and cultural needs of Hispanic families also had to be factored into the planning for the Even Start program in this district.

The program primarily serves the residents of two mobile home parks, Poudre Valley Mobile Home Park and Hickory Village Mobile Home Park, located about a mile from each other. These sites were selected because this is where the majority of dropouts from school are living. The students who live in the mobile home parks attend two elementary schools, one junior high school, and one high school. The Even Start Learning Center is located in a double-wide mobile home in the Poudre Valley Mobile Home Park.

The paid staff of the program includes three codirectors,

a coordinator of the Learning Center, a secretary, and a number of part-time employees, including mentors, child care staff, social workers, and university students.

The Even Start program focuses on children from birth to age 7 and their parents, and also creates an opportunity for other educational and social services to be provided to the whole family. A total of 400–450 families reside in the two mobile home parks at any given time. Forty families participate in the Even Start component, 16 children are in the preschool group, 15 in the Campfire program, and 10–15 students are receiving tutoring services. A total of 100 families participate in the various program components. About 50% of the families served are Hispanic; 95% of the population is low-income.

Components of the Even Start Program

Instructional Home Visits

Once a week, an Even Start Family Mentor visits the home in order to assist the parents in learning how to provide educational experiences for their preschool-age children. The visit begins with a general conversation about what is going on in the home with the family. A story is read by the mentor or parents to the children. Language lessons are designed for the educational needs of each family.

The lesson is developed around a theme, for example, how to build family confidence. The lessons may be conducted in Spanish or English, as needed. Both children and parents are involved in the instruction, which always focuses on preparing the child for school. The Even Start Mentor distributes practical and attractive materials, available in both English and Spanish, appropriate for the developmental age of the child.

Once a week there is a staff meeting to review the home visits, discuss additional lesson topics, and improve instructional materials. Parents and children are also asked what they liked, what they learned, and what they would like to learn in the future.

Learning Center Classes

These are held several times each week and focus on family-identified needs and interests. Center classes bring families together for social interaction, mutual support, and learning. Some of the classes are for adults only, and cover topics the parents have suggested, such as crafts, cooking, making holiday cards and gifts, and creating Halloween costumes.

Tutoring Program

Education students from Colorado State University are available from 5:00 p.m.-7:00 p.m. on school days. They assist children with homework, practice basic skills, computer learning, and provide mentoring and educational counseling. The Even Start and university students read together and play games which promote language development and learning.

Family Enrichment Activities

These are scheduled monthly and are planned to include the whole family. The objective is to provide families with a wide range of experiences. Many children have lived in isolation and poverty all their lives, and, therefore, may be considered to have an experiential deficit. These activities include trips to the zoo, attending a play or football game at the University, and visits to the library. Family excursions provide an opportunity for all Even Start families to be together.

Preschool Children's Group

Even Start community adults are hired as child care staff to work with the children whenever adults need to meet separately. A special group time for children only is held weekly. This preschool experience involves arts, crafts, stories, games, and other activities. Children practice group sharing, taking turns, school routines, and social skills.

Camp Fire Boys and Girls Program

Fifteen children participate in this program, supported in part by Anheuser Busch Corporation. This group is run by university students and serves to enhance positive self-esteem, independence, and social responsibility in K through 6th grade students.

GED Program

Volunteers trained by the Larimer County Adult Literacy Coalition conduct classes to prepare parents who have not graduated from high school for the GED test.

ESL (English as a Second Language)

An Even Start Family Mentor conducts weekly ESL lessons in the homes of Hispanic families.

PLAN NOW Families

This component of the program is funded by grants under the Carl Perkins Act and assists teen parents to plan for the future. The emphasis is on exploring nontraditional careers, parent education, and employability skills.

Student Literacy Corps

In conjunction with Colorado State University, this program provides one-on-one tutoring in the home for parents in basic literacy skills and preparation for the GED test.

Printed Material and Publications

An Even Start newsletter is published every 6 weeks, including program updates, recognition of achievements of parents and families, and other community news. A "user friendly" community resource directory for parents has been compiled. A Training Manual on "Effective Family Outreach" is available. It is written in a very readable question and answer format, and offers many practical suggestions about building trust, effective home visits, reaching families through flyers, notes, and phone calls.

Parent Involvement in Planning, Operating, and Monitoring

Parents are encouraged to volunteer at the Center. The goal is to train them so that they can run the program themselves. A volunteer coordinator provides training for parents so that they can volunteer in the class. The staff encourages feedback from the parents about the curriculum of the home instruction visits, and utilizes parent suggestions to shape future lessons. Another role played by parents is to teach staff to speak Spanish so that they can communicate with Hispanic parents.

When the Even Start project began, a parent advisory committee was formed, but the Even Start directors soon realized that it was more structure than substance. They concluded it would be more helpful to hire parents and others from the park and involve them in the program as part of the staff.

Strengths and Weaknesses

One of the most visible outcomes of this program is the change in the way parents interact with their children as a result of the instructional home visits. They are being taught how to become teachers of their own children, thus empowering parents to take a more active role in their children's education.

One parent talks about how, before participating in Even Start, she would go to a parent/teacher conference and just listen; now she asks questions of the teacher so she can help her daughter do better in school. When the parent shows an interest and becomes involved in school, her children are more interested and more committed to school work. This parent expresses herself in these words:

> I am somebody! I can go and ask questions and speak for myself. I am improved in my language. I feel confident. They've (Even Start) gotten me back to getting my GED.

Prior to the opening of the Even Start Learning Center, the mobile home park was a high crime area. Families who resided there were negatively stereotyped and, therefore, had little self-confidence or self-respect. The presence of the Learning Center, and its many activities for families, has resulted in a positive change in the attitudes of the residents toward their community and an improved perception of mobile home parks by those living elsewhere.

One of the tangential effects of this program was the establishment in the mobile home park of a substation of the Sheriff's Department. This was done in response to the high crime rate and had some unexpected benefits in addition to the reduction of the incidence of crime. The Sheriff's officers spend much time walking and driving through the park and, consequently, have become acquainted personally with the youths and their families.

The Learning Center has had some difficulty getting parents and other adults to come to the Center for classes. Many parents were at-risk learners themselves and see the Center as part of the school bureaucracy which they dislike and/or mistrust: they call it the "escuelita" or "little school." Many of the families are very traditional in their values, expecting the woman to stay at home. They tend to view education as the school's responsibility; they will help their children with education at home, but do not want to become involved outside the home.

Extensive outreach and purposeful community building activities have been needed to build a sense of trust between the Learning Center and the parents and other adults in the mobile home parks. The program has utilized very active outreach strategies, regular home visits, leaving flyers door-to-door, and promoting community-wide activities. The Center is furnished to look, feel, and smell like home, in order for people to be comfortable, "mi casa es su casa." The bulletin boards at the Center are filled with pictures of the families. There are many resources and opportunities for those who drop in to the Center; flowers are on the table and food is always available.

The staff is sensitive to the need to be available and helpful to parents who may require assistance on a moment's notice. They are always alert to taking advantage of "teachable moments," when a family member needs to learn something at a particular time. If a parent is having difficulty using a directory, a staff person will take the opportunity to drop what they are doing and show the parent how to use the directory.

Since the inception of the Even Start program, the curriculum has undergone much change. At the beginning, the staff were repeating lessons learned at the Center during their home visits. Experience taught them to base curricular instruction in the home, as many parents were reluctant or unable to attend classes at the Center. The activities at the Center are now primarily used for enrichment.

Testing of both the adults and children is mandated in the Even Start program; this creates a barrier for many adults. Parents are not upset with the children being tested, but often do not want to take the adult literacy test required if they are to participate in the program. Past negative school experiences have made test taking an uncomfortable and difficult experience. Even Start staff have developed special home lessons and support strategies to assist parents through the test taking process.

As this project has developed, the staff had to learn that many of the parents come from a different cultural orientation, particularly those who are not literate. These parents feel very uncomfortable communicating with the schools their children attend. One of the objectives of the Even Start program is to prepare the parents to talk to the teachers and administrators at their children's schools. The staff often accompanies parents to school meetings and tries to build a bridge of collaboration between home and school. The school officials call on the staff at the Learning Center when they have particular concerns about one of the families living in the mobile home parks.

One important lesson Even Start staff have learned is the importance of taking "ego ownership" out of what they are doing. Staff place emphasis on being flexible, open, and able to change instructional approaches if necessary. The Learning Center staff sees a critical need to get away from the deficit model, start where families are currently functioning, and build upon their positive attributes. Staff training emphasizes the importance of patience in working with families and emphasizes that process is as important as product. Staff do not consider themselves as experts, with all of the answers, but as collaborators with parents to learn to work together and to be able to say with honesty, "I have learned as much as I have given."

Another aspect of staff development is to assist staff members in becoming aware of their own feelings and taking responsibility for them. Staff is encourage to *not* take on roles such as persecutor, victim, or rescuer, but to be able to work with their colleagues, parents, and community leaders as equals, treating others with respect, and recognizing the value of everyone's contribution.

One of the barriers to greater attendance at the Learning Center is the distance between the two mobile home parks. Though they are only a mile away, that is a long distance for a family with preschoolers and no car. Free bus passes, car pools, and center-provided transportation have been an important support service.

Evaluation and Outcomes

As a federally funded program, Even Start is required to collect data with which to evaluate the effectiveness of the program. In addition, staff keep journals to document events and progress in a qualitative way. Every 6 months the staff is responsible for writing reports which include their observations and conclusions. A formal evaluation of the national Even Start program is being conducted by Abt Associates of Cambridge, Massachusetts, and the RMC Corporation, of Portland, Oregon; results are not available at this writing.

The staff have noticed many changes and improvements in attitudes and practices which can be attributed to the presence and activities of the Learning Center. There is a much more positive attitude on the part of schools and community toward the parents and children from the mobile home parks. Before Even Start existed, principals and teachers were reluctant to visit families in the mobile home parks because of fears about safety. The stereotypes about families who reside there are changing as Even Start assists the professionals in working through these stereotypes and seeing the strengths of families. The Even Start program has trained parents to be teachers of their own children, and has, therefore, empowered them to take on new roles and responsibilities.

Improvement in K-12 student achievement may not be evident for a number of years since the program is working with preschool age children. However, there is evidence of success on the part of the tutoring program, which has enabled about 80% of the students participating in the tutoring program to be placed on the honor roll.

Budget and Funding

For the 1992–1993 school year, this program is funded by a $200,000 grant from the Department of Education matched by $135,000, consisting of other grants, donations, and in-kind services from the school district, Colorado State University, and the Fort Collins community. The program began in January 1990; the federal grant is for a period of 4 years. For the first year, a 10% match in funding was required from the district and/or community. In subsequent years, the proportion of the match to be provided by local funds increases. To continue the program after the 4-year grant period has ended, other sources of funding are being sought.

Even Start is a partnership between Colorado State University, the Poudre School District, and the Fort Collins community. The program has been included as part of the long-range strategic planning for both the University and the school district. There is much support from the mobile home community for continuation of the program, and a citizens' group in Fort Collins is lobbying to convince the district to support the operating costs from their budget.

For Further Information Contact

Carol Miller, Robert Williams, Cathy Love—
  Co-Directors
Marilyn Thayer—Coordinator of the Learning Center

Even Start	Colorado State University
Poudre School District R-1	School of Occupational
2407 La Porte	and Educational Studies
Fort Collins, CO 80521	209 Education Building
(303) 490–3653	Fort Collins, CO 80523
(Ms. Miller)	(303) 491–5526
(303) 484–2580	(Mr. Williams)
(Ms. Thayer)	(303) 491–7343 (Ms. Love)

WOONSPE TIOSPAYE (FAMILY EDUCATION)
Takini School
Howes, SD

Major Components:
- Early Childhood Education
- Adult Education
- Parent Time (Parenting Skills)
- Parent and Child Time (PACT)
- Home visits

Special Features:
- Holistic Education
- The Learning Wheel

Profile of Cheyenne River Reservation:

Population of Reservation	12,000
Number of students enrolled in school	250
Number of schools on Reservation	5
Schools for K-8	3
Schools for K-12	2
Number of families participating in program	59
Number of adults	76
Number of children	115
% from Native-American families	99%
% from low-income families	100%

The **goals** of the program are:

- To provide parents with opportunities to be involved in their children's education;
- To promote the importance of a culture-based, developmentally appropriate learning program for children, from birth to 5 years;
- To network with existing agencies to enhance the coordination and continuity of support resources for children and families; and
- To empower parents and children to provide an appropriate functional home learning environment which promotes culture, literacy, and wellness.

BACKGROUND

The Takini (Survivor) School is located in the southwest portion of the Cheyenne River Reservation, one of the largest reservations in the U.S. with 3.2 million acres within the reservation boundary lines which extend 100 miles long and 60 miles wide. The Reservation is located in a geographically isolated area in the north-central portion of South Dakota. The majority of the students attending the Takini School are bilingual (Lakota and English) and are members of the Cheyenne River Sioux Tribe.

The name of the Takini (Survivor) School is significant. The community members and their children are "survivors" within a social and economic environment that lacks many of the material resources common to other populations in other areas. The residents have "survived" the coercive assimilation policies and efforts of society through maintaining their cultural uniqueness and language. The residents of the Takini School area have "survived" the extreme geographic isolation of the area, and have begun the process of working together in harmony to support the educational and other needs of the youth and other residents in the area.

In 1990, the Office of Indian Education Programs, U.S. Bureau of Indian Affairs, developed an Early Childhood/ Parental Involvement Pilot Program. It was based on three models: Missouri's Parents as Teachers (PAT) model, Parent and Child Education (PACE) as adapted by the National Center for Family Literacy, and the High Scope Curriculum for Early Childhood and K-3, developed by the High Scope Foundation in Ypsilanti, Michigan. The concepts and components of these programs were combined into a new program, implemented as a pilot program at six Native American Schools, one of which was Takini. In 1992, the program was renamed and became Family and Child Education (FACE).

The Learning Wheel of Woonspe Tiospaye (Family Education) includes four components: Children, Grandparents, Parents and Caregivers. The spokes of the wheel are Adult Education, Early Childhood, and Parents as Teachers. Takini School outcomes are placed on the seven feathers attached to the wheel, which represent the seven council fires of the Lakota People. On the feathers are the learning processes and expected outcomes. One feather represents the four values of the Lakota people: Respect, Generosity, Courage, and Wisdom.

The program is intended to be flexible and adaptable to the needs of the family participants, reflecting the cultural traditions and values of the community. Therefore, every program is unique. The Takini School program emphasizes a holistic approach to Family and Child Education, addressing learning and development from physical, environmental, cultural, social, and spiritual perspectives.

DESCRIPTION OF THE PROGRAM

The FACE programs are designed to implement a family literacy program through the use of a home base and a center base. The FACE program has four components: Early Childhood, Parent Education, Parent and Child Time (PACT), and Adult Education. It serves Lakota families in three communities—Bridger, Cherry Creek, and Red Scaffold. The center-based components are located in the Takini School, which is about 15 miles from the three communities.

The program serves about 59 families, with services for children from birth to 5 years of age and their parents or other caregivers. Eight staff members are responsible for operating the program. Seven of the staff members are Native-Americans; one, the early childhood teacher, is not.

Components of the Program: Center-Based

Early Childhood Component

Children, ages 3–5, attend a preschool program 3 days a week, from 9 a.m. to 2:00 p.m. The Early Childhood program is conducted by a teacher and an aide who are knowledgeable and sensitive to the culture of the community, and engage the children in active learning based on the developmental level of the child. The High Scope Curriculum is utilized in the classroom; culture-based curriculum is incorporated into the daily schedule of the class. Since the majority of the children are bilingual, speaking both Lakota and English, vocabulary development is an important component of the curriculum. Twenty children are enrolled in the early childhood program.

Adult Education

During the 3 morning hours, while the children are receiving instruction in the Early Childhood classroom, the parents or other caregivers participate in adult education. Courses to prepare for the GED are offered; study skills for college or employment are available; and the adults learn life skills and build self-esteem.

Parent Time

Time is set aside to discuss ideas and concerns about the school, family, or life issues.

PACT (Parent and Child Time)

After spending the morning in their separate activities, parents and children come together for ½ hour of physical exercise in the gym and *Circle Time* with songs, exercises, dancing, and role playing. During PACT time, the adults participate in the early childhood program with their child and practice what they have learned in parenting skills time. The activities are chosen by the child, supported by the parents, and shared by the teaching staff. The activities include reading, active learning, or learning through playing.

Home-Based

Home visits

Three Parent Educators are available for home visits to families with infants and toddlers, from birth to 3 years of age. Two visits, each 1–1½ hours long, are made each month to each family. The Parent Educators assess and observe the growth and development of the baby, and share this information with the parents. PACT is part of the home visit, to help parents realize that they are the first and most important teacher for their children. The Parent Educators refer the parents to health and social services organizations, as appropriate, if they see a need for additional assistance. About 40 families are provided with services from this component of the program.

Group/Community Meetings

Meetings of parents and community leaders are held monthly in each community, to provide opportunities for families to share successes and common concerns about their children's behavior and development. Outside speakers might be invited to present information on topics of interest; food is always available; and each meeting includes some recreational, fun activity.

Parent Involvement in Planning, Operating, and Monitoring

Parent Time and monthly Parent Meetings provide an opportunity for parents to suggest topics for discussion and to raise issues for future consideration.

Strengths and Weaknesses

The group meetings for parents and community leaders have been very successful. Buses are made available by the school system to bring the parents and return them home after the meetings. At the October meeting, those attending carved pumpkins. In November, a turkey dinner was served, followed by traditional stories and singing. At one meeting, the elders from the tribe shared experiences from their childhood. Many of the programs emphasize outdoor activities and environmental concerns. Often the staff provide child care for the children attending.

One difficulty has been scheduling home visits at times when the parent and child will both be there. Attendance of the parents and children at the school for the early childhood program and adult education is often erratic; they may come only 1 or 2 days a week. Bad weather and distance are often factors affecting attendance.

Outcomes and Evaluation

As the children complete the early childhood program and enter the regular kindergarten, the parents who have been active in their children's education often continue to be involved in the regular school. The High Scope curriculum is also used in grades K-3 in the public schools, so the parents are familiar with that approach and feel more comfortable communicating with the teachers about learning problems. The parents are not afraid to go into the classroom, to raise questions about the curriculum.

The staff have observed that parenting skills have changed and improved as a result of the parents' participation in the program. Punitive attitudes and behavior toward children have been noticeably reduced; patience toward children is emphasized every day.

The Family Education Staff participated in a brainstorming session for the 1991–1992 school year, and identified the following as successes:

- Better attendance

- Parents are recognizing little learning experiences

- Learned patience

- Parenting skills are improving

- Bigger room for Early Childhood classroom

- Staff has developed trust, team building skills

- More parent participation/interest high

- Tribal endorsement

Additionally, the staff identified their parental successes:

- Two parents received GED

- Parental involvement in school activities

- Fundraising efforts

- Attendance at "Healing through Unity"

- Involvement with community activities

Budget and Funding

This program costs about $200,000 per year. The funds are provided by the federal Bureau of Indian Affairs.

For Further Information Contact

Linda Hunter, Coordinator
Takini School
HC 77, Box 537
Howes, SD 57748
(605) 538-4399

WARRENSVILLE HIPPY
Warrensville Heights City Schools
Warrensville Heights, OH

Major Components:
>Home visits
>Group meetings
>Field trips

Special Features:
>Parents as Aides
>Referral to community services
>Self-sufficiency for families
>Parent empowerment

Profile of Program and School District:

Public School Enrollment	3,000
Number of schools in district	6
Elementary (K-4)	3
Middle (5–6)	1
Junior high school	1
Senior high school	1
Number of families in HIPPY Program	75–80
% from African-American families	99%
% from low-income families	75%

The **goals** of Warrensville HIPPY are:

- To provide sound basic preschool education to the children;
- To help families become self-sufficient and self-reliant;
- To serve as a referral source for families to community services and social service agencies; and
- To empower parents as their children's first and primary teachers.

BACKGROUND

In February 1989, a local businesswoman expressed her concern, at a Chamber of Commerce meeting, about education in the community and proposed various approaches to improve the schools and school readiness of the children. The Superintendent of Warrensville Heights City Schools was present at one of the meetings where this issue was discussed and was impressed with the interest and concern of the business community. Along with the Cleveland Section of the National Council of Jewish Women (NCJW), the school system agreed to implement HIPPY (Home Instruction Program for Preschool Youngsters).

HIPPY, a project of the NCJW, was developed in Israel, in 1969, to enhance the education and enrich the lives of culturally and educationally disadvantaged children, many of whom were immigrants. HIPPY programs currently serve over 22,000 families and exist in South Africa, the Netherlands, Mexico, Germany, New Zealand, Israel, and the United States. The first program in the U.S. began in 1984; HIPPY is now being implemented at 60 sites, in 17 states. The largest number of programs is in Arkansas, which has 31 programs benefiting approximately 5,000 families.

Gayle Hart was hired in 1989, to organize and initiate the HIPPY program in Warrensville. She participated in 14 days of training at Hebrew University in Israel, and started the first class of children in the fall of 1989. The first year began with 45 children (43 African-Americans, 1 bi-racial, and 1 Caucasian).

DESCRIPTION OF THE PROGRAM

This program is open to families living in the city of Warrensville Heights and the villages of North Randall and Highland Hills. The majority of the children enrolled in the HIPPY program reside in the city of Warrensville Heights, which is predominantly black. Warrensville Heights was formerly a middle-class, white, suburban community that gradually changed to a middle-class integrated neighborhood and has now evolved to a predominantly black community with numerous multi-family dwelling units, heavily populated by low-income families. Banbury Village is one of the main areas targeted by the HIPPY program; it is a multi-family dwelling cluster where living conditions have declined severely over a period of about 15 years.

HIPPY begins with the basic tenet that all parents want the very best for their children and that all children can learn. However, not all parents know how best to develop their children's potential. HIPPY seeks to empower parents, and provide for and create opportunities for positive educational interactions between parent and child. The role of the parent as the child's primary educator is intrinsic to the program. The HIPPY system is designed so that both children and parents can achieve success.

HIPPY's other goals include strengthening the parent/ child relationship; promoting the concept of family; developing increased self-esteem, self-awareness, and self-confidence; encouraging the participating parent's educational and employment goals; early dropout prevention; and serving as a referral source to both community services and social service agencies.

The official sponsor is the Warrensville Heights Board of Education; however, the district does not provide any direct funding. The program is directed by the Warrensville HIPPY Corporation, which has a 16-member Board of Directors to oversee the operation of the program. The Cleveland Section of the National Council of Jewish Women provides members to serve on the Board, in addition to their continuing financial support.

The coordinator is the only full-time staff member of the HIPPY program; her primary responsibilities are selecting parents, organizing meetings, developing enrichment activities, training and supporting the paraprofessional staff, and raising funds to support the program. She is assisted by a part-time secretary. The HIPPY program is staffed by 5 aides who have themselves been mothers in the program.

A total of 75–80 families are active in the HIPPY program each year, with children enrolled in either the 4- or 5-year old class. The participants are 99% African-American, with one or two children each year from Caucasian or Latino families.

About 75% of the families are considered low-income or lower middle class working poor; 25% are middle class by income, but with limited educational backgrounds.

Families are recruited through flyers sent home with children in school, distributed in housing projects, and delivered door-to-door in some neighborhoods. Families are selected to participate in the program based on information gathered during an in-home interview. Criteria for enrollment in the Warrensville Program include economic and cultural factors, educational level of the parent, single parent status, and the educational skills and abilities of the child. Families enrolled in the program participate for 30 weeks a year, for 2 years. The program begins when the child is 4 and continues for a second year while the child is in kindergarten. This is done to stress the importance of the parent being involved in the child's education after the child has entered school.

Components of the Program

Home Visits

Each paraprofessional aide visits the homes of her assigned 12–15 families every 2 weeks, 30 weeks a year, for the 2 years the family is enrolled. Through role playing, the aide instructs and motivates the parent to work with his/her child. This method of instruction fosters a comfortable nonthreatening environment, and promotes empathy for the child who will be doing these same activities during that week.

During each visit, the parents are provided with activity packets which serve as lesson plans, and with instructions outlining parent-child activities step-by-step. By guaranteeing success and offering immediate gratification for teaching efforts, this structured approach gives parents the confidence to take on increasing responsibilities in their roles as educators.

Parents are asked to work with their children for 15–20 minutes a day, 5 days a week. The parent is continuously reminded to create a positive learning environment—never saying "you're wrong"—only giving and/or reinforcing the correct answer.

Group Meetings

Every 2 weeks (alternating with the home visit schedule) the parents meet in a local church. The parents of the 4-year olds comprise one group; those with 5-year olds meet at a different time. Mothers are most likely to attend these meetings, though fathers occasionally are present too. At the meetings the same role-playing techniques are used to demonstrate how parents can play with and teach their children.

A portion of the meeting is reserved for speakers, group discussions, or demonstrations about topics of interest to parents, on such issues as positive discipline, parenting techniques, black history, family communication skills, kindergarten readiness, budgeting tips, gardening, and job opportunities. Information is available on school district services, adult basic education, recreation department classes, and arts, crafts, and fun activities.

Ongoing instruction in good nutrition is part of the group meeting experience and is reflected in the refreshments served to the parents and children. Child care is provided for children accompanying their parents to the group meeting. Educational toys and games, time for creative expression, and story hour are part of the curriculum.

Field Trips

This component is not included in the regular HIPPY program, but has been added in the Warrensville program as an extracurricular feature. Field trips are held on a regular basis for both parent and child. Parents are allowed their input in selecting locations, which are chosen for the educational stimulation and cultural benefit to be derived. The goal is to expose the child and parent to events and attractions that stimulate, provide a basis for future learning, and broaden their concept of the world. Locations of field trips have included the Cleveland Children's Museum, Cleveland Health Education Museum, Warrensville Branch of the County Library, Malley's Chocolate Factory, the Sanctuary Marsh, and Hale Farm.

Summer Program

A 6-week summer program is offered to all current and former HIPPY families and other school district residents with children between 3–8 years old. The program takes place 1 day a week, for 3 hours. At the 1992 summer session, the adults participated in a series of discussions to examine current issues that affect the safety of children and to explore what parents can do to make them as safe as possible. The facilitators for the discussion group were social workers from the N.E. Ohio Parenting for Peaceful Families Association.

The children in attendance for the 1992 summer program participated in simple science experiments designed to stimulate their interest in the world around them, educational play, arts and crafts, and exploring on school grounds.

Publications

A monthly calendar, showing the schedule of group meetings, field trips, and school district activities is sent to each participating family. A newsletter is prepared and distributed twice a year. In addition, pamphlets, flyers, and activity sheets are obtained from other organizations or prepared by the Warrensville HIPPY program to distribute to parents.

Parent Involvement in Planning, Operating, and Monitoring

The HIPPY paraprofessional aides are chosen from the community and are current or previous parents of children enrolled in HIPPY. The aides are able to identify with the parents in the program, understand the challenges they face, and develop a relationship of trust with them. The home visits enable the aides to get to know each family well and learn about their individual situation. The coordinator and aides meet weekly to discuss the previous week's activities, plan the next program, and share experiences and concerns. Family problems are raised and suggestions made as to appropriate referrals to community agencies for assistance.

Strengths and Weaknesses

Since the first families enrolled in Warrensville HIPPY in September 1989, the program has been successful in its efforts to strengthen the educational and social foundations of the families. A total of 45 children and their families started in the first year, 42 were added in the Fall of 1990, and an additional 50 children joined the program in 1991. A total of 54 children and families families have "graduated" from HIPPY.

The HIPPY program staff have experienced several frustrations in their efforts to meet program goals. Since this area was traditionally a middle class suburb of Cleveland, social service agencies are not located in the Warrensville Heights area. Residents must utilize services offered by agencies in downtown Cleveland, about 20 miles away. HIPPY parents lose jobs, face evictions, or seek drug rehabilitation, but the program has nowhere to refer them and no method of providing the temporary support they need.

A second area which needs to be strengthened is publicity. Limited media opportunities exist in the community. As a suburb of Cleveland, it is difficult to reach Warrensville families through the print and broadcast media from the city. There is a perception that this community does not need additional services, but this conclusion is not supported by the demographic data gathered by the schools.

Lack of transportation is another barrier. The school system does not provide buses or other transportation to enable parents to attend the biweekly meetings. This is a particular challenge for residents of Banbury Village, located at the extreme southeast portion of Warrensville Heights, diametrically opposite the meeting site. Some other sites do utilize jitney services for parent transportation, although this has proven not be an option for Warrensville HIPPY. The aides are able to drive some parents to the meetings.

The Warrensville HIPPY program would also be strengthened if it had its own facility. Currently the meetings are held in local churches, but some parents will not attend meetings at a church because of religious reasons. The coordinator and aides favor a space devoted entirely to the program so that they could develop a Parent Drop-In Center. This would give the program a stronger identity and facilitate additional activities centered around parents.

The Warrensville HIPPY program is not an official program of the school district. The School Board subcontracted the operation of HIPPY based on a recommendation of a school district lawyer who felt this particular structure would prevent certain legal issues which might arise with the schools. However, the program might be stronger if it were more closely tied to the school system, in terms of funding, space, transportation, and collaboration between parents and schools.

Outcomes and Evaluation

There is much anecdotal evidence of program effectiveness. The aides have observed changes in parental attitudes and practices during their home visits. Parents are definitely more active in their children's education and very supportive of the HIPPY program and the public schools. Teachers have expressed acknowledgment of and appreciation for the abilities of HIPPY students.

The experiences from the first 2 years of the program indicate that both parents and children have benefited from the HIPPY activities. Data compiled on the first 25 families to complete 2 years of HIPPY has shown the following results: two mothers are taking or have taken college level courses; 10 previously unemployed mothers are working (four of these were previously receiving public assistance); three previously unemployed mothers have started their own businesses; two mothers went from part-time to full-time employment; and five mothers became active within the community, serving as officers for various organizations.

Their children are doing well in school, though academic performance should be monitored for several years to determine long-term gains. Longitudinal studies in locations which have been in existence a longer period of time have shown that HIPPY students are well-prepared academically, have less need for special educational services, and have better retention records. One student from the first group of Warrensville HIPPY families was selected as a SPUR (Scholastic Performance Uniquely Recognized) Student of the Year.

Several measures of program effectiveness are being developed and implemented: Each child is given a basic test prior to entering kindergarten to measure the child's abilities in HIPPY skill development areas such as logical thinking and problem solving activities. A parent questionnaire is filled out by the participating parents at the end of the 2 year HIPPY program. Data is being gathered on the personal growth of the parent, the level of parent/child bonding, and the community involvement of the parent and child.

The Warrensville school district is designing a procedure to code the children who have been in the HIPPY program so that it will be easy to track the children through the school system. The academic achievement, national test results, retention rates, and any need for special services will be among the areas monitored.

Several efforts to assess and evaluate the program are in progress. Dr. Susan Turben, a psychologist with the Department of Education at John Carroll University, has agreed to donate her services to review and critique existing evaluation and to make appropriate suggestions for future implementations.

Budget and Funding

The annual cost of the Warrensville HIPPY program is approximately $70,000. This includes all budget items except the in-kind contributions from the schools. The school district contributes office space, basic office furniture, telephone, photocopier use, and storage space. The coordinator of the program also serves as the fund-raiser, and must make regular, frequent contacts with foundations and businesses in the area to raise the funds necessary to operate the program. Some of those contributing to the Warrensville HIPPY program are Lander area Kiwanis, the local Chamber of Commerce, the Cleveland Section of NCJW (National Council of Jewish Women), the George Gund Foundation, the Cleveland Foundation, and Edward J. DeBartolo and several of his business holdings.

For Further Information Contact

M. Gayle Hart, Director
Warrensville HIPPY
Warrensville Heights City Schools
4500 Warrensville Center Road
Warrensville Heights, OH 44128
(216) 663-2770

Chapter 3

Programs in Elementary Schools

It is widely believed, and generally true, that parents are the most motivated and reachable when their children are young. However, the changing life situations of families which involve job insecurities, marginal housing, rising violence in neighborhoods, and diminished "quality time" with their children make conventional involvement efforts of the past "a thing of the past." Parent-family involvement efforts for parents and guardians of young children now require creativity, insight, sensitivity to new lifestyles and pressures. Most of all, the times require a willingness by school personnel to see the involvement of parents and guardians as activities that increasingly take place outside the school and focus more than in the past on the needs of parents and families as legitimate and contributing concerns of the school.

Until recent times there has been a reluctance on the part of school personnel to become involved in the out-of-school social problems of the child and his family. The always demanding schedules and expectations of teachers, principals, and other administrators made this understandable. However, committed professionals also have a large investment in the success of the children for whom they are responsible. The increasing complexity of life outside the school has impinged more and more on how much the child succeeds in school.

The programs and project descriptions that follow underscore the growing realization and acceptance by school personnel that for children to succeed in school, school personnel must also now understand and be involved with what goes on outside of school. These programs tell an exciting story of how school personnel are both moving out to serve children, parents, families, and communities, and designing new ways to make moving in and out of school more supporting, comforting, and esteem building. All of these new and different efforts end up as important forms of support for children in their efforts to succeed in school. What you, the reader, may be looking at when you think about the innovative efforts that follow is the way elementary schools of the future will need to operate in order to form adult partnerships needed by young children to both achieve academically and succeed as human beings.

PROGRAMS IN ELEMENTARY SCHOOLS

Atenville Elementary School, Harts, West Virginia

Parents as Educational Partners

Balboa Elementary School, San Diego, California

Parent Institute for Quality Education,

Bergen Beach School–P.S. 312, Brooklyn, New York

Parents, Teachers & Children Working Together

Graham & Parks Alternative School, Cambridge, Massachusetts

Hawthorne School, Oakland, California

Families Together

Rockaway New School, Rockaway, New York

Rolling Fork Elementary School, Rolling Fork, Mississippi

      Quality Education Project (QEP)

Sterne Brunson Elementary School, Benton Harbor, Michigan

      School Development Program

Tomasita Elementary School, Albuquerque, New Mexico

Vaughn Street School, San Fernando, California

      Vaughn Family Center

Wapato Primary School, Wapato, Washington

      FOCUS—Focusing our Community and Uniting
      for Success

SUMMARY OF PROGRAM CHARACTERISTICS
Elementary School Programs

Name of Program	Population Served	Components	Beginnings	Special Features
Attenville Elementary School Harts, WV Parents as Educational Partners	K-6 Enrollment—203 99% White 76% low-income	Family Center Parent Phone Tree Parent Workshops Home Visits Tutoring Centers Welcome Wagon	Started by principal in 1989; member of League of Schools Reaching Out	Action Research Committee Portfolios for students, families and school Community Involvement
Balboa Elementary San Diego, CA Parent Institute for Quality Education	K-6 Enrollment—1,190 83% Latino 98% Low-income	Parent Institute Training Course Parent Room Parent Coordinator Governance Team	6-week Parent Training Classes provided each year by Vahac Mardirosian from the Parent Institute for Quality Education	Parent Empowerment Communication between parent and child
Bergen Beach School-P.S. 312 Brooklyn, NY Parents, Teachers, & Children Working Together	K-5 Enrollment—843 65% Whites 30% African-Amers. 37% low-income	Family-School Mtg. Family-School Workshops Teacher/staff Training	Principals and teachers trained by Ackerman Institute to promote greater parent involvement	Inclusion of child in all conferences Student empowerment

Graham & Parks Alternative School Cambridge, MA	K–8 Enrollment—380 48% White 14% African-Amer. 25% Haitian 10% Latino 3% Asian-American	Parent Involvement in Decisionmaking, Classroom Parent Council Parent Coordinator	Started in 1972 by group of parents, first school of choice in Cambridge	Democracy Parent Empowerment Outreach to Haitian families
Hawthorne School Oakland, CA Families Together	K–6 Enrollment—1,320 58% Latino 23% Asian-Amers. 18% African-Amers. 90% low-income	Outreach ESL Classes, Mien, Vietnamese, Cambodian, Spanish Primary Language & Literacy Support Family Stories Parenting Classes	Sponsored by ARC (Art, Research, and Curriculum Associates) with grant from federal government	Support Services for immigrant and refugee families Multilingual staff Multicultural Communication
Rockaway New School Rockaway Beach, NY	K–6 Enrollment—187 75% African-Amer. 15% Latinos 10% White 100% low-income	Parent volunteers Open and accessible classrooms Steering Committee Parent Meetings	Started by teachers and parents in Fall 1991; parents organized by ACORN	School within a School

(continued)

SUMMARY OF PROGRAM CHARACTERISTICS
Elementary School Programs *(continued)*

Name of Program	Population Served	Components	Beginnings	Special Features
Rolling Fork Elementary School Rolling Fork, MS QEP Parent Involvement Project	K–6 Enrollment—725 80% African-Amer. 90% low-income Rural community	Parent Pledge QEP Student Folders Parent Seminars Back-to-School Night	Principal and teachers trained by QEP Project, San Francisco	Staff training Resource manuals Monitoring Evaluation
Sterne Brunson Elementary School Benton Harbor, MI School Development Program	K–6 Enrollment—582 99% African-Amers. 98% low-income	Parent-in-Training Program Parent Volunteers School Advisory Committee School Support Team	Implemented School Development Project in 1986 as part of court-ordered desegregation plan	Parent Leadership training
Tomasita Elementary School Albuquerque, NM	K–5 Enrollment—476 50% Latinos 36% Whites 6% Native-Amers. 4% African-Amers. 52% low-income	Parent volunteers Preschool program "Families in Partnership" Prog. Before/after school child care Summer day camp Kinderproject	Principal committed to high level of parent involvement since 1987; member of League of Schools Reaching Out	Clothing Bank Parents as Substitute Teachers Food Co-op Program

		Service Delivery		Service Exchange
Vaughn Street Elementary School San Fernando, CA Vaughn Family Center	K–5 Enrollment—1,085 89% Latinos 11% African-Amers. 40% low-income 78% LEP	Service Delivery Child Care and Preschool Prog. Parent Education	Demonstration site for FamilyCare, started in 1991; sponsored by LA Educational Partnership & United Way	Service Exchange Bank Block leaders Family Advocates Parent Empowerment
Wapato Primary School Wapato, WA FOCUS—Focusing our Community and United for Success	K–2 Enrollment—780 50% Latinos 32% Native-Amers. 17% White 86% low-income	Parent Meetings Recruiting efforts FOCUS Committee	School Team participated in Leadership Training at Citizens Education Center (CEC) in Seattle, WA	Concurrent English and Spanish sessions Outreach to Native-Americans (Yakima) Certificates of Attendance

PARENTS AS EDUCATIONAL PARTNERS
Atenville Elementary School
Harts, WV

Major Components:
>Family Center
>Parent Phone Tree
>Parent Educational Workshops
>Home Visits
>Satellite Tutoring Centers
>Welcome Wagon

Special Features:
>Action Research Committee
>Portfolios for Students, Families, and School
>Extensive Community Involvement

Profile of School and School District

Located in rural Lincoln County, in coal mining community	
District Enrollment	4,564
Number of Schools in Lincoln County	
School District	20
Elementary (K-6)	15
High Schools	4
Vocational School	1
Enrollment at Atenville	203
% from White families	99%
% from low-income families	76%

The **goals** of the program are:

- To provide parents with training and knowledge so they will become more involved in their child's education; and
- To improve student achievement.

BACKGROUND

Atenville Elementary School is located in a small, rural mining community with few businesses. There is only one traffic light in the county and none in the community of Harts. Most of the residents are employed in coal mining. The school is one of 15 elementary schools, for Grades K-6, in the Lincoln County School District. Most of the students are bused because of the distance from their homes to the school. The county is in the Appalachian foothills and the majority of the students come from low socioeconomic homes, are descendants of people who have lived in the Appalachian Mountains for generations, and possess an abundance of family commitment and mountain heritage.

The focus on parent involvement in this small school in West Virginia was spearheaded by the former principal, Peggy Adkins. She had read the education journals and studied the research, and realized the importance of parent involvement. In 1989, she formed a committee with teachers, staff, and parents to plan and design a stronger parent involvement effort within the school. In the initial stages of the program, the school began to recruit parent volunteers by "opening our doors" to welcome parent and community involvement. Each year they tried to increase the quantity and quality of parent involvement, but due to the absence of a formal plan and adequate funding, the level of parent/community participation remained low.

In the spring of 1991, they began to intensify efforts to develop a formal plan and seek funding for implementation. They were accepted into the League of Schools Reaching Out, and received a small grant from the Institute for Responsive Education to implement the program. The Family Center was opened in September, 1991, and a Parent Coordinator was hired in December, 1991, to organize the various components of the program. Peggy Adkins was named as Assistant Superintendent in 1991. Darlene Dalton became the principal of Atenville Elementary School and has continued to administer, guide, and develop the program.

DESCRIPTION OF THE PROGRAM

The program is staffed by a Parent Coordinator, whose duties include:

- Scheduling, planning, and conducting parent workshops;

- Serving as liaison between home and school;

- Encouraging active involvement of parents through positive, informational public relations efforts;

- Assisting in writing and distributing school newsletters;

- Organizing homework hotline;

- Making home visits;

- Arranging for child care and transportation so parents can attend meetings at school; and

- Coordinating the telephone tree.

The School Improvement Council serves as the advisory committee for the Parents as Educational Partners project. This group is made up of three professional staff members, two support staff members, one business partner, three parents, and one delegate at large. The staff members and parents are selected by their peers, while the business partner and delegate at large are appointed by the faculty senate. The council is responsible for preparing and monitoring the annual school improvement plan, assessing program effectiveness throughout the year, and assisting with the development of new projects.

Components of the Program

Family Center

Located in a former classroom, the Family Center provides a central location for parent-staff interaction. The furnish ings for the room were donated by the Twentieth Street Bank of Huntington, the Matewan National Bank of Logan, and local residents. It is equipped with a phone line, copying machines, refreshment center, and furniture for meeting and conferences. The Center has a small library with resources and reading material for parents. This serves as the hub of all parent/community activities: it is used for parent training sessions, faculty senate meetings, PTA meetings, and many parent volunteer activities.

Parent Phone Tree

Parent and school communication has been greatly increased through the activities of the phone tree. Seven parents, one from each of the attendance areas, operate the phone tree. They call all parents once or twice monthly to update them on upcoming events, to extend invitations to parents to visit the school, and to inform them when emergencies occur.

Parent Educational Workshops

Workshops are conducted to assist parents in such areas as homework, self-esteem, basic skills, educational jargon, and teaching strategies.

Home Visits

During the first year of the program, home visits were made by the parent coordinator and other parent volunteers to a random sampling of parents, most of whom were not involved in the school. The purpose was to meet the parents, start to build the relationship between home and school, and to learn about attitudes and barriers which have kept them from being involved. The home visitors also exchanged ideas with parents to determine what direction the parent involvement program needed to take to be successful.

During the second year, teachers are assisting in the home visits, which are targeted toward families of at-risk children. School personnel gain insight into the home environment and a greater understanding of the child's family life. They establish a relationship with the parents, provide the parents with information on services the school can offer to them and their child, and discuss the child's progress and what the parents can do at home.

Satellite Tutoring Centers

Outstanding students from the local high school and parent volunteers, working under the guidance of professional educators, provide instruction for "at-risk" elementary school students. The first Center is located in a local church. The sessions are conducted twice a week and throughout the summer months. The tutoring is coordinated with the classroom teachers, who review progress and suggest further assignments.

Welcome Wagon

A committee of parents act as hosts/hostesses the first day of school and during kindergarten registration, to make parents welcome and comfortable. The concept of the Atenville "family" begins the first day of school and continues throughout the year.

Parent Teacher Association

The PTA is an active organization, sponsoring programs and contributing money to the school. They conduct a semiannual book fair; plan, organize, and conduct the annual fall carnival; assist with Mountain Heritage Week; and assist with school beautification activities.

Parent Volunteers

In addition to traditional activities such as providing support services for various school events, tutoring, and assisting in the classroom, parents are actively involved in decision making, serving on school committees, and being consulted regularly on all aspects of school governance.

Student, Family, and School Portfolios

The portfolios are designed to provide an alternate means of assessment for students, a technique for keeping information about the family, and a record of events and accomplishments for the school.

The student portfolios are used as a supplement to report cards. They include examples of the student's academic work, lists of books he/she has read, information about cocurricular activities, and school records on attendance and discipline. Also included are self-portraits drawn by the child, biographical statements, examples of the child's writing, and a reflection of the portfolio prepared by the student.

The family portfolio contains a record of home visits made by school personnel, information on the parent's volunteer activities and on his/her attendance at various school events, a log of the contacts made by members of the Phone Tree, records of telephone calls made by teachers, and copies of correspondence between home and school, such as letters from the principal or memos from the teachers.

The school portfolio is a combination scrapbook and journal of the school's activities and accomplishments. It includes information on student achievements, such as which students were successful in the regional competitions and the percentage of students on the Honor Roll; documentation on the climate of the school, such as records of telephone calls and positive notes to parents; a journal of activities, parent training workshops, staff development training, and staff presentations to workshops at schools in the district or at the state level; the percentage of parents participating in each type of activity; and data such as the number of suspensions and the percentage of students promoted to the next grade.

Action Research Committee

This committee is comprised of three professional staff members, two parents, the parent coordinator, the principal, and the project facilitator. Professor Stan Maynard from Marshall University is serving as a consultant to the committee to assist in their data collection and analysis. The Action Research Committee meets monthly to assess the project's current status and to determine its direction. The task of the committee is to develop an assessment plan of the goals and objectives of the "Parents as Educational Partners" project. They will collect data to determine the impact of parent and community involvement on student achievement.

One of the parents who serves on the Action Research Committee tells about her reluctance to speak out to the principal or anyone else at the school. When she was asked to join the Action Research Committee, she was hesitant because she was not sure she would be comfortable there. After a few meetings she says she began to feel confident about speaking. Everyone is so open and honest and she is no longer shy about joining the discussion. Others may disagree with her, but they treat her ideas seriously and with respect.

Involving the Total Community

Many community agencies, businesses, and individuals have been recruited to provide a number of services to the school, including:

- The Community Mental Health Center conducts peer counseling groups;

- Senior citizens instruct students how to churn butter;

- WV Children's Health Project mobile unit teaches students about health care;

- Employees from the John Amos Power Plant teach students about energy conservation and the production of electricity;

- Miners from the Beckley Exhibition Coal Mine provide instruction about the history of coal mining;

- University students teach children how to play stringed instruments;

- Firemen from the Volunteer Fire Department instruct children on fire safety; and

- Heartland Coal Co. and Manns Lumber Co. contribute financially to various programs and assist with enriching the curriculum.

Parent Involvement in Planning, Operating, and Monitoring

From the very beginning, parents were an integral part of the planning and implementation of the program. They have an important role in the School Improvement Committee, the Action Research Committee, and of course the PTA. Parents are asked to be at every meeting convened on any topic related to the school. At first, the parents were coming to the school for specific activities, committee meetings, etc. Now parents are continually in the school and may be called upon to do any number of tasks to assist with the operation of the school, including review and revision of policies and practices. They also play an important role in suggesting what is needed to improve the school and the Partnership.

The original design of the Partnership was to increase parent involvement in traditional, narrow roles—volunteers, PTA, telephoners. As parents began to take more responsibility with committees and project assignments, it became clear that the role of parents in the school should be *much* broader than traditionally conceived. The Principal began to request that parents attend every meeting in the school, including faculty meetings. This type of involvement began to influence school policies and practices, and curriculum and teaching strategies.

Strengths and Weaknesses

The two programs which have proved successful beyond initial expectations are the Phone Tree and the Satellite Centers for tutoring. The seven parents who operate the Parent Phone Tree meet at the school at least once a month, sometimes more often. Not only are they conscientious in disseminating information to all parents about school events and emergency situations, but they also use the phone call as an opportunity to learn from the parents called about any problems, concerns, or needs. They bring these matters back to the committee and then to the principal. This provides continuing feedback from parents who may not be especially active in the school. The telephone calls from the Phone Tree have greatly increased the communication between home and school—with parents serving as the communicators.

The Satellite Center was established during the summer of 1992. It is located at a local church which donated the space. Two high school students and one college student provide tutoring 3 mornings a week to students who are having difficulty at school. There has been a turnaround in performance and attitudes from these students; their parents have also expressed appreciation for the help given. Plans are to open several more Satellite Centers, striving for a total of 7 centers, one in each of the attendance areas.

One of the barriers which the Parents as Educational Partners has encountered is the difficulty of establishing and realizing full equality between parents and teachers. In order to work as a team, the teachers must be willing to accept the parents as equal partners, which is difficult for many teachers who have been trained as professionals accustomed to a high degree of autonomy in the classroom.

A number of efforts are being made to move beyond this barrier. The school has sponsored a 3-day retreat each year, where parents and teachers spend the day discussing mutual goals and objectives. Whenever conflicts occur between parents and teachers, Mrs. Dalton and the parent coordinator act as mediators in order to solve them before they cause difficulties. Communication is a key element: face-to-face meetings, newsletters for parents and teachers, encouragement of "teaming." The process of building trust and a working relationship between parents and teachers is an ongoing one.

Evaluation and Outcomes

As a member of the League of Schools Reaching Out, Parents as Educational Partners established the Action Research Committee to monitor the parent involvement programs and propose actions to improve them. The Committee is using several traditional means of measurement along with the information gathered for the student, family, and school portfolios to determine the effect of parent/community involvement on student achievement.

Many changes have been observed during the several years of this project, especially with regard to increased parent/community support of education and the school. Teachers have become more accepting of parent involvement. The curriculum has undergone changes as a result of the Parents as Educational Partners project and a variety of teaching strategies are being used to help children who have diverse learning styles.

Parents have changed their attitudes and behaviors as well. They are more willing to speak out on issues of concern, since the Phone Tree callers encourage them to express their opinions. The Chapter 1 Parent Advisory Committee, which typically had only a handful of active parents in past years, counted 36 parents at a recent meeting. They believe that the Parents as Educational Partners project has established a school climate where parents feel welcome and, therefore, will attend more meetings.

The following are quantitative indications of the effectiveness of the Parents as Educational Partners Program:

Number of parent volunteers
1990–1991   14
1991–1992   63

Number of parent volunteer hours
1990–1991   2,028 hours for the year
1992–1993   1,465 hours for months of September, October

Family attendance at Honors Assembly
1990–1991   25 families
1991–1992   60 families

PTA Membership
1990–1991   11 families
1991–1992   21 families
1992–1993   36 families

Number of student suspensions
1990–1991   12
1991–1992   0

Budget and Funding

The budget for last year's Parents as Educational Partners project was $10,000, which supported the part-time Parent Coordinator and any incidental expenses needed for the various components of the project. Funds were obtained from a grant from Schools Reaching Out and money from the Chapter 1 program. Added to this were in-kind contributions from various local businesses and companies; an estimated $600.00 worth of food was contributed for various meetings and social events. A local coal company has become a business partner of Atenville School and has made a contribution of $1,000.

For Further Information Contact

Mrs. Darlene Dalton, Principal
Atenville Elementary School
Rte. 2, Box 28
Harts, WV 25524
(304) 855–3173

PARENT INSTITUTE FOR QUALITY EDUCATION
Balboa Elementary School
San Diego, CA

Major Components:
> Parent Institute Training Program
> Parent Room
> Parent Coordinator
> Governance Team

Special Features:
> Parent empowerment
> Communication between parent and child

Profile of School:

Enrollment in Balboa Elementary School	1,190
% of students from Latino families	83%
% of low-income families	98%

The **goals** of the program are:

- To help parents understand the school system in the U.S.;
- To help parents help their children at home;
- To establish better communication between parent and child, help parents recognize the needs of the child, and show them how to empower the child;
- To help parents communicate better with the school, to talk with their child's teacher at least once a month to monitor the progress of the child; and
- To improve the achievement level of minority children.

BACKGROUND

Balboa Elementary School is located in an isolated community. The school provides the only recreational area in the community, since the one park in the area cannot be used by children because of drug activity. The social service agencies needed by the population are located outside of the area.

One of the major activities in Balboa's parent involvement program is the 6-week parent training course, offered by the Parent Institute for Quality Education. The course was offered twice in 1989, once each in 1990 and 1991, and a fifth session is scheduled for the 1992–1993 school year.

The Parent Institute for Quality Education is directed by Vahac Mardirosian, whose family fled from Armenia to Tijuana, Mexico, to escape Turkish persecution. Mardirosian became a minister in the Mexican Baptist Church, and has been active as a parent advocate and parent trainer since retiring from his church in 1986. His "passion is to teach dispossessed parents the ins and outs of America's educational system so they won't be afraid to be active forces in it."

Since 1987, the Parent Institute for Quality Education has provided training to nearly 3,000 parents, the majority of them Latino. In 1991, the San Diego City School District signed a 3-year contract with the Parent Institute to work with 6,000 Hispanic parents in 32 southeast San Diego schools.

DESCRIPTION OF THE PROGRAM

The Parent Institute invites all parents in the school to attend 6 weeks of classes. Traditionally, 20%-40% respond and are present at the training session. During the fall 1992 session, a total of 132 parents, including mothers and fathers, completed the program.

All of the studies in the parent involvement literature demonstrate that when parents participate in school their children do better. Since two out of three Latino children are below grade level, parent involvement can be a potent force in improving student achievement and encouraging Hispanic students to stay in school and not drop out.

Components of the Program

Parent Institute Training Program

Staff from the Parent Institute begin their work with a meeting of the entire school to inform administrators and teachers what they will be doing and to enlist their support and assistance. They schedule two planning meetings with parents to find out their major concerns. The six topics provoking the most interest become the subjects of the classes. The subjects covered might include child growth and development, how to discipline children, teaching at home, how the school works, parents' rights, how to help children succeed in school, self-esteem, drug abuse, and how to work with teachers.

The Parent Institute conducts a very intensive effort to get parents interested in attending the sessions. They compile a list of all parents and send a letter to each family informing it about the program. Every parent also receives a phone call to urge him/her to attend. The Parent Institute recruits parents from other schools who went through the program to give testimonials about its effectiveness.

At the sessions parents are provided with handouts of material to read and use. The classes have been offered in Spanish and Cambodian, depending on the needs of the parents involved. Child care is provided during the sessions, which are scheduled during the day and in the evening.

At the end of the course, parents receive a diploma at a formal ceremony attended by many leaders and educators in the community.

Following the Parent Institute sessions, the teachers and administrators are requested to follow a specified course of action to build on what the Parent Institute has begun and keep parents involved in the school. Principals are expected to invite parents to the school regularly to discuss their children's progress. Parents are encouraged to visit their child's classrooms. School nurses and counselors will work with parents on such subjects as behavior modification in their children and health maintenance. Workshops and home learning activities are sponsored by the school to reinforce the education of the child.

The Parent Institute also provides follow-up for each parent who graduates from the program. A newsletter, containing news, testimonials, and items of interest to parents, is sent each month. If invited, staff from the Institute will return to the school to conduct further training.

Other Parent Involvement Activities

In addition to the Parent Institute series, the school has the following parent involvement activities:

- Paid parent coordinator;
- Parent Room at the school, where parents come to meet other parents and share ideas;
- Governance Team, consisting of 24 members (12 parents and 12 teachers and principals), to address school programs and policies;
- Parent Club, led by a community volunteer (this organization was formed because the PTA is considered too formal);
- Volunteer program, including training for work in the classroom.

Parent Involvement in Planning, Operating, and Monitoring

Parents are involved in the planning meetings for the training, and have substantial input on the topics to be covered in the course. Parents comprise half of the membership of the Governance Team formed to discuss school programs and policies. They have discussed the school's discipline policy, and are also considering efforts to raise student achievement levels.

Strengths and Weaknesses

The most successful aspect of the program is the better communication between home and school. The parents are now more involved with the classroom teacher; they come in prepared to ask more and better questions. The Parent Institute emphasizes that if the child is not succeeding, it is the parent's responsibility to get involved. It is hoped that the training for more parent involvement at the elementary school level will carry over into middle school and high school where parent participation tends to decline.

The Parent Institute has been successful in reaching some parents which the school could not. It makes many personal calls to parents, and, as an organization outside of the schools, is able to convince parents to attend the meetings and become more involved.

The program often has difficulty finding enough space to serve all the parents who are interested in attending. The Parent Institute could run four or five classes in the building at once. The daytime classes often have 100–150 persons in attendance. The night classes for working parents may attract as many as 150 persons. Better facilities are needed to reach all of the parents who might benefit from the program.

Evaluation and Outcomes

No formal evaluation of the Parent Institute program has been undertaken, although parents are constantly praising the program. Many improvements in attitudes and practices have been observed, as a result of the parent training by the Institute. The teachers have begun to welcome parents into the classroom—there is now an extra chair or two for visitors. Teachers now realize that the parents are very interested in their children's education and, therefore, feel positive toward the parents.

As a result of attending the Parent Institute sessions, parents are better informed about school policies and practices. They attend more school events and visit the school more often than before the training.

Budget and Funding

The Parent Institute bills the schools a minimal amount for the parent training sessions and raises the remainder of the money it needs from private donations. The Parent Institute has received $5,000 to provide the program at a single school. The 3-year contract with the San Diego School District places the cost of training at 32 schools at $600,000.

The only cost to the individual school is the purchase of refreshments for the parents and costs of child care during the classes.

For Further Information Contact

Margarita Carmona, Principal
Balboa Elementary School
1844 So. 40th St.
San Diego, CA 92113
(619) 263–8151

PARENTS, TEACHERS & CHILDREN WORKING TOGETHER
Bergen Beach School–P.S. 312
Brooklyn, NY

Major Components:
>Family-School Meetings
>Family-School Workshops
>Teacher and staff training

Special Features:
>Inclusion of child in all conferences
>Student empowerment

Profile of School and School District:

Number of students enrolled school district	26,500
Number of schools in district	
Elementary schools	21
Junior high schools	5
Number of students enrolled in school	852
% from African-American families	30%
% from Latino families	3%
% from Asian-American families	2%
% from White families	65%
% with limited English	2%
% from low-income families	37%
% bused from other neighborhoods	25%

The **goals** of the program are:

- To train teachers, guidance counselor, and administrators to be able to work with parents and students, in a nonconfrontational, problem solving way;
- To change the attitudes of teachers and parents away from an adversarial perspective to one of partners and team members; and
- To enhance learning and student achievement.

BACKGROUND

This program was started in 1988, when P.S. 312 was invited to participate in a training program, sponsored by Family-School Collaboration Project of the Ackerman Institute of New York City, to promote greater parent involvement in the school. The Ackerman Institute is a private, nonprofit organization for training and research. The school district contracted with the Ackerman Institute to make the program available to those principals who chose to participate. The principal of P.S. 312 was pleased to have the opportunity to participate, and requested that all of the teachers at her school take part in the training. In September 1988, the principal, teachers, and guidance counselor began to put the ideas learned from the training sessions into practice in the school.

DESCRIPTION OF THE PROGRAM

P.S. 312 is located in a middle class neighborhood with a majority of white, traditional two-parent families living in single family homes. In addition to serving the children from the area, P.S. 312 also enrolls a number of children from outside of the neighborhood who are bused in. The total enrollment of 852 for the 1992–1993 school year includes 150 children in special education classes. About 25% of the children attending the school arrive by bus from other areas, as a result of an open enrollment policy which allows parents to choose P.S. 312 and an effort to alleviate overcrowding in other schools in the district.

The parent involvement program emphasizes ways in which teachers and administrators can approach parents in order to promote partnerships between school and family. The partnership concept is implemented both at the individual level and at a group or school level. It is put into practice through interactions between teacher, parent, and student in meetings called to solve a problem or face a difficult situation. It is reflected in group meetings, planned and attended by all members of the school community.

This is an ongoing program. Ackerman Institute staff may conduct additional training of teachers and other school personnel. The program does not require additional full-time, regular staff, since all persons at the school are expected to utilize the process for establishing and nurturing partnerships with parents.

One of the major features of the partnership efforts at P.S. 312 is the inclusion of the child in all school meetings, including those dealing with problems associated with the students and meetings where social events for families are being planned.

Components of the Program

Teacher and Staff Training

The training, provided by the Ackerman Institute, emphasizes two key ingredients for improved family/school relationships: (1) family-school meetings as problem solving techniques; and (2) climate building activities intended to improve the atmosphere of the school and raise the morale of the teachers and parents.

Those participating in the training learn techniques for conducting successful meetings, how to put the parent and child at ease, ways to discuss a problem without the need to place blame on anyone, and ideas for constructive solutions.

Family-School Meetings

These are held when an individual child is having a behavior problem or an academic problem. Present are the teacher, the parent(s), the child, and the principal or principal's designee (guidance counselor, assistant principal, or school psychologist). The parent is expected to talk with the child before the meeting to prepare him/her to address the issue.

The meetings follow a plan intended to help the parents and child feel at ease and encourage everyone to speak honestly. The meeting begins with an introductory statement that this is not a meeting because the child was "bad," but rather to consider a situation which may be impeding the child's education. A brief report of what is going well with the child is followed by a discussion of the "concern," what is not going well with the child.

The meeting ends with a proposed plan specifying what all those present, including the child, are going to do to help solve the problem. The student plays a key role in the process, both in expressing his/her explanation of the reasons for the problem and in proposing a solution. Incentives are planned as positive reinforcement for the child's following through on the actions agreed to at the meeting. These might include special privileges at home or school, such as working on the computer, being a lunchtime monitor, or working as an office monitor. Material incentives are discouraged.

After the meeting, thank you notes are sent by the principal to those participating. The parent is asked to complete an evaluation of the meeting, what he/she liked and disliked, and how it could have been improved. A follow-up meeting is scheduled for a time 4–6 weeks in the future to review the progress made in solving the problem.

Family-School Workshops

This component of the program was designed by the P.S. 312 staff as a strategy for improving the school climate. Six or eight workshops are scheduled for the school year, intended for parents, children, and teachers. A Planning Committee, composed of parents, teachers, children, and administrators, meets once a month to plan the workshops. They conduct a survey of parents at the beginning of the year to gather suggestions for topics for the workshops. The purposes of the workshops are to increase parent involvement, to enhance parent support of the school, and to build partnerships between families and the school.

No one is required to attend the Family-School Workshops, but the number of persons present may total from 250–500. The flyers sent home to families announcing the meetings ask the parents to register if they are planning to come so that the Committee has an idea about how many sessions to plan.

The workshops are scheduled from 6:45 p.m. to 9:00 p.m. The participants meet altogether for a few minutes at the beginning of the meeting to learn about the plan of the workshop. From 7:00 p.m. until 8:30 p.m. parents, children, and teachers are participating in the workshop they have chosen. The last half hour is for refreshments and socializing.

All members of the family are invited; children who attend with their parents are excused from homework for the next day and teachers are careful not to schedule any tests following the workshop night. The workshops are not lectures, but include presentations, discussion groups, and activities designed to appeal to the family and to the teachers at the school. Workshops may be led by teachers, parents, or persons from the community, depending on the topics covered.

The attendance at the first Family-School Workshop totaled 500, far higher than the 150 expected by the school. The Committee realized that it must plan for a number of workshops to accommodate the large number of participants. One of the topics for the Family-School Workshop during the 1992–1993 school year was Family Science Night. Those attending were divided into workshops corresponding to the grade levels at the school: K-1, 2–3, 4–5, and a combination one for parents with several children in the school. The parent(s) and child both attend the workshop. The content of each is designed to be appropriate to the grade level of the children participating.

Parent Involvement in Planning, Operating, and Monitoring

Parents are involved with the planning of the Family-School Workshops and some parents assist with the presentations or activities at the workshops. Parents are consulted at the beginning of the year, through the survey, concerning the topics to be addressed at the workshops. Parents, of course, are present at the Family-School Meetings, convened to discuss a problem situation with their child. The traditional approach to parent involvement would include parent and teacher in such meetings; the unusual factor in this approach is that the child is always present at the meetings. If there are siblings in the school, they attend the meetings also.

In addition to the Family-School Workshops Committee, other groups are active in the school, including a Curriculum Committee and a Parent Liaison Committee which works with the Parent Association.

The principal does not support the idea that the school should be run by a committee. She is the leader of the school and intends to make final decisions and take responsibility for them. However, she is committed to the concept that everyone who might be affected by a decision must be consulted, and insists that all committees set up in the school have parent and student representation.

The acceptance of parents and students on all committees and the presence of students at family-school meetings has taken a long time to realize. It is a gradual process; it represents a major shift from traditional, conventional parent involvement and cannot be rushed. Some of the schools which originally participated in the training provided by the Ackerman Institute have not been able to implement the components successfully. The commitment of the principal at P.S. 312 has been a major factor in convincing the teachers to accept children as part of the family-school partnership and to include parents and students in all school committees and decisions.

Strengths and Weaknesses

The Family-School Workshops have been a huge success; everybody is involved in the planning and many assist on the night of the workshop. The topics are chosen by all, and reflect what families are interested in learning about. The teachers support the workshops, often attend them, and also adjust the homework and tests for their classes to accommodate the fact that children are expected to attend the workshops.

The Family-School Meetings are also considered an effective way of dealing with problems individual students may be having. At the beginning, there was opposition from both teachers and parents to having students present at the meetings. Both groups were accustomed to talking about the child's problems without his/her presence. As parents and teachers see the positive outcomes of this process, as they see that the child's problem is alleviated, they become supportive of the process.

One example of the type of problem addressed by the

Family-School Meeting concerns a preschool-age child who regularly cried at the beginning of school. At the meeting the child told those present about a frightening experience her family had during the summer, where they were robbed at gunpoint. Apparently, she was still upset by this event and very anxious about being left by her parents at school. Following the meeting, the child did not cry before school again.

A second example concerns the issue of homework, which is one of the common topics for the family-school meetings. The 4th grader was rarely doing her homework, so a Family-School Meeting was arranged. From the discussion at the meeting, it became clear that there was no set routine at home to provide a structure to encourage the completion of homework. The parent and child both agreed to the suggestions from the teacher about procedures and routines to institute at home. The objective was to have the child take the responsibility for the homework, but to have a set of structures to support the process.

One of the problems encountered in the implementation of this program is the difficulty in scheduling Family-School Meetings. The principal attempts to plan them during daytime hours, but must then have a substitute in the classroom for the teacher who attends the meeting. Coverage is sometimes arranged through support personnel. Additional funding would make the scheduling of the meetings easier.

Because of overcrowded schools in parts of the school district, a number of students, all from minority families, are bused into P.S. 312. Efforts are being made to increase the attendance of these families at the Family-School Workshops by using a school bus to pick up family members for the workshops.

Another group of families whose participation in the school should be strengthened are those with children in special education classes. Many of these children are bused to P.S. 312 from other parts of the district. The principal is considering proposals and ideas for increasing the involvement of those parents in the school.

Outcomes and Evaluation

There has been a large increase in the number of parents attending programs; previously about 5–15 parents were expected at the Parent Association meetings. Now the number attending the Family-School Workshops is in the hundreds. Those present, including parents, students, and teachers, are asked to evaluate the workshops, and make suggestions which are used in planning future programs.

Both parents and teachers have begun to accept the presence of students at meetings. Student attitudes toward the school and academic achievement of those students involved in a Family-School Meeting have shown marked improvement. Parents feel more comfortable in the school and may learn more effective ways of listening to their children and working with them to solve problems, as a result of their experiences in the Family-School Meetings.

Budget and Funding

Teachers at P.S. 312 volunteer to assist in planning and running the Family-School Workshops. Parent volunteers also help with all aspects of the programs. The Parent Association provides some funds for expenses associated with the Workshops. Additional funds would be useful to pay for substitute teachers in the classrooms while the teachers attend Family-School Meetings, and to provide transportation so that families living a distance from the school could attend the Family-School Workshops.

For Further Information Contact

Ellen Flanagan, Principal
Parents, Teachers & Children Working Together
Bergen Beach School
P.S. 312
7103 Avenue T
Brooklyn, NY 11234
(718) 763–4015

GRAHAM & PARKS ALTERNATIVE SCHOOL
Cambridge, MA

Major Components:
> Parent involvement in decision making
> Parent Council
> Parent and community involvement in the classroom
> Parent Coordinator

Special Features:
> Democracy
> Empowerment
> Outreach to Haitian Population

Profile of School and School District:

	Cambridge Public Schools	Graham & Parks School
Total Students	8,023	380
% White	46%	48%
% African-American	31%	14%
% Haitian		25%
% Latino	16%	10%
% Asian-American	8%	3%

Number of Schools in Cambridge	15
Elementary Schools (K-8)	14
High School	
(2200 students in 6	
administrative houses)	1

% on Free Lunch	60%
% from outside neighborhood	50%

The **vision** of the Graham & Parks Alternative Public School is: "Building a Democratic School Community."

The **mission statement** of the Graham & Parks Alternative Public School includes:

> We build the school in the only way it can be built: out of the relationships of the people who live and work and interact here, out of our ideas, out of our work, and out of our struggles. . . .

BACKGROUND

The philosophy of this parent involvement program was developed by a group of parents in the early 1970s. Their preschool-age children had been in cooperative nursery schools and they wanted to continue the same kind of involvement as their children entered the public schools. This was before the current emphasis on parent involvement, so these parents had to design their own system to achieve their goal of involving all of the parents in the school. An article by Gary Putka, in the December 30, 1991, issue of *The Wall Street Journal*, describes the inception of the school:

> The school was launched in 1972 . . . to answer the demands of liberal parents who wanted a place for student "cooperation, not competition," where "parents . . . are welcomed and urged to contribute to the classroom," and where a "definite policy" would ensure "ethnic, social and economic diversity."

In 1981, the current Graham & Parks Alternative Public School was created, the result of joining two schools, the Cambridge Alternative Public School (a small, magnet school which was the original program) and the Webster School, a small, traditional neighborhood school. This alternative school was the first school of choice in Cambridge, even before a comprehensive choice plan was implemented.

DESCRIPTION OF THE PROGRAM

The Graham & Parks Alternative School is part of the Cambridge, MA, public school system, and, therefore, enrollment is a result of parental choice. The school serves students in grades K-8, and enrolls about 380 students. Half of the students come from outside of the neighborhood and are bused.

The mission/vision statement of the school includes the following:

> We are responsible for building, developing, making our school. The "we" includes staff, parents, admin-

istrator, students, and community people; the "we" involves cooperation and collegiality. . . .

We believe in *democracy*, in participatory and representative democracy. This involves developing *structures* that enable shared decision-making among administrator, parents, staff and students to occur so that all parties are fairly represented in an equal manner, in a system of checks and balances.

Parent involvement is completely integrated into all aspects of the school program; it is not viewed as a separate aspect. The school was conceived by parents, and parents continue to play a major role in the day-to-day operation of the school. "Parents have eyes and ears and hands; they have skills, ideas, and connections with the business and political communities."

The Parent Coordinator has major responsibility for the parent involvement program, but all staff at the school are constantly looking for ways in which parents can be involved in the classrooms as well as in the administration and decision making of the school.

Components of the Program

Parent Involvement in Decision Making

The Steering Committee is the school's policymaking body. It is composed of five staff members, five parents, the principal, and the Parent Coordinator. The five slots each for parents and staff are designed to promote a balanced view. One slot of each is for a bilingual person, one for a minority, two for majority, and the fifth may be from any of the above categories. They are selected at an election held in January. Any and all topics can come to the Steering Committee for discussion: hiring, curriculum, grade structure, student placement, discipline, building and grounds, program evaluation, and many other issues. Each member has one vote, and the principal cannot override the committee's decision, though most are reached by consensus.

This committee meets twice a month, in the evening,

and sets policy for the school, consistent with provisions in the teachers' contract and policies determined by the district's School Committee (the local school board). The Steering Committee has created various committees to help with the work; each committee usually is composed of equal numbers of staff and parents. Committees include Fund Raising, Hiring, Curriculum, Program Evaluation, Building and Grounds, Bilingual, School Literary Magazine, Arts Collaborative, and Race and Class.

Recent activities of the Race and Class Committee demonstrate the type of issues addressed by the school. This committee was set up to examine questions related to social class, race, and achievement. They brought in a consultant to make sure that the children from working class families and minority families are achieving up to the level of middle class children.

The Hiring Committee has the responsibility for interviewing and participating in the selection of all staff in the school, from the secretary to the principal.

Parent Council

The Parent Council is a monthly meeting of only parents, equivalent to the PTA in many schools. It is intended as a structure to balance the monthly staff meeting. All parents are voting members. The Parent Council plans and designs programs to meet the needs of the parents. This might include a presentation from a teacher on how a particular subject is taught, an outside speaker on child development, and a seminar on how parents can help with the education of their children at home. The bilingual parents have a separate Bilingual Parent Advisory Committee (PAC) which discusses issues relevant to the bilingual classes.

Parent and Community Involvement in Classroom and School

Classrooms at the school routinely have parents and other volunteers on hand, reading to children, working with computers, tutoring one-on-one, or running art projects. In kindergarten classes, the teachers have a regular schedule of parents who come in to provide special help for children. There is a special art program for grades K-2, in which two parents per class are trained to help the art teachers. Around holiday times, parents from different cultures are invited to do projects or make presentations about their customs.

Parents are consulted by the principal and teachers about decisions concerning their child's placement in school. Two parent/teacher conferences are scheduled yearly for each student to provide an opportunity for a formal review of the child's progress in school. The report cards do not contain traditional grades, but each teacher writes a narrative progress report sent to the parents prior to the parent-teacher conference.

At the 7th and 8th grade levels, parents play an important role in helping to identify and arrange for apprenticeships and/or community service for the students. Many parents offer their worksites for students to learn about and participate in a particular work experience.

Teachers are always being encouraged to design new ways for parents to be involved in the classroom. Parents have been included in the development of thematic units in grades 1 and 2. Parents assisted staff in designing social studies units for the 7th and 8th grades.

Parents have been very active in raising money for the school, raising a total of $15,000-$25,000 each year. One of their most successful projects is selling Christmas trees, which raises $5,000-$6,000 a year. A separate foundation has been formed as a mechanism for raising funds for the school. The parents have also helped prepare a proposal for a grant to provide science equipment for the school.

The Graham & Parks Alternative School benefits from the involvement of a number of persons and organizations from the community. When district budget cuts resulted in the cutting of the counselor position at the school, the principal recruited 15 graduate students from a local university to come in and assist with the counseling needs. The school has a business partnership with LOTUS, and also collaborates with the Harvard Law School on the Big Brothers and Big Sisters program and with MIT on a Computer Design Lab. Thirty-five graduate students from the Kennedy School of Government at Harvard volunteer at the school each week. A number of educational consulting agencies work with the school on a variety of science and math projects. The community volunteers include many participating in the Foster Grandparents Program.

Parent Coordinator

The role of the Parent Coordinator is mainly one of support for the parents: orienting new parents to the school, assisting parents with a concern or complaint to resolve the situation, and placing all volunteers. She also is the one responsible for reaching out to parents reluctant to take an active role in their children's education. The Coordinator works closely with the Principal and the Staff Developer, and serves on the Administrator Committee, the Steering Committee, the Parent Council, the Grievance Committee and the Fund Raising Committee. Each classroom has its own Room Parent, who reports back to the school's Parent Coordinator.

Communication

Dialogue between parents and teachers is a major objective of the parent involvement program at the school. Two or three notices are sent home weekly. "Notice" refers to the frequent communications from teacher to parents to give parents a better understanding of the classroom, assist them to find ways in which they might help, and allow them the chance to share or participate in their children's education. The Parent Coordinator is responsible for the parent notices at the school-wide level.

The classroom meeting is another means for communication. The first meeting is held early in the school year: the teacher talks about homework expectations, curriculum, ways parents can help at home or in the classroom, and other topics pertinent to that grade/class. This meeting also gives parents the chance to know each other and set up an informal network for support.

Outreach to Haitian Population

At the present time the large number of Haitian families with children in the school has necessitated different approaches. The notes from the school to the parents are prepared in three languages—English, Haitian-Creole, and Spanish. Meetings specifically for the Haitian parents are scheduled monthly on Sunday evenings, the most convenient time for that group. Out of the 60 Haitian families in the school, there are usually between 20 and 50 in attendance at the meetings. A Haitian Parent Liaison provides assistance with translations back and forth at the meetings. A dozen staff members speak Creole, so they are able to communicate with the Haitian parents.

Many of the Haitian students come to this country from conditions of extreme poverty, often suffering from malnutrition, with no previous education, limited literacy in Creole, and no knowledge of English. The principal, teachers, and parent coordinator have learned that they have to make an extra effort with the Haitian parents, due to their apprehensiveness about authority figures. School officials are also aware of the tradition of harsh discipline in the families and try, through parent education, to provide parents with suggestions and support for discipline policies which are less physical and less severe. The teachers have introduced courses and classes to the whole school in Haitian language and culture. English classes are also offered in the evening to the Haitian parents.

Strengths and Weaknesses

Those in the school believe that parent involvement in the school has led to a high quality school. They are proud of the achievement of their students, who score in the 85–95 percentile in math and reading on the CAT tests. An impressive 90% of the students pass all the state basic skills tests. The attendance rate is 97%.

In the early 1970s, the principal of the school, the teachers, and the parents were called upon to recruit students for the school. They made many presentations at day care centers, churches, and other community gatherings to promote the school and its philosophy. Now the Graham & Parks Alternative School is oversubscribed and has a waiting list consisting of 3 times as many students as the school has space for.

The decision making structure is considered to be a key factor in the school's success. Since it is responsible for hiring, setting policy, funding, curriculum, and all other aspects of the functioning of the school, the Steering Committee is a crucial structure. It serves as the skeleton or the framework and everything builds upon it.

The school has met some resistance from the bureaucracy and hierarchy in the school district, which has not always given full support to the way the school was being operated. It took about 6 years to convince the central administration of the importance of parents and their full participation in all aspects of the governance of the school. The school district officials eventually were impressed both by the success of the students and also by the commitment and intensity of the parents. Many parents whose children attend the Graham & Parks Alternative School became active in school district politics. At one point, four elected members of the School Committee (school board), out of the total of seven, were parents with children in the Graham & Parks School.

The principal, Parent Coordinator, and other staff are continually working to increase and improve parent involvement. They admit that shared decision making is difficult, and results in many clashes and conflicts between diverse points of view, but they remain committed to their vision, and work continually to manage the conflicts and achieve agreement, and often consensus, on the issues.

They are concerned about how parents can become more involved in the curriculum; there have been remarkable successes with some efforts, but others have not met expectations. One difficulty in a school such as Graham & Parks Alternative is that there is no standardized curriculum, only general guidelines, which makes it more difficult to find a specific place for parent participation.

Evaluation and Outcomes

Over the years the characteristics of the families whose children attend the Graham & Parks Alternative School have changed, necessitating a change in the activities and mission of the parent involvement effort. In the case of parents from working class families, transportation and day care are provided to encourage the parents to be involved in the school. It is not always enough to send a note home—often it has to be pinned on the child's shirt. Sometimes a phone call home is necessary.

It is estimated that the proportion of parents actively involved at the present time is about 55%. About 10 years ago, 80% of the parents were actively involved, according to a survey conducted by the Institute for Responsive Education. The decline may be the result of changing family composition and significant increase of mothers in the work force.

Another factor responsible for some of the erosion of parental input is the tension between the teachers' union and the parents. In the early days of the school, parents were active in evaluating the performance of the teachers; however, this practice was eliminated in 1985 after a successful union grievance brought by some of the teachers.

Budget and Funding

No extra school system funds have been available to support the school. Every school in Cambridge has a parent support person, supported by state grant funds, while Graham & Parks' Parent Coordinator is full-time and paid by district funds. However, overall funding for each school is comparable. The Fund Raising Committee has been extremely successful in its efforts and brings in funds which double the materials and supplies budget received by the school from the district allocation.

For Further Information Contact

Dr. Leonard Solo, Principal
Graham & Parks Alternative School
15 Upton St.
Cambridge, MA 02139
(617) 349-6612

FAMILIES TOGETHER
Hawthorne School
Oakland, CA

Major Components:
> Outreach
> ESL Classes—Spanish, Vietnamese, Mien, Laotian, Cambodian
> Primary Language and Literacy Support
> Family Stories
> Parenting Classes

Special Features:
> Support services to immigrant and refugee families
> Multilingual staff
> Multicultural communication and awareness

Profile of School:

Number of children enrolled (K–6)	1,320
% from Latino families	58%
% from Asian-American families	23%
% from African-American families	18%
% from Native American families	1%
% on Free Lunch	90%

The **goals** of the project are:

- To help families overcome language, literacy, and sociocultural difficulties that prevent their full participation in school programs and in U.S. society;
- To promote language and community skills through the writing, recording, publishing, and sharing of family stories; and
- To enhance parenting skills and multicultural understanding.

BACKGROUND

Families Together, started in August 1991, is a Family Literacy Project (FELP) funded by a Title VII grant from the U.S. Office of Bilingual Education and administered by Art, Research, and Curriculum Associates, Inc. (ARC), and the Oakland Unified School District. ARC is a private, nonprofit agency, founded in 1977, and based in Oakland, CA. It provides technical assistance to school districts in Northern California in the area of multicultural education and programs for limited English proficient students. Its mission is to promote educational excellence and equity for students of diverse racial, ethnic, cultural, and linguistic backgrounds.

Families Together is located in Hawthorne School, a neighborhood elementary school, with grades K-6. The project was designed by ARC staff who have extensive experience in multicultural and multilingual programs and staff from Hawthorne School—the principal, the nurse, and several teachers. They utilized knowledge gained from the research on second language acquisition and whole language programs to plan the Families Together program.

DESCRIPTION OF THE PROGRAM

Families Together provides instruction and support service to immigrant and refugee families from Latin America and Southeast Asia. The families of children in the Hawthorne School are targeted for the program, but the classes and workshops are also open to parents and older youth (18–25 years of age) throughout Oakland and the Bay Area, who can benefit from the language, literacy, and parenting classes. The populations served include Latinos, Vietnamese, Mien (a group from Laos), Laotian, Cambodian, African-American, Chinese, Caucasian, Native American, and Filipino.

The staff of Families Together includes a director, outreach coordinator, and instructional assistants. School staff members, including the parent involvement coordinator and the school nurse, serve as liaison between the school, the Families Together program, and the parents, and assist in setting up and conducting the parent workshops. They have experience working with the families in the area, and fluency in the languages of the families in the program. Parents and community members also volunteer for the program.

Components of the Program

Outreach

Information about Families Together and the programs and services it offers is distributed by the school, the teachers, letters sent home with the children, posters in the school and community, and community groups. The effort is made to reach parents through their children in the classroom or by visits and phone calls to the homes. Before the program began, a needs assessment survey was undertaken to learn about the families and what services would best accommodate them and to provide them with information about the programs to be offered. A second survey was conducted following the first year of the program to find out parents' attitudes toward the program and if there were additional unmet needs. The information gained from talking with parents was used to design the program and choose the topics for the parent workshops.

ESL Classes

These are held both during daytime and evening hours, for the convenience of the families. Four different classes are offered—day and evening, beginners and intermediate—but there is still a waiting list. Between 60 and 80 parents attend the classes regularly.

Primary Language and Literacy Support

These classes are designed for parents who have not learned to read or write in their primary language, and are currently offered for Spanish speakers. The literacy skills they learn in their primary language can assist in their learning English. A special support class is held for the Mien parents, since they do not have a written language; they work on the lessons they are learning in the ESL classes.

Family Stories

About 15 persons are active in this group, where parents and family members tell their stories which are then written down and published. The first book published is entitled *Stories and Life Experiences*. This book, printed in both Spanish and English, will be used in adult ESL classes.

Parenting Classes

These are held once a month. Parents are most often grouped into separate language groups and discuss topics of their choosing. Two of the most successful workshop topics are "How to Motivate Your Child," and "Helping Your Child with Reading and Writing." Other topics include "Discipline for Self-Esteem," "Drug and Alcohol Awareness," "Gang Influence," AIDS Awareness and Prevention," and information on school policies and practices.

Summer and Interim Activities

During the summer months and between 10-week sessions, Families Together offers parents and families opportunities for computer training, field trips to such places as the Academy of Sciences in Golden Gate Park, learning American folk songs, playing American board games, and learning about filling in various government forms. A Potluck Supper, organized by parents, included foods from all parts of the world; more than 600 persons attended, including families and teachers.

Special Services for Immigrants and Refugees

These include translation services, providing interpreters between families and schools, and referrals for legal help and social and mental health services.

Parent Involvement in Planning, Operating, and Monitoring

Parents have major responsibility for planning such events as the summer Potluck. They serve as the authors of the books published as a result of the Family Stories effort. Parents in the intermediate and advanced ESL classes are being encouraged to prepare and distribute a newsletter, to use their skills and also improve communication with families and the community.

Strengths and Weaknesses

All of the components have been successful; the number of parents wishing to take the ESL classes exceeds the available openings. Some of the success in attracting parents to the classes and services is attributable to having staff which can speak their language. Cambodian parents began to attend workshops and classes after a staff member was employed who spoke Cambodian and had contacts with organizations and groups in the Cambodian community.

The program has experienced some difficulty in attracting Asian-Americans to the services and classes, because of the cultural differences in the way Asian parents respond to the outreach techniques. The strategies used for Cambodian, Laotian, or Vietnamese parents are different from those for Hispanic families. Staff must be sensitive to those differences and willing to adjust accordingly.

Asian-Americans tend to be shy and reserved at the classes and workshops, whereas Latino parents are more outgoing and talkative. The staff has also noticed gender differences in attendance patterns; men from Asian-American families have been less likely to participate in the Families Together activities. Some Latino men seem to become active and attend more when the teacher of the language or literacy classes is male.

Because of the large demand for additional ESL and literacy classes, instructional assistants have been trained to assume some of the teaching duties, and the Oakland Adult School is providing an instructor. It is important that new staff receive training in how to work with people from several diverse cultural backgrounds. Two other personnel issues are (1) that all of the staff are employed on a part-time basis and (2) that ARC is the sponsoring organization and, therefore, the employer of the staff of Families Together. Both of these factors make supervision and coordination of classes and programs a challenge.

Staff at ARC are constantly encouraging the Families Together program to expand, to develop collaborations with many local community groups, and to bring more outside services into the program. This is necessary if the program is to continue after Title VII funding ends in 1994.

Outcomes and Evaluation

Changes in attitudes and behavior of both teachers and parents have been observed as a result of the Families Together project. The teachers in the Hawthorne School are supportive of the program and are becoming more aware of which parents are active in the classes and workshops. Many teachers inform the staff of Families Together about incidents and events concerning the children of those parents.

Some of the parents are able to go into the classroom of their children as a result of the workshops which provide them with information about the school and their rights and responsibilities. One parent relates that she always dreaded going to school herself and would have headaches and a knot in her stomach every time she was near the school. These physical symptoms are no longer present, and she can enter her child's school and classroom without fear and dread.

Budget and Funding

The Families Together program is currently funded at $145,000 per year, through a Title VII (Bilingual Education Act) federal grant to ARC. In addition, the Oakland Unified School district provides in-kind contributions, including space in the library of Hawthorne School, and pays for a portion of staff salaries.

For Further Information Contact

Angela Barra
Families Together
Hawthorne School
1700 28th Ave.
Oakland, CA 94601
(510) 261-3257

ROCKAWAY NEW SCHOOL
Rockaway, NY

Major Components:
> Parent volunteers
> Open and accessible classrooms
> Steering Committee
> Parent meetings

Special Features:
> School within a School

Profile of School:

Number of Children Enrolled in P.S. 183	650
Number of Children Enrolled in Rockaway New School	187
% from African-American families	75%
% from Latino families	15%
% from White families	10%
% from low-income families	100%
(Majority are from public housing projects.)	

The **goals** of the school are:

- To improve the educational process;
- To improve the dialogue between parents and teachers; and
- To share a vision and develop a working relationship of joint partnership between teachers and parents.

BACKGROUND

During the summer of 1990, ACORN (Association of Community Organizations for Reform Now), a private, non-profit community organization, began building an organization of low- to moderate-income parents on the Rockaways Peninsula in Queens, NY. An ACORN organizer contacted several of the local school Parent Associations and began the process of knocking on .doors in every low-income housing project and neighborhood in the area. One-by-one residents were asked how they felt about the schools and given a chance to join ACORN. As more and more people joined, parents recruited other parents with petitions at supermarkets and more door knocking.

A series of meetings were scheduled—in community centers, churches, homes—to discuss complaints and criticisms of the educational process and to plan strategies for action to improve the schools. Groups were organized with parents from six elementary schools; 30–40 persons regularly attended the meetings.

During the winter of 1991, ACORN members participated in training sessions, utilizing material from effective schools research and the Chicago-based Designs for Change. In addition to leadership development, the sessions explored such issues as reading, testing, tracking, and other academic concerns of parents. Some of the parents were able to visit restructured schools. From their discussions and school visits, ACORN members developed a list of "key ingredients" they wanted in their children's schools. The list included alternative forms of assessment, heterogeneous groupings instead of tracking, hands-on learning, collaboration among teachers, and other qualities of the schools parents had visited.

ACORN members took this list to the then Acting Superintendent Josephine Schwindt, asking her to work with them to establish a school, mini-school, or section within a school reflecting these principles. Mrs. Schwindt told the parents she shared their vision of quality education. She circulated the parents' proposal to principals throughout the district, encouraging them to meet with parents. Most importantly, she identified a group of four teachers who had been working collaboratively in one school, but wanted to expand their efforts to higher grades and were looking for a new home school. She suggested P.S. 183 as a potentially supportive school, with several empty classrooms. The principal, while unenthusiastic about the proposal, was ready to retire and did not actively oppose the mini-school. The PA president was an ACORN member and supported the idea.

In addition, the superintendent offered the assistance of a staff person from the district office, Kathleen Woychowski. Ms. Woychowski, an experienced staff developer, had originally brought the four teachers together and worked extensively with them to develop the mini-school at their previous site.

Leslie Mahoney, a teacher already at P.S. 183, was recruited to join the mini-school and became teacher-director of the school. The teachers, the school Parents Association president, and several ACORN parents formed the School Planning Committee. They refined their plans at a week-long Summer Institute sponsored by The Center for Collaborative Education, and began recruiting students by going door-to-door in the neighboring housing projects and by talking to people outside a local supermarket. After only one day, they had signatures from 300 parents who wanted a change in the schools and the names of 100 children, grades K-5, whose parents were interested in enrolling them in a new alternative school.

There are many characteristics which the parents wished to see in their new school: open classrooms, collaboration between parents and teachers, cooperative learning, multigrade classrooms, a high level of parent involvement in the school, and shared decision making within the program.

DESCRIPTION OF THE PROGRAM

In the 1992–1993 school year, the Rockaway New School has 187 children enrolled in grades K-6. Students are enrolled on a first-come, first-serve basis. The parents of those who apply and are accepted are expected to be active participants in the school. The staff at Rockaway New School are supportive of the New York City choice plan which is being implemented in the fall of 1993, because it will mean that students from outside their attendance zone will be permitted to enroll in their school.

The New School expects to add about 15–20 students each year for the next 2 years and to extend the program through grades 7 and 8, but does not want total enrollment to exceed 250 children. They have multigrade classrooms, open classroom structure, and utilize cooperative learning.

One teacher-director and six other teachers are responsible for the academic program. A parent involvement coordinator from ACORN assists with organizing parent volunteers and working with community groups.

Components of the Program

Parent Volunteers

A total of 30–35 parents are active volunteers in the school. Groups of parents work with children in the classroom on such activities as cooking and reading. They are also asked to assist the teachers when groups of students go on field trips.

Open and Accessible Classrooms

Teachers are available to talk with parents before and after school. Parents are welcome in the classroom at any time.

Steering Committee

Parents and teachers (five to six of each) volunteer to serve on this committee which meets once a month to set the policies for the Rockaway New School.

Parent Meetings

The parents meet once a month to discuss topics of interest, including curriculum.

Community Issues

These are addressed by the teachers and parents as a school/community collaboration.

Family Outreach Worker

This job has been performed by a parent volunteer, but it is proposed that the position be formalized and paid, with a parent working on it 4 hours a day.

Communications

In addition to regular newsletters, frequent notices are sent home to parents to keep them informed on everything that is happening in the school. The report cards for the children are more than just forms with letters on them; they include long, detailed observations about the child's strengths and weaknesses.

Parent Involvement in Planning, Operating, and Monitoring

Parents are included in every aspect of the Rockaway New School. They can help in the classroom, be a part of shared decision making on the Steering Committee, and be a partner with the school to ensure that their children succeed in school. Some days the number of parents wanting to help out exceeds the space available and there are not enough appropriate activities for all volunteers.

The teacher-director is learning that the parent involvement may have to be more structured and scheduled than she originally had planned. Some thought and planning is being devoted to specifying how many parents are needed for which duties at what hours of the day. As parents begin to understand the school schedule more fully, they will be able to be present when they are most needed.

Ideally, parents will be able to take over some of the instructional duties; the school has been experimenting with parents teaching lessons as the head of the classroom. Some parents have the talent, background, and skills to do this, but others do not. More time and training are needed in order to achieve the team approach, with both parents and teachers participating.

Strengths and Weaknesses

The most successful and satisfying aspects of the program come from listening to parents: they are supporting the school, they are excited as they see their children succeed in school, there is hope in their voices as they talk about their children's education. It is wonderful to hear parents defending Rockaway New School when something derogatory is said about it. It is also exciting to watch parents take responsibility for the school, by participating in decision making.

Some parents are extremely dedicated to the school and stay involved continually. Others do not have the time, energy, or confidence to be regular volunteers in the school.

The least successful experiences have been in trying to get the administration and teachers in P.S. 183, in which Rockaway is housed, to understand and accept the new school-within-a-school. The teachers in the new school have observed much division and conflict between the "main" school and themselves. Those in the regular school say inaccurate and uncomplimentary things about the children who attend the new school; they imply that this is a school for slow children, perhaps because the majority of the children are from public housing projects.

The P.S. 183 educators are not accustomed to the many parents who regularly come to the Rockaway New School to assist in the classroom. There has been some resentment on the part of P.S. 183 staff toward the parents over the use of the copy machine. The P.S. 183 staff consider parents as an inconvenience and, therefore, are not cordial and welcoming to those working at the Rockaway New School.

The parents, teachers, and students at Rockaway New School use their own stairway, located close to the front door, to go to their part of the building. They do share the lunchroom, but the students from the New School tend to eat at separate tables from the P.S. 183 students. New School parents

serve as lunchroom supervisors for their students, while the
P.S. 183 students are largely unsupervised.

District officials, including the new superintendent and
the school board president, are extremely supportive of the
Rockaway New School and have regularly offered to help.
They have asked that one ACORN employee and an ACORN
parent member join a task force formed to restructure the
middle schools in the district. These school officials also
provided support and assistance to the Rockaway New School
when it was expanded to include additional grades.

The teachers union (United Federation of Teachers-
UFT) has expressed concerns over how jobs are posted at the
school and whether union representatives were consulted in
the process of developing the Rockaway New School. The
leadership of the union supports some of the school reform
efforts, particularly at the high school level.

One difficulty the school has had is in finding space for
the evening meetings of parent groups and committees. The
school will not remain open in the evenings; they often hold
their meetings at the ACORN office, located in a little building
near the school, and sometimes they meet in the homes of
parents.

Outcomes and Evaluation

Before the Rockaway New School was started, there
was little participation from the parents of the students who
attend; now there is much parent involvement. Before there
were very few meetings for parents, and very few parents in
attendance. Now there are typically 30 parents at the meetings.
The parents have pride in their school and in their children;
they had definitely not felt this before the new school was
opened. The parents believe that what they say makes a
difference; they have become empowered to take responsibility
for the education of their children. Their self-confidence and
self-esteem have improved.

The teachers are specially selected and strongly support
the concept of parents as partners. Although there has not been
a formal evaluation of the program, it is evident that student
achievement has improved: about 30% of the children are

performing significantly better; 40% are showing some progress; but for 30% of the children, the achievement is still marginal.

The Rockaway New School is affiliated with the Center for Collaborative Education in New York City, which has provided training for parents and teachers, and will be documenting and monitoring the design and operation of the school.

Budget and Funding

The Rockaway New School receives its basic funding from the regular school budget. It has also been given a $25,000 grant from the Diamond Foundation. The ACORN Organizer assists with the parent organizing activities of the school; her salary and expenses are paid by the ACORN organization.

For Further Information Contact

Leslie Mahoney, Teacher-Director
Helene O'Brien, ACORN Parent Organizer
Rockaway New School   NY ACORN
2–45 Beach 79th Street   845 Flatbush
Rockaway Beach, NY 11693   Brooklyn, NY 11226
(718) 634–9458   (718) 693–6700

QEP PARENT INVOLVEMENT PROJECT
Rolling Fork Elementary School
Rolling Fork, MS

Major Components:
> Parent Pledge
> QEP Student Folders
> Parent Seminars
> Back-to-School Night
> Parent Resource Center

Special Features:
> Training for administrators, teachers, and parents
> Resource manuals and other printed materials
> Monitoring; Evaluation

Profile of School and School District:

Number of children in school	2,000
Number of schools in district	4
Elementary schools (K–6)	2
High schools (7–12)	2
Number of children in Rolling Fork School	725
Number of families	350–400
% from African-American families	80%
% from White families	20%
% on free/reduced lunch	90%

This project, designed and sponsored by the Quality Education Project, has identified seven key **objectives**:

- To get parents actively involved in the support of their children's education;
- To institute systems which keep parents informed about their children's progress and curriculum activities;
- To train school administrators to implement parent involvement strategies;
- To train teachers to generate at-home parent support that will reinforce classroom instruction;
- To train parents to support their individual child's education at home and at school; and
- To strengthen the community by involving leaders from the business, medical, and religious communities in support of local schools.

BACKGROUND

The Quality Education Project is a private, nonprofit organization headquartered in San Francisco, CA, whose mission is to stimulate meaningful parent involvement in the schools. QEP offers schools a field-tested, professionally supervised, and site-tailored parent involvement program, consistent with current parent involvement and school effectiveness research. After a period of needs assessment at the school, the QEP Field Director works with the school to design a program adapted to the ethnic identity, cultural diversity, language backgrounds, concerns and goals of each school community.

The implementation phase of the program is an ongoing collaboration between the district and QEP. School principals and lead teachers are trained to implement program components, coordinate QEP activities, and provide parent involvement workshops for parents and teachers. When the program has been successfully integrated into the schools' operations, the program is monitored by QEP personnel until there is agreement that the district can sustain the program without additional consultant services.

During the 1991–1992 school year, QEP services involved over 210,000 children in 355 schools in California, Mississippi, and Indiana.

The Quality Education Project was introduced to the state of Mississippi in 1989, at the invitation of former Governor Ray Mabus and former state Superintendent of Education Richard Boyd. QEP secured a grant from the U.S. Department of Education to initiate the program in seven Mississippi school districts. In the fall of 1989, the 3-year implementation phase of project was commenced at Rolling Fork Elementary School. The school is making every effort to continue the project components on an ongoing basis.

QEP staff interviewed administrators, teachers, school board members, parents, and community leaders from the school and the district, to determine if the district was ready to get parents involved, if parents were ready to participate, and if the community was ready to support such an effort. Following a thorough assessment of the school district's strengths and needs, a report was presented to the superintendent, discussing the district's priorities, needs, strengths, and weaknesses.

QEP field directors worked directly with teams of school staff members to customize all elements of the program to fit the special needs of the participating school. Regular school staff members were trained to coordinate program implementation and sustain the program after QEP withdraws.

DESCRIPTION OF THE PROGRAM

The QEP program was selected for implementation in seven school districts in Mississippi as a strategy for increasing parent involvement as a key factor in promoting school success. Two lead teachers from Rolling Fork Elementary were selected and trained by QEP; they serve as the primary staff for the parent involvement project.

Components of the Program

Parent Pledge

This contract identifies basic ways parents can support their children's education. It includes:

- Making sure the child gets to school on time;
- Communicating with the teacher about the child's progress;
- Attending Back-to-School Night and parent/ teacher conferences;
- Following school rules; and
- Providing the child with a quiet place for study and supporting learning activities in the home.

QEP Student Folder

This folder contains a child's corrected work and results of any tests, with a space for the teacher to write additional notes to the parents. It is sent home weekly for parent review;

the parent signs it, adds comments if he/she wishes to, and sends it back to the teacher. This keeps the parent current on the child's progress.

Parent Seminars

The school sponsors six parent education workshops in the evening on such topics as homework, children's self-esteem, testing, and parenting skills.

Back-to-School Night

This event inaugurates the home-school partnership early in the year. Strategies are developed to maximize parent attendance and provide parents with vital information about the school, the staff, and their children's classes.

Education Sunday

This is one of the community events encouraged by QEP. Congregations are asked to voice their support of education and encourage parent involvement. Teachers from Rolling Fork School attend and speak at different churches.

Parent Resource Center

Parents and teachers use the Center to make materials for the classroom. Parents volunteer at the Center to assist in preparing materials for teachers.

Staff and Parent Training

The program includes inservice training to help teachers work more effectively with parents and workshops to help parents monitor their children's progress and support learning at home.

Newsletters

QEP encourages the principal to develop effective monthly school newsletters to provide parents with clear information about school programs and policies. Classroom teachers are trained in the use of newsletters to explain classroom activities and curriculum to parents, and to suggest home activities which reinforce what children are learning.

Parent Involvement in Planning, Operating, and Monitoring

By expanding the concept of parent involvement beyond participation in volunteer activities at the school site, schools can teach families how to encourage learning and support the school curriculum during the hours they share at home with their children.

Whenever the QEP newsletter is sent home, parents are asked about their opinions and concerns, and they are encouraged to respond in writing to the school. Parent representatives are included as members of the Superintendent's Advisory Committee. Parents have also been involved with the Curriculum Committee which was formed to deal with the many concerns related to the consolidation of the Sharkey Issaquena and Anquilla school districts in 1991.

Parents are encouraged to participate in the PTA. The attendance of parents at school board meetings has increased; they are more involved and more willing to speak out now.

Strengths and Weaknesses

The QEP folders have been one of the most successful aspects of the program. They have helped the school communicate with every family; the child's work is taken home and seen by the parents. Parent response to this has been positive.

The Mississippi QEP Program Director reports that Education Sunday has been embraced by many Mississippi school districts. However, it was one of the least successful components in Rolling Fork. It appears to be a good idea, but logistically it is difficult to carry out where there are so many little towns and churches. Recruiting parents who attend each congregation to be spokespeople for the school would make this activity more effective.

This is a community where change does not take place rapidly. While parents have been slow to increase their attendance at school activities and respond to invitations to participate, the program leaders must be careful not to become discouraged. They need to persist in their efforts, as each year more people do become involved.

The school serves a large geographic area and, thus, the distance from many homes to the school may be as far as 30 miles. Some of the parents do not feel a relationship between school and home, because the school is located so far from them. No transportation is provided for attendance at the Parent Resource Center.

The hours for the parent seminars have been shifted to an earlier time, because parents are less likely to come to a meeting when it is dark. They are now held at 6 p.m.

Outcomes and Evaluation

A number of activities have been undertaken to assess the effectiveness of the QEP parent involvement program. QEP assists the district in developing and administering a home survey to assess the parents' perceptions of the program and their knowledge of learning strategies for use in the home.

QEP has identified several key areas which activate and support effective home-school partnerships. Success of the program is measured by yearly comparisons of current levels of parent involvement in these key components with the amount of parent involvement present before the project was implemented. Gains in student motivation, attitude, attendance, school completion, parenting skills, and parent and community support for the school are also reported.

Staff have observed many changes in attitudes and practices as a result of the QEP parent involvement activities. Prior to this effort, teachers perceived that parent/teacher conferences were times for parents to complain. Teachers now welcome parent/teacher conferences and view them as opportunities for positive conversation and problem resolution. Teachers also are sending more positive notes home to reinforce the partnership between home and school.

Parents are no longer as intimidated by school officials as they were before this program. They are volunteering to help in the school more often.

An increase in community support of the schools has also been observed. A local bank is helping the school sponsor an art contest in the 5th grade.

The impact of a parent involvement program on student achievement is difficult to isolate, and changes in student test scores may become more apparent over time. Although test scores of the higher achievers have not changed, there has been a significant positive change in test scores of the low achievers over the past 3 years. The QEP parent involvement program may be one of the factors responsible for this improvement.

Budget and Funding

The QEP program was implemented at Rolling Fork Elementary School through funding from a federal grant from the Department of Education. One of the technical assistance services provided by QEP staff is helping the districts obtain funding for the program from private foundations or through state or federal grants.

For Further Information Contact

Mrs. Ethel Brown, Principal
QEP Parent Involvement Project
Rolling Fork Elementary School
600 South Parkway
Rolling Fork, MS 39159
(601) 873-4849

STERNE BRUNSON SCHOOL DEVELOPMENT PROGRAM
Benton Harbor, MI

Major Components:
>Parents-in-Training Program
>Parent volunteers
>School Advisory Committee
>School Support Team

Special Features:
>Parent leadership training

Profile of School:

Number of students enrolled in school	582
% from African-American families	99%
% from low-income families	98%

The **goals** of the program are:

- To encourage more parents to take an active part in the education of their children; and
- To provide parents with information about the schools and education so they can be a positive advocate for the school within the community.

BACKGROUND

In 1981, Judge Douglas Hillman ordered the Benton Harbor Area School District to adopt the School Development Program as part of a comprehensive desegregation plan. In the fall of 1982, the program was implemented in four schools; in 1986, the model was adopted by all elementary schools, including Sterne Brunson Elementary School.

Benton Harbor is an economically depressed area where over 50% of the students are eligible for the school's free or reduced federal lunch program. Judge Hillman mandated the implementation of the program in an effort to improve the climate and academic conditions in the schools.

The model used for the court-ordered School Development Program was developed by Dr. James Comer, Professor of Child Psychiatry at the Yale University Medical School and Director of the Yale Child Study Center. Its purpose is to build an active partnership between school staff and parents by creating a family-like environment within schools, one that emphasizes caring, social responsibility, and academic achievement.

The School Development Program was first planned and implemented, beginning in 1968, at two inner-city elementary schools in New Haven, CT. The goals were to improve academic performance and school success of poor minority students; build parent-staff collaborations to develop trust and reduce the sociocultural gap between home and school; and use developmental principles to improve schools' responsiveness to children's needs. To administer the project, a governance and management team, with representatives from families and school, was organized; school committees and teams were set up; and a parent program was developed to provide training and opportunities for school involvement.

Joyce Johnson became the principal of Sterne Brunson in 1984. She had been assistant principal in another school which had already adopted the School Development Program. After receiving approval from the superintendent to implement the Comer Process at Sterne Brunson, the principal made the decision to implement the program more slowly than was done in some of the other schools in order to avoid the mistakes they had made. She spent the first year developing a School

Advisory Team and a school improvement plan, building an atmosphere of trust between the teachers and parents, developing a strong collaboration between the PTO and the school, and establishing the position of parent liaison.

DESCRIPTION OF THE PROGRAM

The School Development Program provides important roles for parents in the schools, working as classroom aides or support staff in the library or main office. Parents organize, run, and attend a number of school events designed to bring the school and community closer together. The School Advisory Committee identifies problems and opportunities related to school climate, staff development, and the academic program. A third critical component of the School Development Program is the School Support Team which assists teachers in developing social and academic programs that address child development needs, especially social and emotional needs.

The Sterne Brunson Elementary School provides education for 582 children in preschool classes through the 6th grade. In past years, as many as 21 parents were given stipends to work during the year as helpers in the school. However, due to budget constraints, the stipends for parents were terminated in the spring of 1992. Therefore, the parents and teachers who work in the School Development Program are volunteers. One of the preschool teachers has volunteered to serve as parent liaison, a link between the school and parents when problems arise.

Components of the Program

Parents-in-Training Program

As many as 21 parents each year were provided with stipends in compensation for their work in the school and the classroom. These helpers worked in the school 5 days a week for 3 hours a day. They worked with classroom teachers, listened to children read, assisted with preparation of the bulletin boards, decorated the walls of the school and the gym.

Reading and math courses were offered to the helpers by the school district so they would improve their knowledge and skills in these subjects and could be more effective in the classroom. Once a month they attended inservice training on a variety of topics.

As indicated earlier, budget problems resulted in the number of parent helpers on stipend being reduced each year from 21 to three, until finally, in the spring of 1992, this component of the program was ended.

The parents who were fortunate enough to have participated in this program gained knowledge, skills, and confidence through their work in the schools. Many of them have found regular jobs as lunchroom supervisors in the schools, and working in local factories or retail stores. Four have gone back to school and are working to complete their GED certification.

Parent Volunteer Program

A total of 42 parents serve as volunteers at Sterne Brunson. They usually have flexible schedules, and many do not work every day. Some fulfill their responsibilities through tasks they can do at home. Academic courses are offered to them through the school system, but are not mandatory for the parent volunteers.

Parent-Teacher Organization (PTO)

The PTO is active in recruiting and selecting members to be parent representatives on the Committees and Subcommittees of the school. The PTO is also a fund-raising organization for the school. Some of the activities organized to raise money are selling popcorn, a bake sale, and selling gifts at Santa's Christmas shop.

School Advisory Committee

Teachers, parents, and noninstructional staff are represented on the School Advisory Committee, which serves as an advisory board to the principal of the school. The broad membership of the committee allows everyone with a stake in the school to have a voice in decision making, leading to consensus planning, cooperative implementation, and a sense of ownership and trust between home and school.

This Committee has up to 12 members and meets once a month. The parent representatives are chosen by parents at a PTO meeting. Teachers are elected so that all grade levels at the school have a spokesperson on the Committee. One teacher represents the preschool, kindergarten, and first grade; one teacher represents grades 2 and 3; and a third represents grades 4, 5, and 6.

The School Advisory Committee identifies problems and opportunities related to school climate, staff development, and the academic program. It develops a school improvement plan that details objectives in each area, strategies for meeting these objectives, and a process for monitoring and evaluating the plan. The committee prioritizes concerns, identifies and allocates resources, governs program implementation, and evaluates and modifies strategies and program elements.

The Committee has designated four subcommittees, each of which has teachers and parents. All of the teachers are asked to serve on at least one subcommittee, which includes the Academic Subcommittee, Social Subcommittee, Public Relations Subcommittee, and Staff Development Subcommittee.

School Support Team

This group, which is another subcommittee of the School Advisory Committee, consists of the school psychologist, teacher-consultant, social worker, principal, and two teachers, one a specialist in reading. In the original Comer schools in New Haven, this group was called the Mental Health Team, but educators in Benton Harbor did not like that name so received permission from Dr. Comer to change it to School Support Team. The purpose of this Team is to provide support to teachers and students, both in academic and social issues.

A broad range of subjects is discussed by this Team; it makes the decisions concerning referral of students for special education testing and placement. It discusses issues related to school climate and safety, such as the plan developed for better control in the lunchroom. The principal often takes her personal concerns before this group for advice and assistance.

Parent Involvement in Planning, Operating, and Monitoring

Parents are involved in this project as employees, volunteers, and members of committees and subcommittees which are working on school improvement. Parent involvement has undergone some revision since the beginning of the project; parents are encouraged to participate in school activities. It is recognized that activities completed at home in support of the school should be given acceptance and recognition.

Educators have traditionally said that many parents do not care about their children's education. The School Development Project provides evidence that parents do care, and they will become active in the schools if they are given a substantive role to play in the classroom or the school.

The stipend program for parent helpers was a successful aspect of the School Development Program. However, even without regular pay for their assistance, parents continue to volunteer in the school and in the classroom. They realize that their services are needed by the school, and that parent involvement is a critical element in school improvement.

Strengths and Weaknesses

Parents feel welcome at the Sterne Brunson Elementary School; they know they have a right to be there, to speak up about concerns they have, and to be listened to by teachers and administrators. Through the training sponsored by the school district, parents have developed a rapport with each other and now have a network and support system among them.

The lack of funds to pay stipends for the parents-in-training has been a disappointment, since that program has demonstrated its effectiveness in providing the participants with confidence, knowledge, and skills as parents, as school employees, and for future career potential. However, many of the parents who would be participants in that program continue to serve as volunteers at the school.

One of the challenges has been to convince the teaching staff that parents have contributions to make to the classroom and school, despite their low educational level and current low-income status. Teachers are beginning to accept parents and not be threatened that parents might expect to takeover their classrooms. Teachers also have learned that they cannot expect parents to have the same skills as they do.

Outcomes and Evaluation

Longitudinal evaluations of the two schools in the School Development Program in New Haven indicate that both schools attained the best attendance records in the city, greatly reduced student behavior problems, minimized parent-staff conflict, and achieved near grade-level academic performance. Students at one of the New Haven schools (King) rank ahead of all other inner-city schools in reading and math skills, and moved from 20th in reading and 31st in math to 10th place in both subjects among all New Haven schools.

Many positive outcomes have been evident as a result of the School Development Program at Sterne Brunson. Teacher attitudes are changing toward more acceptance of parents' strengths and weaknesses. Many teachers go to their students' homes to find out why a child is not in school. Parents feel more at ease in the school; they no longer feel inferior to the teachers, who are open and responsive to them. Parents attend and speak at school board meetings more frequently than in the past. Improvement in student test scores and in social behavior has been evident partly as a result of this program.

Since the school began implementing the model over 100 parents have participated in some capacity. Large numbers of family members regularly attend school events. The school has an 85%-90% attendance rate at parent/teacher conferences.

The Benton Harbor School District has kept records of student achievement as measured by the MAEP (Michigan

Assessment of Educational Progress) tests, administered to four grades at the schools. The results are listed below:

	Reading	Math
1980 MAEP Scores		
4th Grade	33.1%	41.1%
7th Grade	40.5%	28.2%
10th Grade	38.2%	16.9%
1987 MAEP Scores		
4th Grade	68.6%	92 %
7th Grade	50.5%	59.7%
10th Grade	69.2%	45.5%

The scores and grades are not as high as the school would like for them to be, but they certainly demonstrate an upward movement.

Budget and Funding

The lack of funding for stipends for parents-in-training has weakened the School Development Program at Sterne Brunson. Some of the other components of the program which cannot be implemented due to lack of money are district training of teachers, the social skills unit, field trips, and guest speakers for the school.

For Further Information Contact

Joyce Johnson, Principal
School Development Program
Sterne Brunson Elementary School
1131 Columbus
Benton Harbor, MI 49022
(616) 927-0734

TOMASITA ELEMENTARY SCHOOL
Albuquerque, NM

Major Components:
Parent volunteer program
Preschool Program
"Families in Partnership" program
Before and After School Child Care
Summer Day Camp
Kinderproject

Special Features:
Clothing Bank
Parents as Substitute Teachers
Food Co-op Program

Profile of School:

Enrollment in Tomasita School	476
% from African-American Families	4.3%
% from Latino Families	50.5%
% from Asian-American Families	3.2%
% from White Families	35.9%
% from Native American Families	5.7%
% of students on free/reduced lunch	51.6%
% of students with limited English	5.5%
Attendance Rate	94%
Promotion Rate	99.8%

The **goals** of the program are:

- To provide opportunities for both parents and family members to interact with school in a meaningful way; and
- To enhance self-esteem of the children and parents through involvement of family members at the school.

BACKGROUND

The principal at Tomasita Elementary School does not call this a parent involvement *program*; parents have been involved since 1987, and the principal holds a strong belief that this should continue. When parents are involved, you have good communications between home and school, and a common sense of shared goals. Parents need to feel they belong in the school and the school belongs to them. Schools exist to serve the community and will be successful if and when they assess the needs of the community and take action to address those needs.

When people are involved in planning and operating a program they feel a sense of ownership, which results in a more responsive program.

DESCRIPTION OF THE PROGRAM

Tomasita Elementary School is located in Northeast Heights, in the middle of the city of Albuquerque adjacent to "the hub." The neighborhood served by Tomasita Elementary School is a microcosm of the city of Albuquerque, with families from diverse socioeconomic situations, ranging from below the poverty level to significantly above. The majority of families are blue collar and reflect the cultural diversity of the city, including African-Americans, Native Americans, Latinos, and Anglos. The neighborhood is located in a high crime corridor, but the parents are going the extra mile to make sure their children are safe and receive a good education.

The Tomasita Elementary School enrolls children from preschool to Grade 5. They are located in a "temporary" trailer, which has been their home for the last 20 years. A new building has been constructed and is scheduled to be ready for occupancy in 1993.

The parent involvement program has no paid staff, but is located in a parent center within the school. A total of 100–125 families participate in the activities listed below each year. More than 200 parents are volunteers in the school, and 12 community members volunteer regularly at Tomasita.

Components of the Program

Parent Volunteer Program

The principal of Tomasita had previously worked in the central office and saw many resumés of women returning to the work force listing experience from many volunteer activities. She realized that volunteering in the school could greatly assist the school program and also provide parents with skills and experiences which could be used in qualifying for regular, paid employment, either within the school system or in other types of organizations. It is her belief that parent volunteers should be used in some meaningful way since they are giving their time to the school.

In the spring of 1988, the school developed a document on volunteerism, which defines various types of jobs volunteers can do. The principal and teachers begin volunteer recruitment during school registration, by direct one-to-one grass roots contact. Parents sign up for a particular type of job and it goes to the Parent Faculty Organization for review and assignment to a specific teacher, classroom, or PFO officer and/or chairperson. The school has no secretary, so the front office is run by the health aide and four parent volunteers.

Volunteers are considered as part of the staff and receive the same folder about the school at the beginning of the year (including staff lists, map, evacuation information). A list of written expectations is provided to each volunteer. Any volunteer who works for the school will receive references from the principal for regular employment in the future.

Preschool Program (Birth to Age 4)

This program was begun by the principal and a parent. It provides a preschool experience to children 2 mornings a week, from 9 a.m. until noon. The program is run completely by parents and is totally free. The children are fed lunch and then parents/guardians take them home.

One significant requirement of the program is that an adult (parent, baby-sitter, guardian) must stay with the child during the program. This provides on-site training in parenting

skills, early childhood readiness skills, and adult social interaction skills. The parents, grandparents, other relatives, and
baby-sitters who bring the children to the program thoroughly
enjoy being with one another, as well as having the benefits for
their children. The success of this component relies on planning and organizational skills. The adult participants take pride
in developing these skills early on in the program each year.

The program operates on $150 a year for materials and
supplies. Transportation for field trips is provided by a city
van.

"Families in Partnership" Program

This is a collaborative effort between the City of Albuquerque and the Albuquerque Public Schools to provide a
comprehensive child development program for children and
families. Families who have children 3-5 years of age, live
within the designated program site areas, and fall within the
Federal poverty guidelines are eligible to participate. This
program also attempts to hire workers for the day care center
from the community.

Before and After School Program

This program, sponsored by the City of Albuquerque
Parks & Recreation Department, begins at 7:00 a.m. and ends
at 6:00 p.m. The cost is minimal to allow low-income workers
to receive quality child care for their school-age children.

Summer Day Camp

This is a collaborative effort between the City, the Girl
Scouts of America, and the Albuquerque Public Schools. The
Day Camp runs 7 weeks during the summer months, Monday
through Friday from 9:00 a.m.-3:00 p.m. It is a free program
with a minimal registration fee; child care is available before
and after camp hours, and breakfast and lunch are served
daily. The Summer Camp places an emphasis on hiring adults

from the community. It is uncertain whether this program will be able to continue in the future due to funding problems.

Tutoring Program

Individual tutoring is available twice a week for Tomasita students during after-school hours. Parents, high school students, and middle school students are hired as the tutors. This not only provides employment opportunities, but the tutor training program enables the tutors to gain skills which might be transferable to other employment in the future. This program relies on supplemental funding and is offered when funds are available.

Parents Involved in Education (P.I.E.)

P.I.E. teams consist of the classroom teacher and parents of children in that particular class. They meet once a month to plan the instructional focus and support activities for the class. The "lead" parents organize field trips, special events, and guest speakers for the class. They also enlist other volunteers for each activity. This is a voluntary program; it is left up to the discretion of the teacher whether or not to participate.

Emergency Substitute Program

Parents are hired as substitute teachers whenever the district runs out of substitutes. In order to qualify, parents must fill out the application form and have a TB test. This program provides employment for parents and enhances both the parents' and students' self-esteem when the child sees the parent valued and accepted by the school as the "teacher-for-the-day."

Tomasita Clothing Bank

Parents are in complete charge of this program. They conduct a clothing drive within the community and then distribute the clothing to families. Through the collaborative efforts of the parents, the school nurse and nurse assistant, and the local WalMart, they are able to clothe the 51% of the families who fall below the federal poverty guidelines.

At the beginning of the drive, the parents ask teachers to be observant and try to identify families who might benefit from this service. The nurse contacts the families by phone or letter, to let them know clothing is available. The parents are very receptive, and their situation is kept confidential.

In order to raise money to purchase underwear and shoes for these families, the parents and students sell various items in the school store. The profits from this and from the soda machines are used to buy shoes and underwear. The WalMart Store has been very cooperative in this effort and arranges for a certain number of families to visit the store to obtain clothing without charge.

This program provides a great opportunity for parents to share their resources and feel supportive of their community. Everyone's self-esteem is enhanced through this program.

Life Link Program

This is a Food Co-Op program available to parents and citizens who volunteer in the community, in any capacity, for a minimum of 2 hours per month. They may purchase approximately $45.00 worth of groceries for $15.00. This is run entirely by parents; they receive the groceries, check them in, separate them into individual boxes, receive payments, and deliver boxes each month. Through this activity the parents receive training and experience in organization of time and materials, in problem solving, critical thinking, mediation skills, and negotiations. The Life Link Program is in operation only when they have the magic combination of *space* and volunteers.

Foster Grandparents Program

Older citizens from the community serve as helpers in the classroom, working with children on class assignments, playing games to reinforce skills, and reading to children.

Kinderproject

Instead of pulling kindergarten children out of regular class time for remedial help, Chapter 1 teachers and aides work with the children during the afternoon. The help received during the first year of school has resulted in a significant decrease in Chapter 1 referrals in the first grade.

Parent Involvement in Planning, Operating, and Monitoring

Of the 11 components of the Tomasita parent involvement program, parents are in charge of the Program for Preschoolers, the Clothing Bank, and the Life Link program; they participate either as paid workers or volunteers in the Program for Preschoolers, the Families in Partnership program, the Summer Day Camp, the Tutoring Program, the P.I.E. program, and the emergency substitute program. Thus, the parents not only receive services from the components of this effort, but are integral to the operation of each of these programs. The parents participating in these activities are not simply providing clerical or menial assistance, but their presence is critical to the effectiveness of the program.

Tomasita is a school-based management site and the staff and parents are directly responsible for planning and implementing the curricular program and all of the support programs, such as Chapter 1 Reading, the Kinderproject, and the multicultural program. They are also directly responsible for the extracurricular programs such as the Student Council, the Multicultural Club, the Computer Club, and the Young Astronauts' Club.

The school has been in the process of restructuring since 1987. The School Restructuring Council is made up of parent or staff representatives from each of the federally funded programs and the preschool program. Their aim is to propose improvements to be made at the local level.

Staff and parents are responsible for designing and reviewing the annual budget. Staff, students, and parents have been involved with the design of the new school building, the selection of furniture and equipment, and the planning and implementation of a community party to celebrate the permanent facility. By 1995, the staff and parents will be trained to become involved in the evaluation of staff, both paid and unpaid (volunteer). Involving staff, students, parents, and the community-at-large in all issues affecting programs and services encourages accountability of the school toward the community.

Strengths and Weaknesses

The preschool program has proven to be one of the most successful ventures, since it has provided multifaceted assistance directly to the families. The parent or other adult who brings the child to the program learns parenting skills and how to offer educational experiences to infants and toddlers. The P.I.E. (Parents Involved in Education) program has not been utilized by many teachers since it involves extra time and effort. This is a voluntary program and requires the initiative and leadership of the classroom teacher to be successfully implemented. The budget cuts throughout the district have meant that teachers cannot receive extra compensation for the time they spend on the P.I.E. program.

The temporary buildings and the lack of space have been a continuing frustration to teachers and parents, but everyone has adjusted to it with a "catch as catch can" attitude. In the new building there is a parent room with a library, coffee pot, furniture, and equipment. A washer and dryer will be located there for use by parents operating the Clothing Bank, who up until now have had to take the clothes home to launder them.

There continues to be a need for a Parent Coordinator and, if possible, an assistant, for the Parent Center. As of the present time, however, the tight budget situation does not permit new staff to be hired.

Outcomes and Evaluation

Changed Teacher Attitudes and Practices

Teachers feel very good about parent involvement and are cooperating with efforts to keep the doors of the school and classroom open to parents, figuratively and literally. The teachers also feel the need to be treated as professionals and want to be compensated for their efforts. Before the budget cuts, the school was able to pay teachers for participation in after school programs; 90% of the teachers were involved. Now that the school can no longer compensate them for the extra effort, the participation has dropped to 10%.

Changed Parent Attitudes and Practices

Parents are in and out of the classrooms all the time. More and more people become involved every year. A total of 200 volunteer certificates were given out in the 1991–1992 school year; this indicates that parents from about half of the families are active in some capacity at the school.

Reformed School and District Policies

The principal and teachers were unhappy several years ago about the way in which the Chapter 1 program was run in the kindergarten. The Chapter 1 teachers would either pull the child from the room for 45 minutes or work with the child in the room. Since kindergarten only is scheduled for 2½ hours a day, Chapter 1 cut into the child's day too much. The principal, reading teacher, parents, and Chapter 1 teacher developed a project called Kinderproject, their alternative to the Chapter 1 arrangements.

Kinderproject is scheduled in the afternoon. At the beginning of the program, the principal of Tomasita worked on development skills with a group of kindergarten students for 1 hour twice a week. The program has now expanded to four times a week and employs a full-time teacher and aide. The Kinderproject services 34 of the 70 children in kindergarten and now serves as a model for the rest of the school district.

Increased Parent/Community Support

Tomasita receives support from many businesses and community organizations. The school does not have to call them, they are calling the school to ask what they can do to help. These partners include WalMart, The Olive Garden, International House of Pancakes, Wendy's, McDonalds, and Church of Good Shepherd.

Increased Student Achievement

The scores on the standardized tests are improving every year, but there is no way to determine how much of this increase is due to the parent involvement program.

Budget and Funding

Most of the parent involvement projects are operated with volunteers and, therefore, have no dollar costs to the school. The Kinderproject has a budget of $50,000 from federal Chapter 1 funds. Other costs include such things as expenditures for awards and certificates, and these are paid for with money from fund-raising activities at the school and donations from organizations such as the Optimist Club.

For Further Information Contact

Ms. Terry Toman, Principal
Tomasita Elementary School
701 Tomasita N.E.
Albuquerque, NM 87123
(505) 293–1230

VAUGHN FAMILY CENTER
A SCHOOL READINESS NETWORK AND
INTEGRATED FAMILY SERVICES PROJECT
Vaughn Street School
San Fernando, CA

Major Components:
- Service Delivery
- Child Care and Preschool Program
- Parent Education

Special Features:
- Service Exchange Bank
- Block Leaders
- Family Advocates
- Parent Empowerment
- Parent Involvement in Governance

Profile of School:

Number of students enrolled in Vaughn Street	1,085
% from Latino families	89%
% from African-American families	11%
% of families earning under $15,000/yr	40%
% of families with limited English	78%

The **goals** of the Vaughn Family Center are:

- To enhance school readiness through developmentally appropriate programs for children birth to 5 years of age;
- To improve social and academic competence for elementary school children;
- To provide a center which is customer-driven, focused on prevention, and adaptable to diverse communities;
- To create a community partnership focused on building a safe neighborhood and strong families; and
- To facilitate the renewal of larger delivery systems.

BACKGROUND

The FamilyCare Initiative was started in Vaughn Street Elementary School in May, 1991. The program is sponsored by the Los Angeles Educational Partnership (LAEP) and United Way-North Angeles Region, together with the Los Angeles Unified School District, the Child Care Resource Center, and scores of public and private collaborators. FamilyCare was designed by over 200 parents, teachers, service providers, community members, and public/private partnerships to address the needs of children and families who are economically disadvantaged, diverse, and multilingual. Their vision was influenced by the changing demographics of the school population and the recognition that the social service delivery system is too fragmented to provide comprehensive, adequate, and effective services for families.

DESCRIPTION OF THE PROGRAM

The first FamilyCare Center, the Vaughn Family Center, is housed in the Vaughn Street Elementary School. The center is designed to be a "one-stop" service-exchange center which links the community to the school. Those eligible for services are children from birth to age 12 living within the school's boundaries, their older siblings, and parents or guardians. Referrals come from teachers, the school counselor, and parent volunteers; parents also contact the Center on their own.

The services are delivered primarily by professionals from private and public agencies together with a small, bilingual, culturally sensitive core staff. The core staff, hired by the Los Angeles Educational partnership, includes a director, administrative assistant, family counselor, and three family advocates. Family Advocates work face-to-face with parents to assist families in on-the-spot problem solving and accessing resources as needed. Twelve block leaders are planned for the program; these will be parents living in the community, who are trained to keep in touch with families in their neighborhood, especially those without a telephone, and to make referrals to the Center.

Staff from other agencies typically work at the Center

for several hours once a week. Services include health and dental, after-school youth activities, gang prevention, child care, employment and job training, housing, drug and alcohol treatment, family counseling, and legal aid. Off-site services are linked to the Center through agreements designed collaboratively by community agencies and the Center's governing commission, and are monitored by the Center Director.

The Family Center is governed by a 40-member independent Program Commission, including 20 parents and 20 service providers and community leaders. Two teachers and the school counselor serve on the Commission. The Director attends the school's site-based management council and also participates on the school's initial inquiry team, study team, and attendance team.

Components of the Program

Service Delivery

Basic health and social services, including prevention, treatment, and information, are available at the Family Center at Vaughn Street School. In cases where the needed service cannot be offered at the Center, a referral is made to off-site providers.

Child Care and Preschool Program

The Center coordinates a School Readiness Network to provide parents with information on and referrals to early childhood programs in the community (Head Start, state funded Children's Centers, etc.). The Network serves to establish professional links among these Early Childhood Education providers, to share resources, to improve transitions for children who move among the different types of care, and to facilitate training and licensing of Family Day Care Providers.

Service Exchange Bank

Parents reciprocate for services consumed by contributing time and skill in tasks such as construction, transportation, language translation, Center governance, committee work, gardening, baby-sitting, reading aloud to their own children, and coaching recreational activities. For instance, in the case of computer classes for parents, those in the advanced computer class are asked to serve as teaching assistants for the beginning or intermediate classes (in return for the instruction received in their own class); parents enrolled in the intermediate class may be asked to type the school bulletin or perform other clerical tasks; and those parents in the beginning computer class might be asked to provide child care for the parents in the higher level classes.

Parent Education

Parents are offered intensive training in issues related to the school budget, governance of the school, leadership, ESL, job skill development, and parenting skills.

Family Advocates

Family advocate staff members provide case coordination and service integration for families with multiple problems.

Block Leaders

Parents who live in the neighborhood served by the school will be recruited and trained as block leaders to keep in touch with the families in their immediate area, encourage them to utilize the services of the Family Center, and provide the school and Center personnel with information about family and neighborhood conditions and needs. They may also provide in-home instruction of the 4-year olds on the waiting list for a school readiness program, and serve as community liaisons to help with specific Center functions such as food distribution and drop-in child care.

Parent Involvement in Design, Operation, and Monitoring

The parents are involved with the Family Center in all aspects of the governance and operation. The FamilyCare Program Commission, which sets policies for the Center and selects staff, is made up of 50% parents and 50% service providers and community leaders. The Parent Service Exchange Bank encourages all parents receiving services through the Center to contribute their time, energy, and skills in reciprocation of the benefits they are receiving. The Block Parents serve as outreach workers for the Center, and as communicators between school and home.

Empowerment of parents has been a major focus of this project, but parents also must be able to accept limitations on their roles. They learn that major change requires much time and energy, to plan activities, to reach consensus decisions, and to collaborate across languages and cultures. Parents have been asked to set policy and to participate in the selection and hiring of staff. Originally, plans were to hire parents from the neighborhood as family advocates. However, when the complex needs of the families were considered, along with the traditional shortcomings of the service-delivery system, it was decided that persons with more professional training and experience would be more appropriate and effective as case managers.

Strengths and Weaknesses

One of the most successful aspects of the FamilyCare Program has been the Commission which governs the program. It has been most effective in the design of the program, hiring of staff, and operation of the Center.

A component which is not yet in place is the Block Parents, whose selection is expected during 1993. Currently, parents function informally as Block Parents. The high rate of mobility and transiency in the neighborhood may present obstacles, but the project staff are convinced they are not insurmountable. It has been a challenge to develop an organization composed of members from diverse backgrounds who strive to make their decisions based on consensus, rather than on voting. Their collective decisions should benefit the whole organization, not any special interest group. Sometimes individuals or groups are more concerned about their power and turf than they are with the overall purpose of the organization. Leadership has focused on developing and strengthening the collective vision, to work toward the common good. Through sensitive teamwork and understanding of locally determined priorities, the collaboration has been remarkably effective.

A number of techniques and strategies have been used to build an organization of members who can put the needs of the group ahead of their own short-term interests. Common goals, trust, and effective communication are critical; training has included mentoring, modeling, skilled facilitation, conflict resolution, role playing, and lots of working side-by-side on tasks to develop competencies and to build the cohesiveness of the organization, all focused on enhancing the chances of remaining productive and achieving desired outcomes.

Outcomes and Evaluation

In order to monitor and assess the program, the Family Center Director and Family Advocates are keeping logs to document the process and progress of the various activities. Stanford Research Institute has been selected to conduct the statewide evaluation of the FamilyCare program.

Budget and Funding

The cost of the Family Center in FY 1993 is $302,000, including funds for the Director, the Family Counselor, three Family Advocates, the Block Parents, the telephones, operating supplies, equipment, and major contributions to the school to pay for relocation of bungalows (for school functions that formerly occurred in Family Center's classrooms). The school district supplies the space and utilities free to the Center.

Financial support for the initiative comes from United Way, Stuart Foundations, Primerica Foundation, Mervyn's Corporation, RJR Nabisco, CITIBANK, Kaiser Permanente/ Paramount, the California Child Care Initiative Project, Chan

Family Relief Fund, the California Educational Initiatives Fund, Irvine Foundation, Blue Cross of California, Healthy Start (SB 620), and School Restructuring (SB 1274).

In April 1992, Vaughn Street Elementary School was awarded a $321,120 grant from RJR Nabisco Foundation. The school was one of 14 chosen nationwide from 1,100 applicants. The funds will be used in part to pay for additional equipment and services for the FamilyCare Center.

For Further Information Contact

Dr. Yvonne Chan, Principal
Vaughn Family Center
Vaughn Street School
13330 Vaughn Street
San Fernando, CA 91340
(818) 896–7461

FOCUS—FOCUSING OUR COMMUNITY AND UNITING FOR SUCCESS
Wapato Primary School
Wapato, WA

Major Components:
> Parent meetings
> Recruiting efforts
> FOCUS Committee

Special Features:
> Concurrent English and Spanish Sessions
> Outreach to Native Americans
> Certificates of Attendance

Profile of School and School District:

Number of students in school district	3,000
Number of schools in district	5
Primary school (K–2)	
Intermediate School (Grades 3–5)	
Middle School	
High School	
PACE Alternative School	
Number of students enrolled in Primary School	780
% from Latino families	50%
% from Native American families	32%
% from White families	17%
% eligible for free/reduced lunch	86%

The **goals** of the FOCUS program are:

- To reach parents of high-risk students;
- To provide parents with information about their rights and responsibilities in the education of their children; and
- To make them feel more comfortable in the school.

BACKGROUND

The FOCUS program was initiated in the spring of 1991, with the assistance of the Citizens Education Center in Seattle, WA. A team of administrators, teachers, parents and community leaders participated in the design and planning of the program.

DESCRIPTION OF THE PROGRAM

The Wapato Primary School is located in a rural farming community. The school district also includes the Yakima Indian Reservation within its boundaries. Many Latino migrant workers live in the area and are involved in seasonal farming.

The FOCUS Program is planned and operated by the FOCUS Committee, a volunteer team including parents, teachers, counselors, and community representatives. All parents are welcome to attend the FOCUS meetings, but a special effort is made to design them to attract those parents who do not typically become involved in the school.

The Wapato Primary School has about 780 students enrolled; the target group of parents (minority, low-income, at-risk) is estimated to be 400–500. The largest proportion of students at the school are from Latino families, many of whom are migrant workers who come to the county for seasonal farm work. Data collected in 1989, indicate that more than 900 students in the schools were from migrant worker families; during the year 25% of those families moved from the area.

Components of the Program

Parent Meetings

The FOCUS program consists of six parent meetings each year. There are two concurrent sessions, one in English and the other in Spanish. Child care is offered during the meetings and refreshments are provided.

Incentives are offered to both the parents and the students to encourage them to attend the meetings. A door prize is given out to parents at the meeting; students whose parent(s) attend receive a small toy with educational value. At the end of the year, every parent who has attended one or more meetings receives a certificate, with stars placed on the certificate to indicate how many meetings they attended.

During the 1991–1992 series of programs, a total of 237 different parents participated in the parent meetings. A total of 74 different staff members, including teachers, paraprofessionals, counselors, and administrators, participated in the programs. They assisted in many capacities—welcoming and registration, serving as discussion leaders, helping with refreshments.

The topics covered in the FOCUS meetings are chosen by the FOCUS Committee. These include:

- Rights and responsibilities of parents;

- Information about school support staff who can help children succeed (counselor, nurse, speech therapist, etc.);

- Parent-teacher conferences—skills for parents;

- Ages and stages—child development material for children grades K-2;

- Support agencies in the community, such as the Department of Health, Department of Social Services; who they are; who is eligible to receive services; how to obtain services;

- Home learning activities.

Recruiting Efforts

Two fliers are sent home with the students—one a week before the meeting, and the second a day in advance. However, the most successful recruitment technique for this parent population is the personal invitation to parents from their own child, not the printed materials. Many parents do not read, and others do not pay much attention to printed notices, but rely instead on "word of mouth" information. Recruitment actually takes place in the classroom. A committee member goes from room to room to inform the students about the parent meeting and remind them to encourage their parents to attend. The counselors also take an active role in recruiting parents to the meetings.

When Wapato parents were asked how they had heard about the FOCUS programs and what made them decide to come, most responded that they came because their child had asked them to come and said it was important. This was the result of the "pep talk" given to the students in the classroom by team members.

FOCUS Committee

The FOCUS Committee has 8–10 members, volunteers representing parents, teachers, counselors, and community representatives. An effort is made to be sure the Committee is ethnically representative of the population of the school. The FOCUS Committee plans the meetings, disseminates publicity, encourages students to persuade their parents to come, and conducts the meetings. They meet at least once a week to design the FOCUS meetings and discuss feedback from previous meetings.

Parent Involvement in Planning, Operating, and Monitoring

Parents are active members of the FOCUS Committee which is responsible for planning the parent meetings. They help at the meetings and assist in collecting the information used to assess the effectiveness of the programs.

The FOCUS Committee has concluded that parents feel more comfortable and will be more supportive in a group with others similar to themselves. Two of the positive dynamics which occur in these sessions is parents reacting to other parents' concerns and parents starting to teach others at the meeting. Though the FOCUS meetings are open to all parents, special efforts are made to encourage attendance from families of at-risk students and those who have often been underrepresented in the schools.

The facilitators strive to be open to *all* parent comments and concerns. At one meeting parents were asked to compare the school they attended to their child's school. Parents of all

ethnic groups openly shared their frustrations and their negative or confusing experiences at their school and their child's
school. All the parental sharing was accepted and acknowledged as authentic and valid by the facilitators. This open,
nondefensive approach nurtured a cooperative parental attitude that prevailed at all sessions.

Strengths and Weaknesses

The most successful aspect of this program was the
offering of concurrent sessions in Spanish and in English. The
Spanish-speaking sessions consistently had greater attendance
by both male and female parents. Fathers said they would
make sure their wives attended when they could not be there.
It was obvious that these parents wanted to attend, to learn
more about the schools, and become more supportive of both
their child and the school. Most parents also want to take an
active part in the discussions which are part of the Parent
Meetings; at meetings where translations are required they
hesitate to speak up or to ask questions. When the meeting is
conducted in Spanish, parents can take a very active part in the
discussions. Many parents had not had the opportunity to
attend and participate due to language barriers. These parents
attended most or all of the sessions and asked for additional
parent meetings.

Another successful aspect of this program has been the
informal, relaxed atmosphere achieved at the FOCUS meetings, the respect shown to all parents, and the developing
partnership of parents and teachers. In addition to the planned
part of the program, there is an opportunity for informal
conversation during the refreshments. Parents bring up questions, issues, or complaints; teachers or administrators try to
answer their concerns on the spot, but, if that is not possible,
they contact the parents after the meeting with information and
answers as appropriate.

The participation of a significant number of staff members in the parent meetings was another effective factor in the
program. The Committee achieved this level of involvement
because they were so good at giving people specific roles to
play, by encouraging a team effort, by thanking people, and by
making them feel appreciated.

The FOCUS Committee has learned that it is not productive to introduce too many skills or concepts into the meetings, so they are trying to make the contents simpler and cover only one or two topics thoroughly, rather than attempting to be comprehensive about the subject matter.

One of the challenges of this program is keeping all of the FOCUS Committee members committed and energized. Since they are all volunteers, they sometimes feel overwhelmed by the responsibilities of the program. The Assistant Principal, who serves as the team leader, must be sensitive to their energy level and the fact that this is exhausting work and tends to result in burnout. The Committee is trying not to rely on teacher volunteers for too much of the Committee work. It is more important for the teachers to attend the FOCUS meetings, since the parents are very anxious to meet and talk with them.

Outcomes and Evaluation

The teachers and administrators have noticed many positive results of the FOCUS meetings. More parents attended Parent-Teacher Conferences held after the FOCUS session on that topic. Parents who have attended the FOCUS meetings feel more comfortable going into the school. Where teachers have been actively working with parents, an increase in student achievement has been noticed. Parents want much more interaction with teachers; if this can be accomplished, more beneficial outcomes will follow.

Changes in teachers' attitudes and behavior have been noticed. Staff are more cordial—they assist, welcome, or smile at parents who are in the school. The bilingual teachers who do the presentations in Spanish at the FOCUS meetings have developed some very good relationships with the Hispanic parents.

The Citizens Education Center has monitored the first year of the FOCUS program and collected extensive information on its performance, including attendance, staff and parent participation, number of fathers, and number of parents from different ethnic backgrounds. They have also provided a framework for evaluating the effectiveness of the presentations, what works best, and what things can be done to improve the programs. Twice a year, in January and August, persons from all of the schools working with Citizens Education Center come together to share their experiences, positive and negative.

Dr. Beverly McConnell is the Evaluation Consultant for the Citizens Education Center and has collected and analyzed data from the Wapato project and 11 other similar efforts in the state of Washington. She has developed a number of indices to assess the effectiveness of the programs and to compare them with each other including:

- Coverage index—percentage of parents attending;

- Male index—number of fathers participating;

- Economic index—whether the program is reaching low-income families;

- Ethnicity index—which groups are attending;

- Language index—how many parents with limited English proficiency are attending;

- Staff participation index;

- Sustained interest index—how many returned after the first meeting;

- School change index—indicates whether the school is making changes in policies and practices in response to parent participation.

Dr. McConnell's analysis demonstrates that the FOCUS program rated high on several indexes: the Language Index, the Economic Index, Staff Participation Index, and the Male Index. It is estimated that 24% of the families with children in Wapato Primary School do not speak English; however, 50% of the parents attending the parent sessions had limited English proficiency. This attendance was high as a result of the separate session in Spanish, which is very popular among parents.

Approximately 86% of the children attending Wapato Primary School are from low-income families; the proportion of low-income parents attending the parent sessions is about

87%, indicating that the program is attracting those to whom it is targeted.

Wapato School has the highest percentage of staff involvement in the FOCUS program of any of the 12 Washington sites in the evaluation. This may be a result of the teachers being given specific jobs to do before and during the parent sessions. Wapato also provided awards, prizes, and tokens of appreciation for those teachers and other staff who participated.

The FOCUS program scored very high on the Male Index, probably because so many of its parents are Latino and did not grow up in the U.S. The father may be the only one in the family who drives, and as the head of the family may feel that he should be representing the family at the school.

Wapato also was rated at the top is total attendance, as demonstrated by the Coverage Index, with an attendance rate of about 30%. This is considered especially noteworthy because Wapato is a school with a large enrollment. Smaller schools are often more successful in recruiting parents to evening meetings and workshops.

Budget and Funding

It is estimated that the program costs about $750, which is the amount needed for food, door prizes, and toys for children. Some Chapter 1 funds have been allocated to the FOCUS project, and Committee members have also solicited local businesses and organizations for donations to meet their financial program needs.

For Further Information Contact

Kathleen Johnson, Parent Volunteer Coordinator—
(509) 877-2177
Oralia Garza, Paraprofessional—(509) 877-2177
Lila Barnett—(509) 877-4181
FOCUS—Focusing our Community and Uniting for
Success
Wapato Primary School
P.O. Box 38
Wapato, WA 98951

Chapter 4

Programs in Middle Schools

Middle school students are at a difficult and challenging age. The first efforts at being independent and a separate person begin and gain momentum during this time. This has implications for parent-family involvement. This growing, developing person begins to send signals about the parent and school which can easily be interpreted as not wanting parents or guardians to be visible, or at least not as visible as during the elementary school years.

Our advice to parent-families and educators is "don't believe it," or at least take the signals with a large grain of salt. Our experience with even the most worldly-wise, street-smart middle-schooler is that within them lurks a strong need for parents and guardians to be active, involved, and influential. It is a mistake—a big mistake—to "fade," because parent-guardian nurturing and direction is always an irreplaceable gift, but it has a particular urgency now. The rapid physical growth, emotional turmoil, and need to plan for what the child will do in high school and beyond, underscore the importance of parent-family involvement in the school life of the student in middle school.

The student's outward attitude, the work schedule of busy, harried parents, and, to some extent, the attitude of school personnel, combine to make parent-family involvement in the middle grades a tough job requiring extra energy and creativity. If strong patterns or habits of parent-family involvement have been established in the elementary schools, there is no overwhelming reason why they cannot continue in the middle grades. If earlier patterns were not established, there is no compelling reason that should defeat establishing successful contributory involvement.

The program and project descriptions that follow highlight new and emerging ideas of school-parent-family relationships and connections. They present a developing recognition by school personnel that efforts to stretch and reach out in unconventional ways are the operating styles that contain possibilities for increased levels of parent-family-school connections that lead to increased student success and achievement.

PROGRAMS IN MIDDLE SCHOOLS

Calverton Middle School and West Baltimore Middle School, Baltimore, Maryland

TIPS—Teachers Involve Parents in Schoolwork

Crossroads School, New York, New York

Kettering Middle School, Upper Marlboro, Maryland

Kosciuszko Middle School and Parkman Middle School, Milwaukee, Wisconsin

Empowerment Project

Morningside Middle School, Ft. Worth, Texas

Operation PUT—Parents United with Teachers

SUMMARY OF PROGRAM CHARACTERISTICS
Middle School Programs

Name of Program	Population Served	Components	Beginnings	Special Features
Calverton and West Baltimore Middle Schools Baltimore, MD TIPS—Teachers Involve Parents in Schoolwork	Grades 6, 7, 8 Calverton—1,400 99 African-Amer. 71% low-income W. Balt.—1,785 90% African-Amer. 65% low-income	TIPS Homework Projects TIPS packets to teachers Orientation for parents	Program designed by Joyce Epstein from Johns Hopkins University; started in Baltimore in 1990	Prototype interactive homework assignments Certificates of Recognition for Students & Parents
Crossroads School New York, NY	Grades 6, 7, 8 Enrollment—120 37% African-Amer. 36% Latino 24% White 1% Asian-Amer. 60% free lunch	Advisory system Parent conferences Building Bridges "Conversations" with parents Work parties	Started by teacher who wanted to offer alternative education to young adolescents	Multicultural Multiage grouping Untracked Flexible scheduling Cooperative learning Student empowerment
Kettering Middle School Prince George's County Upper Marlboro, MD	Grades 7, 8 Enrollment—932 86% African-Amers. 13% White 6% low-income	Home-School Communication Parent Calendar Parent Volunteers EVERYWHERE Homework Hotline	New principal in 1988; PTA leaders convinced her of need for greater parent involvement	Mentors for Black Achievement Program Teachers in PTA Summer retreat for teachers and parents

(continued)

SUMMARY OF PROGRAM CHARACTERISTICS
Middle School Programs (*continued*)

Name of Program	Population Served	Components	Beginnings	Special Features
Kosciuszko and Parkman Middle Schools Milwaukee, WI Empowerment Project	Grades 6, 7, 8 Enrollment Kosciuszko—740 64% Latino 85% low-income Parkman—520 99% African-Amer. 90% low-income	Home visits Transition from elementary to middle school High Expectation Program Computer Classes ESL Classes	Funded by grant from Clark Foundation; sponsored by Milwaukee Education Trust	Empowerment Brother 2 Brother Sister 2 Sister
Morningside Middle School Ft. Worth, TX Operation PUT— Parents United with Teachers	Grades 6, 7, 8 Enrollment—750 85% African-Amer. 100% low-income	Parent visitation Parent discussion sessions Parent Action Committees	Sponsored by ACT (Allied Communities of Tarrant) and Texas Interfaith Education Fund	Parent empowerment Church recognition of student achievement

TEACHERS INVOLVE PARENTS IN SCHOOLWORK (TIPS)
Calverton Middle School
West Baltimore Middle School
Baltimore, MD

Major Components:

 Developing the TIPS homework projects

 Dissemination of TIPS packets to teachers

 Orientation for parents

Special Features:

 Prototype interactive homework assignments

 Certificates to recognize students' completion of
 homework and interactions with family

Profile of Schools:

Number of students enrolled in Calverton Middle School	1,400
% from African-American families	99%
% from low-income families	71%
Number of students enrolled in West Baltimore Middle School	1,785
% from African-American families	90%
% from White families	10%
% from low-income families	65%

The program **goals** of the TIPS are:

- To increase parent awareness of their children's schoolwork;
- To increase parent involvement in their children's learning activities at home that are linked to classwork;
- To increase students' ability and willingness to talk about schoolwork at home and the frequency of this happening;
- To improve students' skills and homework completion in specific subjects;

BACKGROUND

The implementation of the TIPS program in two middle schools in Baltimore was started in 1990, and is intended to continue as an ongoing program within the schools. The TIPS process was designed by Joyce Epstein from the Center on Families, Communities, Schools and Children's Learning at Johns Hopkins University. Based on her research that showed a subject specific connection between the parents' involvement in learning activities at home in reading and student gains in reading skills, Epstein began to work with teachers to see how to increase parent involvement and student skills in other subjects. The TIPS process for the middle grades extends the earlier work by Epstein with math and science teachers in the elementary grades to develop an interactive homework process to keep families informed and involved in their children's education.

The *TIPS Manual for Teachers: Language Arts and Science/ Health Interactive Homework in the Middle Grades* by Joyce L. Epstein, Vivian E. Jackson, and Karen Clark Salinas, with Language Arts and Science Teachers from Calverton and West Baltimore Middle Schools, was published in 1992. It describes Teachers Involve Parents in Schoolwork (TIPS) as

> a teacher-parent partnership process, in which teachers can help all families stay informed and involved in their children's learning activities at home, and help all students complete homework in order to promote greater success in school. The TIPS activities keep school on the agenda at home so that children know their families believe schoolwork is important and worth talking about. Over time, as TIPS is used each year, students get the idea that their teachers want their families to know about what they are learning and to participate in their homework assignments.

During the summers of 1990, 1991, and 1992, the staff from the Center on Families, Communities, Schools and Children's Learning and 14 teachers from the two middle schools in Baltimore worked together to develop prototype homework activities in Language Arts and Science/Health for grades 6, 7, and 8, adding one grade each year to the project. About 40 activities in each subject and at each grade level were produced, for a total of about 240 examples for the teachers in the demonstration schools to use.

DESCRIPTION OF THE PROGRAM

Homework becomes a three-way partnership involving students, families, and teachers. TIPS Language Arts provides a format for students to share a variety of skills in writing, reading, thinking, grammar, and related language activities with their parents and interact with family members by interviewing, gathering reactions, discussing ideas, reading written work aloud, and exchanging other ideas. TIPS Science provides a format for students to conduct and discuss a hands-on lab or data collection activity related to the science topics they study in class.

The TIPS program has been phased in at Calverton and West Baltimore Middle Schools, first with the 6th grade starting in September 1990, adding the 7th grade in September 1991, and finally the 8th grade in September 1992. The program does not require extra staff, since it is considered a part of the instructional program at the school. The Department Chairs at the schools supervise and guide the teachers in the implementation of the TIPS program. All language arts and science/ health teachers are participating.

A Field Coordinator from the Baltimore Fund for Educational Excellence also assists the teachers with their use of TIPS, and conducts informal evaluations of reactions of teachers, parents, and students to the process.

Components of the Program

Developing the TIPS Homework Projects

The following process is suggested in the *TIPS Manual*:

Teachers cooperate to design and develop TIPS interactive homework assignments to match the curriculum and learning objectives. It helps if two or more teachers work together, discussing, writing, and editing their ideas. Optimally, the length of a TIPS activity is the front and back of one piece of paper. Creating TIPS homework activities is more than cutting and pasting ideas from other homework. Student-family interaction must be built into every activity. In most TIPS activities this means asking students and families to interview each other, play a game, collect data, record reactions or suggestions, apply a skill to real life, or work together in some other way.

Dissemination of TIPS Packets to Teachers

During a departmental meeting in September, the TIPS program is introduced to teachers by the project leader. The goals of the program are explained and the *Manual* and homework activities for the subjects and the different grades are distributed. Guidance is given on the key components of the program and on things the teachers should remember as they use the process.

Orientation for Parents

Parents are informed in many ways about the TIPS program, including letters during the summer from the principal, orientation sessions at the school, material distributed on open house night, information in newsletters, and information from their children.

TIPS Homework Assignments Given to Students

In Calverton and West Baltimore Middle Schools, the language arts and science/health homework activities are printed on different colored paper to distinguish them from each other and from the white paper that fills middle grades students' notebooks. Parents also are alerted to ask students about the TIPS activities on the blue or yellow or green papers each week.

The teachers use TIPS every week or every other week. Most teachers give students more than 1 day to enable them to find time to interact with a family member. Some teachers assign TIPS activities over the weekend to give parents more opportunity to find time to talk with their children about schoolwork.

The homework TIPS activities include:

- Brief message to the parent or guardian stating the topic of the assignment and the skills involved, dated and signed by the students.

- The objectives of the assignments are worded clearly and simply so that the student can read them to the parent or the parent can read them with the student.

- Materials required for the assignment are common, inexpensive, or readily available items in the home. If students do not have or cannot get them, the materials should be provided by the school.

- Step-by-step instructions are included to tell students and parents what to do and whether to write answers or conclusions on the homework paper. In the case of science experiments, the outline of a lab report or data chart is included for students to record their findings. Discussion questions are included to guide students' interactions with parents or other family members.

- A Home-to-School Communication section invites parents to write comments, noting whether their child understood the homework, whether they enjoyed doing the activity with their child, and whether they gained information about their child's work in language arts or science and health.

- A parent's signature is requested on each activity.

Quoting again from the *TIPS Manual*:

When the homework is completed, the teacher conducts a short, stimulating follow-up activity in class to give students opportunities to share their work and their families' responses and reactions. Follow-up activities reinforce the importance of homework, the importance of family involvement, and the contributions of family interactions to enrich thinking about the curriculum. It is up to the teacher whether the TIPS homework assignments are given the same weight in the grading system as the regular homework.

Certificates

After a certain number of TIPS activities are completed, some teachers award students and families certificates for their participation. This may be done at the end of a report card period, or once or twice a year.

Parent Involvement in Planning, Operating, and Monitoring

The emphasis of the TIPS program is to encourage and facilitate interaction at home between the student and his/her parent or guardian or other family member. If the TIPS homework assignments are designed appropriately and introduced well to students in class, the students conduct the interactions at home. Parents are not asked to teach skills, or read or write to complete the students' work. Students complete their homework, including guided interactions to share ideas and information, at home.

As they prepare the activities, teachers must be sensitive to the skill levels of their students, and the students' abilities to explain and share their work. The assignments must take into account the educational level of the parents and the constraints on their time and energy. If a parent is not present at home, the student is encouraged to ask a relative or other adult to participate in the homework assignment.

Strengths and Weaknesses

Reactions from parents during the first 2 years of the TIPS program at West Baltimore Middle School and Calverton

Middle School demonstrate that they have enjoyed completing the assignments. The homework activities are designed to serve as a source of information to parents about what their child is studying in a particular academic subject. Parents become accustomed to the colored homework activities that appear each week. The students learn to schedule their time to complete the assignments and discuss their work and ideas with a parent.

As the program proceeded in its evaluations on the implementation of TIPS, one of the project leaders learned that a few parents misinterpreted the goals and the purpose of the TIPS program. They considered all homework as punishment for the student, indicating that the child did not complete work in class. Project leaders and teachers must overcome such misperceptions about homework and TIPS by improving their communication with parents, during orientation sessions and throughout the implementation process.

Outcomes and Evaluation

Research conducted by Joyce Epstein and her colleagues over the past 10 years, and summarized in the *Manual*, shows that

> teachers in middle grades can implement good practices to involve parents in learning activities with their children. Teachers who actively and frequently use parent involvement include parents with all educational backgrounds, not only well-educated parents. These teachers show more appreciation of parents and report more cooperation from parents (including single parents and parents with less formal education).

> Middle grades teachers who systematically involve families begin to see more parents as allies—interested in their children and in the schools. Parents who receive frequent requests for involvement from teachers report that they learn more about the school program, recognize and appreciate the teachers' efforts, obtain ideas about how to help at home, and

rate the teachers higher in interpersonal skills and overall teaching quality.

Middle grades students report that they learn things about their parents they would not have known without the assignments that require and guide interaction at home. Student and parent communications increase about school, schoolwork, and homework.

Three types of evaluations of the implementation of TIPS were conducted in the first 2 years: (1) interviews with teachers, parents, and students, (2) surveys of teachers on their implementations of TIPS; and (3) the collection and analysis of homework samples to determine the students' and families' uses of TIPS, their successes, problems, and reactions.

The evaluations show that the program goals were accomplished. Large numbers of families, students, and teachers changed their patterns of communication about homework from previous years. In informal interviews, the researchers found that parents, teachers, and students expressed unusually positive attitudes toward TIPS. Students reported that they learned something about their parents that they would not have otherwise known because of their discussions from the TIPS assignments.

In reviewing homework samples over several weeks, the researchers found that large numbers of parents, who were not previously involved with their children's homework and learning at home, were actively involved in TIPS; teachers reported higher rates of return of TIPS homework than regular homework; and TIPS helped teachers communicate with parents.

Budget and Funding

Funding for the development of TIPS in the middle grades, the *TIPS Manual*, and the TIPS homework activities, has come from a grant from the Edna McConnell Clark Foundation and from the Office of Educational Research and Improvement of the U.S. Department of Education. The *TIPS Manual* and prototype activities are available to other middle grades educators. The main cost of the project to schools is in printing or copying the homework activities for the students. Evaluations of the TIPS process and its effects will continue by researchers at the Center for Families, Communities, Schools, and Children's Learning at The Johns Hopkins University, with the assistance of the teachers in the demonstration schools.

For Further Information Contact

> Joyce Epstein or Karen Salinas
> Center on Families, Communities, Schools and
>   Children's Learning
> Johns Hopkins University
> 3505 North Charles Street
> Baltimore, MD 21218
> (410) 516–0370

For information on the TIPS program in West Baltimore and Calverton Middle Schools, contact:

> Vivian Jackson
> Fund for Educational Excellence
> 605 N. Eutaw St.
> Baltimore, MD 21201
> (410) 685–8300

CROSSROADS SCHOOL
New York, NY

Major Components:
>Advisory system
>Parent conferences
>Building Bridges
>"Conversations" with parents
>Work parties

Special Features:
>Multicultural
>Multiage grouping
>Untracked
>Flexible scheduling
>Cooperative learning
>Student empowerment

Profile of Program and School:

Number of students enrolled at Crossroads	120
% from African-American families	37%
% from Latino families	37%
% from White families	24%
% from Asian-American families	1%
% eligible for free lunch	60%
% who speak more than one language	40%
% from outside district	35%

The **goals** of the Crossroads School are:

- To empower children, by providing them with academic skills and a sense of self—who they are, where they want to go, ways to get there; and
- To revitalize parent involvement at the middle school level.

BACKGROUND

Ann Wiener, a teacher in a middle school in Community School District #3 in New York City, had a vision of a middle school which would be staffed and structured so as to meet the needs of children at this critical age. She perceived that the most important aspect of education for children in early adolescence is social learning, and she began to design a program which would appeal to students of this age and keep them in school. In 1989, she wrote a proposal and took it to the local school board and the district educators. There was positive response to her ideas, and her proposal was approved, but there was no help from the district in locating space she might use for her school.

Ann Wiener followed up on many leads to find space, riding her bicycle around the area to look for a facility. In the course of her searching, she met Maggie and John Sears who were in the process of designing and developing a new plan for P.S. 165, located on West 109th Street on the edge of Harlem. The Roosevelt Institute had sponsored a pilot project aimed at empowering the school and parents at P.S. 151 in Manhattan as part of the Better Schools Project. The effort at P.S. 165 was to replicate the P.S. 151 project in another school.

DESCRIPTION OF THE PROGRAM

In the fall of 1990, Crossroads School opened—an alternative middle school, diverse racially, ethnically, economically, and in ability—based on the vision and philosophy recommended by the Carnegie Commission in its report *Turning Points*. This middle school has an untracked core academic program, an advisory system, a diverse collegial staff, multiaged grouping, flexible scheduling, cooperative learning, student self-evaluations, and narrative teacher reports.

The Crossroads School is staffed by a Director-Teacher, six teachers, and a part-time school secretary, who is a parent of two students at the school. The staff is from diverse backgrounds, with several who speak Spanish.

Components of the Program

Advisory System

As children move from the self-contained elementary classroom to middle school where they have many teachers, there is often no adult with primary responsibility for the student. At Crossroads, the advisor provides the anchor for the child. All adults at Crossroads—including aides, administrators, and teachers—serve as Advisors. Each Advisor acts as a liaison between school and home and is responsible for a group of 14–16 children, of different ages and grades, for the year. The Advisor and his/her advisees meet twice a week. The Advisor telephones the parents within the first 2 weeks of school, and maintains frequent phone contact throughout the year. The Advisor is the staff person at the school to whom parents can turn for information on how their child is doing in school and for assistance in solving any problems which may arise.

Parent Conferences

Parent/Advisor/Student conferences are held twice a year, with the students as full participants in the discussions. Participation is 100%. Students "role play" in sessions with their advisor in preparation for an active role in the conferences.

Building Bridges

This program, started in the fall of 1992, was designed to develop stronger partnerships between parents and the school. It recognizes that many parents do not find schools welcoming and do not recognize the importance of school-parent partnerships. The program includes three components:

- A part-time Parent Coordinator;

- A series of small-group meetings or "conversations"; and

- "Work Parties" at the school, where parents, staff, and students engage in such activities as renovating the playground, painting donated chairs, or building needed school equipment.

Monthly parent/teacher "conversations" in Spanish and English are facilitated by staff with an emphasis on sharing viewpoints, feelings, and concerns, and using such techniques as fishbowl, role playing, and simulations. In addition to strategies for supporting academic success, topics include communication problems, teen values, sex, risk-taking behavior, substance abuse, single parenting, reasonable limits for early adolescents, death, nutrition, and how to exist with 10–13-year olds. It is rare that outside experts are brought in; parents have enormous knowledge, and calling upon this knowledge empowers parents.

Staff have found that these meetings, combined with Work Parties and the close advisor/parent relationship, changes the way parents conceptualize their responsibilities for their children's education, strengthen parent/teacher relationships, and increase student academic success.

Political/Community Activism

Parents, students, and teachers can count on each other as a support network to turn to when confronted with troublesome national political events. After the Los Angeles riots, when police officers were acquitted in the beating of Rodney King, the parents came together to discuss racism and what they might do about it. One participant in the discussion was the child of a Holocaust survivor. With parental support, students decided to sponsor a Silent Protest, which was held at noon on the corner of 110th and Broadway. Police were present to protect the students' protest, which lasted 8 minutes. Almost every child at the school participated.

The students in the school became concerned when a group reported that the nearby Woolworth's store appeared to be discriminating against blacks because it would not let several black students from Crossroads into the store. The students planned and conducted test visits to the store and concluded that the policy toward white students was clearly different; white students were permitted to enter and wander through the store, while black students were not. Much discussion about racism and discrimination resulted. The students contacted the District Attorney's office to discuss whether charges can be brought against the store.

Another example of parent/student activism occurred in connection with a leaky roof at the school. Since the school opened in the fall of 1990, efforts had been made to have the school system repair the roof. Finally, in the fall of 1992, the School Construction Committee scheduled a meeting; parents and students planned and conducted a demonstration to dramatize their concerns and to stress the urgency of their demands. They presented the Committee with a list of needed renovations and repairs for both the inside and the outside of the building. Roof replacement has begun and is scheduled for completion by August 30, 1993. Though the School Construction Committee had stated that there were no funds available for any interior repairs, interior repair work valued at $579,000 will be done.

Social Events

This diverse school community develops closer relationships with each other through a number of social events, including Fall and Spring picnics and two potluck suppers, organized around student performances and graduation.

Volunteer and Fund-Raising Activities

Parents are welcome to visit at all times. They have gone on school trips, answered telephones, organized mailings, and put up shelves.

Parents have been very active in contributing money to the school and in raising funds for needs of the school. In 1992, 94% of the parents donated $3,000 for school supplies. In the fall of 1992, they raised over $6,500 from the sale of holiday wrapping paper. They are also working on locating a source of funds to purchase playground equipment.

Steering Committee

Staff and parents have formed a Steering Committee to plan and conduct activities for parents. Participation is open to all. A Steering Committee, rather than a PTA, was chosen as a means of encouraging input from all parents rather than the white, middle class parents who often dominate most PTAs. A diverse group of about 25% of the families are generally present at Steering Committee meetings.

Newsletter

A school newsletter is mailed home regularly. All written materials provided by the school are available in English and Spanish.

Parent Involvement in Planning, Operating, and Monitoring

In middle school parent involvement drops dramatically. Crossroads actively seeks participation, knowing that a parent/school partnership is a powerful and crucial ingredient for student academic success. Parents are involved in many of the aspects of the school on a day-to-day basis. One of the issues in planning for the alternative middle school was how to encourage parents who were very active in elementary schools to continue their interest and involvement at the middle school level. In adolescence, students are reluctant for parents to hang around, and in conventional schools the teachers often view parental participation with skepticism. Many of the parents have had very negative experiences in their relationships with their children's schools, and have not had the cultural background to prepare them for involvement in education. The staff at the Crossroads School constantly looks for ways to involve parents appropriate to ages of the students and the needs of the school.

One example of how parents and staff collaborate to improve the educational program at the school concerns reading. In the 1991–1992 school year, everyone was in favor of the students reading more. To achieve this, staff, with strong parental support, instituted 40 minutes of reading every day. Everyone now accepts this and the children are using the time productively: some are reading novels or other books cover-to-cover and others are looking up information in reference books. All agree that instituting a formal reading period helps students to read more.

Strengths and Weaknesses

Crossroads School parents have become much more involved than is typically the case. They are gaining more information and experience about early adolescence, and are feeling more comfortable in dealing with the ups and downs of children in this age group. Parents have learned to allow their middle schoolers to participate in school activities outside of school hours and away from the home, and to broaden their vision of their child's future. Parents are also working with advisors, learning about various options for their children's high school education.

One unsuccessful effort is asking parents to respond to invitations or surveys in writing. For input, the school has found that they have to contact the parents directly and personally. A phone chain provides parents with notices about what is going on at the school. A survey of parents was conducted in 1991, and provided the school with much information about parents' preferences and interests.

The staff respects parents and constantly strives to achieve a true partnership between home and school. They recognize that parents know their children best and, therefore, have much to contribute to the teachers about their child's personality, learning style, strengths, and weaknesses.

One barrier experienced by the Crossroads School is the lack of real support from the public school system. The school had to mount their own campaign to repair the leaky roof; the state allocates only $25 per student for texts and books; the school system provides very little to the school for supplies, books, paper, pencils.

Outcomes and Evaluation

Many examples of the effectiveness of the Crossroads School could be listed. Although all students can choose to come—or not come—to Crossroads, only three out of 120 did not return after the summer 1992 vacation. Attendance rates are a high 98%. Scores of the students on citywide required tests are good, although Crossroads primarily uses methods of assessment other than tests. Report cards do not include letter grades, but rather are primarily comments about what the student is doing well, what he/she needs to work on, and specific suggestions for improvement.

Crossroads works with others to strengthen the school. In 1992–1993, staff from Crossroads have attended a Bank Street College of Education seminar on alternative methods to assess student achievement. As a member of the Coalition of Essential Schools, Crossroads continually reviews different ways of assessing children and teachers and holding the school more accountable.

The Diamond Foundation funded a documentation of the first year of the Crossroads School. Currently, Michelle Fine, professor at City University in New York City and the University of Pennsylvania, Philadelphia, and several graduate students are engaged with Crossroads staff in a 3-year study of educational policy and school/community issues.

Budget and Funding

The New York Board of Education pays the salaries of the teachers and staff and makes a contribution toward supplies, books, and equipment needed at the school. Currently, Board of Education support is inadequate in providing quality education. Parents have raised $3,000 for supplies. Private individuals have given a grant of $10,000 to the school. Volunteers from Riverside Church donate their time to the school and have performed such tasks as painting the classrooms and cleaning the playground.

The following individuals, organizations and foundations assist with various special programs at the school:

- Roosevelt Institute Better Schools Project

- The Bruner Foundation
- The Diamond Foundation
- New York Foundation for the Arts
- Carnegie Council

For Further Information Contact

Ann Wiener
Crossroads School
234 West 109th Street
New York, NY 10025
(212) 316-5256

KETTERING MIDDLE SCHOOL
Prince George's County
Upper Marlboro, MD

Major Components:
> Home-school communications
> Parent Calendar
> Parent Volunteers **EVERYWHERE**
> Homework Hotline

Special Features:
> Mentors for Black Male Achievement Program
> Communications and Academic Studies Program
> Teachers active in PTA
> Summer Retreat for Teachers and Parents

Profile of School and School District:

Number of students enrolled in district	113,000
Number of schools in district	171
Number of students enrolled at Kettering	932
% from African-American families	86%
% from Asian-American families	1%
% from White families	13%
% from low-income families	6%

The **goals** of the program are:

- To increase home-school communication;
- To encourage greater parent participation in education; and
- To form home-school partnerships which will result in higher student achievement.

BACKGROUND

The Parent Involvement Program started in 1988, shortly after Mrs. Eleanor White was named the new principal of the school. The PTA leadership scheduled a meeting with the new principal, and talked with her at length about the need for greater parent involvement in the school. Mrs. White listened with a sympathetic ear, and began immediately to institute some of the programs proposed by the PTA and to make changes in the response of the school to parents and their concerns.

DESCRIPTION OF THE PROGRAM

Many of the components of Kettering Middle School's Parent Involvement Program have been suggested and are supervised by the school's PTA organization. The dynamic leadership within the PTA, coupled with Mrs. White's energy and enthusiasm, has resulted in an active program which is striving for more parent involvement and, ultimately, higher student achievement. Kettering Middle School serves only two grades—7th and 8th—which presents a challenge to the PTA and the school administration. Each year they greet 500 new parents, whose children are in the school only for 2 years and then move on. There are 932 students in the school, 86% of whom are African-American; most of the families are middle class and upper middle class.

Components of the Program

Home-School Communications

The monthly newsletter is the primary means of written communication between home and school. It includes listings of all the upcoming activities and important dates on the school schedule. A Parent Calendar indicates the dates of all of the social events, cultural events, PTA meetings, progress reports, and report cards. A Message Board at school is another technique for sharing information between teachers, students, and parents.

Parent Volunteer Program

Parents are always welcome at the school, and there are many opportunities for volunteers. The Committee which oversees this component realizes that students in the 7th and 8th grades do not want their parents in their own classrooms, so volunteers are not assigned to their own children's classrooms. Some of the locations and roles for the 50–60 parent volunteers who are in the school each day include:

- Parents who are engineers and scientists regularly assist in the Science Labs;

- Parents assist with materials preparation and clerical work in the Work Room: laminating, cutting out letters, typing, copying;

- Parents work in the TV Studio;

- Parents serve as timers for Team Olympics, Little Competitors, and other physical education activities;

- Parents attend Career Day and share information about their jobs as lawyers, doctors, engineers;

- Parents have redecorated the Health Office; and

- Parents have assisted on field trips.

Parents who are unable to volunteer during the day help out with activities in the evening. Seventy parents served as chaperons at the Sock-Hop; parents helped with the serving and cleanup of the Family Spaghetti Dinner.

Parents also visit the classrooms to observe children who are having special difficulties, and then report back to the principal concerning their observations and suggestions for solutions to difficult situations.

Homework Hotline

Parents can call the electronic answering machine at any time, press the correct extension number, and hear the teacher announcing the homework for the class for that night. Parents can also leave messages or convey their suggestions or complaints to the administrators at the school.

UJIMA

This is a program to promote the achievement of Black male students, to assist them to explore and establish realistic and attainable educational and career goals, and to provide opportunities for them to demonstrate and practice positive leadership behavior. A total of 42 mentors are assigned to students in the school. Some of the parents serve as mentors in this program.

PTA Committees

The PTA Executive Board has formed a number of committees to implement and oversee many of the parent involvement activities at the school. The committees meet once a month.

Summer Retreat

Staff from the three elementary feeder schools, Kettering Middle School, and the local high school attend a retreat every summer to address many issues related to coordination and continuity between the three levels of schooling. About 160 persons attend the retreat, including administrators, teachers, and parents. Twenty-five teachers and five Kettering Middle School parents are invited. The 1991 retreat was entitled "Making the Connection;" this was followed in 1992 by "The Connection is Clear." During the retreat the participants are assigned to smaller groups for discussion of issues; at some sessions they break down into grade levels, in others they form small groups along academic lines.

School-Based Management Steering Committee

This group, including administrators, teachers, and parents, serves as the policymaking organization for the school. It has created 12 subcommittees to study, review, or monitor policies and programs and report back to the Steering Committee with recommendations for action. Parents are represented on many of these subcommittees, including the Parent Involvement Subcommittee, the School-Community Subcommittee, and the Budget Subcommittee.

Homework Assignment Booklets

Homework is an important issue with parents, students, and teachers at Kettering Middle School. Often parents are uncertain about their role in monitoring homework, and students in the 7th and 8th grades often do not place a high priority on homework. In order to assist all parties, the principal purchased samples of various types of notebooks with specially designed pages for recording homework assignments. One format was selected to be used by all teachers, students, and parents. A parent who was involved in the choice of the homework assignment forms offered to provide copies for the whole school. Several days later a truck arrived at the school with more than 200,000 copies of the form, donated by the parent.

Communication and Academic Studies

Both parents and teachers provide tremendous support for this program, designed to provide continuity between the elementary magnet program and the high school academic center. This program concentrates on excellence in basic subjects and focuses on a variety of communications-related curricula and activities. Enriched art, drama and dance as a part of the physical education program, Spanish and other languages, and an emphasis on creative writing and debate, are components of the program which is designed to develop intellectual skills and concepts for academic achievement.

Parent Involvement in Planning, Operating, and Monitoring

Parents play a crucial role in every aspect of this program; the PTA Committees are responsible for many of the components. Every activity within the schools, from classrooms to extracurricular activities, seeks to involve parents in many different capacities. The PTA president and the school principal have developed a strong, trusting relationship and maintain constant communication with each other.

The PTA is striving to achieve a level of parent involvement in the middle school which is comparable to that which most parents experience when their children are in the elementary school. Due to the difference in the children's feelings at this age, and the difference in school structure, the parent involvement cannot be the same. The students want to be independent and do not want their parents in the school. The program has to work around the students and involve parents in ways not directly related to their own children. However, the principal attempts to demonstrate that parents are still wanted, although the activities and tasks are different from the elementary level.

The principal believes that the school must have a strong working relationship with the home, or the school will not be effective and the students will not be successful in their education. She emphasizes that this should be a partnership, not a power struggle, between parents and teachers. One of the steps taken by the principal to increase the confidence of the parents was to take down the counter which parents had to stand behind when they went to the school. This was symbolic of a barrier between parents and the school, and its disappearance was intended to demonstrate a sense of cooperation and partnership and to reduce the distinction between "Them" and "Us."

The intention is to develop a high level of trust between all parents and the school personnel, so that parents will feel free to criticize the school without posing a threat to the teachers and administrators. It is hoped that parents will be supportive of the school and, therefore, willing to be an integral part of what is going on there.

The PTA has taken an active role in issues other than parent involvement in the school. They were involved and vocal in the school board decision concerning the choice of curriculum for the magnet high school. They were supportive of the opening of Kettering Middle School as a community school, open to the neighborhood and the community for meetings and events every night of the week. They have spoken at school board meetings in support of providing a continuity program that bridges academic offerings at the elementary and high school.

Strengths and Weaknesses

The number of parents active in the Kettering Middle School is evidence of a strong parent involvement program. The PTA President has been very effective at finding parent volunteers who will respond to calls for assistance in classes, activities, and clerical tasks. Parent attendance at regular PTA meetings is not high, but parents are sure to come if there is a topic of interest to them. The parent involvement program has had to be flexible; the principal and PTA president must continually be adding and changing in order to serve the needs of both the parents and the school.

The replacement of the rotary telephone system with push-button phones, and the purchase of the answering machines and the fax machine, have had a great impact on communication. The push-button phones and electronic answering machine system have enabled the school to implement the homework hotline and the message system for teachers and administrators.

Outcomes and Evaluation

Over the past 5 years, the Kettering Middle School parent involvement program appears to have been successful, from the standpoint of the numbers of parents volunteering at the school, attending meetings, serving on committees, and contributing time and money to the school.

Several indicators are cited as evidence of school effectiveness. The attendance rate is 94.5% (the goal set by the principal is 97%). Three years ago, there were 30–40 phone calls to the area office with complaints about the school; during the

1992–1993 school year there have been only two. A total of 53% of the students at the school are on the Honor Roll for their academic achievement. Three years ago, 300 students were suspended from school; last year, the number was down to 30. During the 1992–1993 school year, only five students had been suspended during the first half of the year. This means that the school can concentrate on instruction and not discipline.

Budget and Funding

The district funds for education at Kettering are supplemented by fund-raising activities sponsored by the PTA and donations from the parents.

For Further Information Contact

Mrs. Eleanor White, Principal
Kettering Middle School
65 Herrington Dr.
Upper Marlboro, MD 20772
(301) 336-4100

EMPOWERMENT PROJECT: EMPOWERING PARENTS TO IMPROVE STUDENT ACHIEVEMENT
Kosciuszko Middle School
Parkman Middle School
Milwaukee, WI

Major Components:
Home visits
Transition from Elementary to Middle School
High Expectations Program
Parent Center
Computer Classes
ESL Classes

Special Features:
Empowerment
Brother 2 Brother and Sister 2 Sister

Profile of School and School District:

	Milwaukee Public Schools	Parkman Middle School	Kosciuszko Middle School
Enrollment	89,000	520	740
% African-American	56%	99%	15%
% Latino	10%		64%
% Asian-American	3%		3%
% Native-American	1%		3%
% White	30%	1%	15%
% Free/reduced lunch		90%	85%

The **goals** of the Empowerment Project are:

- To enhance student achievement, attendance, and attitudes;
- To develop parent leadership and advocacy in order to take action on educational issues; and
- To inform and communicate with parents so they can become involved in supporting the education of their children.

BACKGROUND

The Empowerment Project was formally started in 1990, following a grant awarded to the Greater Milwaukee Educational Trust by the Edna McConnell Clark Foundation, for the improvement of the quality of education in two middle schools in the city of Milwaukee. The two schools chosen are located in low-income neighborhoods in Milwaukee: Parkman Middle School, an African-American school on the North Side, and Kosciuszko Middle School, a heavily Hispanic school on the South Side.

The program was planned and designed by community leaders and staff from the Greater Milwaukee Educational Trust. In July 1990, two community organizers were hired, one for each of the middle schools in the project. The Trust emphasized that although the organizers would work out of the school, it should be understood that they work for and with parents. At the end of July the organizers initiated a parent canvass to make a personal connection with as many parents as possible and to ask for ideas and suggestions for improving their school. During the next month, the two organizers visited and spoke to 400 parents.

One of the first events of the Empowerment Project was a day-long strategic planning workshop, held in August 1990, at both of the schools involved. A total of 72 persons attended the workshop associated with Parkman Middle School, including 29 teachers and 37 parents. The Kosciuszko Workshop was attended by 49 participants, including 23 teachers and 18 parents.

The purpose of the workshops was to develop vision statements, goals, and objectives to be incorporated in the strategic planning process for the Empowerment Project. The participants discussed attitudes toward parent involvement and practical steps to take to succeed at increasing parent involvement at the school.

DESCRIPTION OF PROGRAM

The Empowerment Project uses a "Community Organizing Model" that is designed to increase the role and responsibilities of parents, families, residents, and students in educational achievement. Two community organizers from the Greater Milwaukee Educational Trust direct the Empowerment Project at Parkman and Kosciuszko Middle Schools. They are assisted by school personnel, consultants, and parent volunteers.

The organizers work out of the Parent Center, established in each school as an access point for information and training, and to provide comfortable parent space in the building where parents can assemble and relax. A phone bank has been installed at Parkman to encourage parents to call the school for information on their child's homework, school policies, or general school and community news.

Components of the Program

Home Visits

During the summers of 1991 and 1992, the two parent organizers have visited the homes of every student entering the 6th grade at Parkman or Kosciuszko Middle School in the Fall. These visits are to make the parents feel welcome at the school, assist with information to make the transition easier, and, most important of all, to find out how parents view the school and what needs to happen in order for them to become more active in their children's education. A form is filled out, to include demographic information and other data about the student and family. They are asked about their hobbies and interests and whether they might volunteer at the school.

Transition from Elementary School to Middle School

In order to facilitate the transition, parents and students are encouraged to go to the school building before school opens. They are shown the building, meet some of the staff, and are made to feel comfortable about the upcoming year.

Parents Organization

Meetings of the parents organization are scheduled each month; about 30 parents attend and discuss such topics as school security, gangs, homework, high school choices, report cards, attendance, student self-esteem, and role model issues. Forty parents participated in a series of four workshops on leadership and planning training.

High Expectation Program—Attendance, Attitude, and Achievement (HEP–AAA)

This is an incentive-based program designed to improve student attendance, grades, and attitudes. In order to participate, the student and his/her parent(s) are asked to agree to a contract, which includes the responsibilities of the teacher, the student, and the parent.

A group of students from each grade (6th, 7th, and 8th) are identified by their teachers as needing extra help. The parent coordinator and parent volunteers visit the homes of students participating in the program to ask the parents to sign the HEP Contract, to volunteer at the school, and to attend and participate in school meetings and events. Each student attaining 95% attendance or an increase of .5 in their GPA (*e.g.*, 2.0 to 2.5) receives a reward and a certificate.

School Support Activities

Parent volunteers are always welcome at the school, to assist in the Parent Center and help with the Hotline. In addition, parents have been hired as part-time Parent Aides. At Parkman, the Aide makes home visits, prepares mailings, and phones parents. At Kosciuszko, one parent aide assists in the Spanish class and others help out in the Parent Coordinator's Office and the Parent Center.

Parent Center

The Parent Center provides physical space for parents to meet, make a phone call, or just stop in for a visit. The Center serves as a resource library for parents and a referral service for family needs. An average of 5–10 parents per week drop in to seek assistance with school or social service problems.

The Parent Center regularly sponsors workshops for parents on education topics they have expressed an interest in: homework, how to make the transition to high school, how to read the report card, how to read and interpret the child's test scores. Other topics for parents are job readiness and relaxation therapy.

Another activity of the volunteers at the Parent Center has been to call all families, encouraging parents to attend the parent/teacher conferences scheduled in March. Flyers and a parent newsletter are mailed to announce the conference days and provide "tips" for effective conferencing.

Parent Hotline

The Parent Coordinator and parent volunteer assistants use the telephone to inform parents about school events and meetings, to check on missing homework, to recruit parents as volunteers in the school, and to provide information on parent classes. In addition, hundreds of flyers and letters are sent home and/or mailed to parents.

Parent Classes

Classes are available to parents in such subjects as computer skills, ESL, and silk screening.

Brother 2 Brother

This program, at Parkman Middle School, is comprised of minority male students, and is designed to address academic achievement needs in the areas of spiritual, social, mental, and physical health. They hope to organize a group of African-American men and women willing to prepare Parkman's male students for manhood. Their goal is to promote brotherhood, build self-esteem, and develop personal and social growth among male students through community service. At the kick-off breakfast, held in March 1992, 72 students, 24 parents, and 15 mentors attended. Sister 2 Sister is a similar organization focusing on African-American women.

Parent Involvement in Planning, Operating, and Monitoring

The Empowerment Project has succeeded in recruiting parents to be involved in many activities within the school. Parents now sit on the Advisory Council. They answer the Parent Hotline, responding to parents who call the school for information and assistance. Parents were active in putting pressure on the superintendent and the school board to hire more African-American teachers for Parkman Middle School. They were not successful in achieving this goal in their own school, but the number of African-American teachers in the Milwaukee Public School District has risen, partly as a result of parent activism.

Those planning and designing the Empowerment Project did not start with a traditional concept of parent involvement. A major emphasis was on the home visits and other communication with parents to find out directly from parents what they are concerned about and how they view the education of their children. Shirley Owens and Daisy Cubias make a conscious effort to be open and honest with the parents, trying to establish a level of trust which will ensure meaningful communications.

Much of the emphasis during the home visits is to diminish the hostile attitudes of the parents about the schools. Many parents are suspicious to see an organizer at their door to talk about education. Some will not open their doors, but talk from a crack in the door or from a window. Some students and their parents are defensive, surprised at visitors from school when school is not yet in session, and expecting bad news or a negative report.

As the project has progressed, it has become evident that contact should be made with the parents before their children enter the middle school. There is a need to reach them at the feeder schools, to emphasize to them the importance of their contribution, and encourage them to become involved at the middle school level.

Strengths and Weaknesses

Much effort has been given to working with the teachers to alter any preconceptions they might have about the inadequacies of parents. The parent organizers have tried to overcome the adversarial aspect of parent vs. teacher, "them against us," and have stressed that this is a "win-win" situation, where teachers and parents will both benefit from increased parent involvement. They have made presentations to teachers at several different training sessions. Parents are now being treated with respect; they have developed self-confidence and, consequently, have experienced changes in how they view the school.

An effort has been made to provide secretaries and receptionists at the school with suggestions about how to treat parents. Training sessions have been held to emphasize that the parents are the "customers" of the school and should always be treated politely and with respect.

The computer classes for parents have been very successful; attendance has been good, and the parents are being trained in a skill which may be useful in their employment efforts. The interest in the ESL class at Kosciuszko is growing; only three parents enrolled when the class was started, but that number soon increased to 13.

It has been very difficult to schedule meetings which both parents and teachers can attend. Teachers find it difficult to attend meetings during the day, and are reluctant to stay late to meet with parents. It is a problem to get teachers to communicate regularly with parents; they rarely call parents unless there is a problem with a student.

Evaluation and Outcomes

Logs are kept of all contacts and activities, calculations of the number of volunteer hours parents have contributed to the school, and counts of the number of parents attending various school functions and activities. Many positive changes have been noticed as a result of the project efforts: changed teacher attitudes, teachers' calling parents more often than before, more positive attitudes toward the school on the part of parents, more willingness to participate in school activities, increased parent/community support, and improved student achievement.

One of the parent volunteers at the school has noticed that the school personnel appear to have more tolerance of parents since the project started. She also notes that her daughter is more interested in school and appears to be learning more since her mother became regularly involved as a school volunteer.

The High Expectations Program (HEP) has been the catalyst for a number of changes in attitudes and behaviors of project participants. When the program was first presented, teachers reacted negatively because they thought the project meant additional work for them. After several meetings where many issues and difficulties were discussed, the teachers now feel more positive. They have stated that they observe improved attendance and attitudes from some of the students. Parents appreciate receiving morning phone calls from the school about their child's absenteeism.

At the Parkman School, attendance for those students in the HEP program has improved from 84% to 89%, and Grade Point Average has increased from 1.7 to 2.04. In the 1991–1992 school year, 27 of the 196 6th grade students in the program achieved 100% attendance and 92 achieved 95% attendance. Of the 147 7th graders, 19 students reached 100% attendance and 73 attained 95%.

At Kosciuszko, a total of 138 students participated in the HEP program during the fall of 1992. After the first 6-week marking period, 22 had achieved 100% attendance and 25 had a 95% record. A total of 53 students had raised their grades at least .5 points; 22 have a GPA of 3.0 or above.

The number of parent involvement hours has increased every year since the project began. During the 1988–1989 school year, about 1,500 parent involvement hours were recorded for both schools. Each year since then this total has doubled, resulting in a total of 9,500 parent involvement hours for the 1991–1992 school year. An orientation session held in August 1992, at Parkman, was attended by 130 parents and 69 students; this was the first orientation session at the school since

1987. A total of 175 parents and 150 students attended an open house at Kosciuszko.

The attendance of parents at the parent/teacher conferences has shown a marked increase due to the efforts of the Empowerment Project. At Parkman Middle School, a total of 24% of the parents attended conferences during the 1989–1990 school year, while in the following year, 1990–1991, after the start of the Empowerment Project, 44% of parents of children in the school were present. At Kosciuszko, the percentage of parents attending conferences rose from 51% in the 1989–1990 school year, to 57% the following year.

Budget and Funding

It is estimated that the Empowerment Project can be operated in two schools for an annual budget between $95,000 and $125,000. This figure does not include all of the costs, since the school contributes space, furniture, telephone, and office supplies.

For Further Information Contact

Shirley Owens, Parkman Middle School
Daisy Cubias, Kosciuszko Middle School
Greater Milwaukee Education Trust
756 N. Milwaukee
Milwaukee, WI 53202
(414) 287-4145

Parkman Middle School
3620 North 18th Street
Milwaukee, WI 53206
(414) 445-9930

Kosciuszko Middle School
971 Windlake Ave.
Milwaukee, WI 53204
(414) 383-3750

OPERATION PUT—PARENTS UNITED WITH TEACHERS
Morningside Middle School
Ft. Worth, TX

Major Components:
Parent visitation
Parent discussion sessions
Parent Action Committees

Special Features:
Parent empowerment
Church recognition of student achievement

Profile of School:
Number of students enrolled in the school 750
% from African-American families 85%
% from low-income families 75%
% in free/reduced lunch program 67%

The **goals** of the program are:

- To encourage parents to become involved in the education of their children;
- To help parents understand the schools, by providing information about the instructional program and school expectations so that they can become supporters of the school;
- To make the school the center of the community by bringing together parents, community leaders and organizations, businesses, and churches;
- To help parents understand their opportunities and responsibilities to work with their children at home;
- To help parents have a positive attitude when they visit the school;
- To reduce the dropout rate;
- To improve student achievement;
- To help parents understand their opportunities and responsibilities to help their children become better students; and
- To help parents have a positive attitude when they visit the schools.

BACKGROUND

The Texas Interfaith Education Fund (TIEF) was established by the Texas Industrial Areas Foundation (IAF) Network. It brings together parents, citizens, church members, business and community leaders, and teachers and administrators to focus on the public school system and how it can be changed and improved to meet the needs of families in the 21st Century. The philosophy of the organization is described and developed in a paper entitled "The Texas I.A.F. Vision for Public Schools: Communities of Learners," published by the Texas Interfaith Education Fund in 1990.

TIEF introduced an education reform initiative early in 1991. It has worked with superintendents, principals, and teachers on over 45 campuses from 22 school districts in Texas and Arizona. It has begun to develop a constituency of parents and taxpayers in those districts who see themselves as stakeholders in education and who will work collaboratively with teachers and administrators in designing major reforms for their local schools. TIEF is recognized as the catalyst in bringing *all* stakeholders in education together to develop a common vision for their school or district.

The Allied Communities of Tarrant (ACT) was formed in 1987, and began organizing the community from the grassroots level to become knowledgeable about education and empowered to take action to improve it. ACT served as the catalyst to bring together the educators from the school, including the superintendent, principal and teachers, Chamber of Commerce representatives, members of the Education Committee for Ft. Worth, Inc. (an organization of downtown business leaders), and church and community leaders. They have strengthened their work by studying the Texas IAF vision paper, *Turning Points*, the Carnegie Commission report on middle schools, and the California state report entitled *Caught in the Middle*.

After many meetings with individuals and organizations, the Morningside Middle School was chosen as a promising site for implementation of a parent involvement program. There were both "good" and "bad" reasons for selecting this school to be the first major effort of ACT. The principal is considered an effective leader and committed to promoting more parent involvement. The students from this school have low test scores, a low level of achievement, and a very high dropout rate. Many ACT churches are located in the neighborhood around Morningside; they can be expected to provide many volunteers for parent organizing. Meetings with parents demonstrated that parents do care about the education of their children, but feel helpless to do anything about school improvement because of their feelings of inferiority and powerlessness, and the many demands on their lives.

The Alliance Schools Project is a partnership between TIEF, the Texas IAF Network, Regional Education Service Centers, the Texas Education Agency (TEA), school district officials, and school staff and parents. Morningside Middle School is one of 32 schools chosen to participate in the Alliance School project, which provides additional resources for staff development and the freedom to design a plan for education at the school that is not restricted by state mandates and regulations. The strong parent involvement effort at the school and the successful performance of the School-Based Management Committee are some of the reasons Morningside was chosen to participate in this effort.

DESCRIPTION OF THE PROGRAM

Approximately 600 families have children attending Morningside Middle School, for grades 6, 7, and 8. About 85% of the students are African-American; it is estimated that 75% of the students are from low-income families and 20% are living in conditions of severe poverty.

The program is a joint effort of ACT and the school staff. The ACT office is located in an office building near the school. Several church committees are active in the educational improvement efforts, including:

- Pastor Education Committee whose purpose is to establish and maintain effective communication between the organizers, the education coordinator, and others active in the project;

- Church Education Committee made up of two members from each church in the neighborhood. It works with the Education Coordinator to further communication between the churches and the project; and

- Church Visitation Group which is responsible for the grassroots organizing efforts, based on door-to-door visits.

The Education Coordinator is the only paid full-time staff working on Operation PUT. She is assisted by many volunteers, who are parents, teachers, religious, business, and community leaders. In addition to organizing the visitation program, the Coordinator serves as staff for the Education Committee of ACT, plans training sessions for the home visitors, and is the main liaison between churches, parents, and the school.

Components of the Program

Parent Visitation

The home visitation efforts came about because the ACT organizers realized that the more conventional means of communication—letters to parents and even telephone calls—were not effective in encouraging parents to attend meetings and become involved in the education process. They concluded that parents should be approached in a personal way, through a home visit from a parent, teacher, community leader, or church representative.

Every year the Education Coordinator designs and implements a plan to visit every family with a child enrolled at Morningside Middle School, and provide them with information about the school, the ACT organization, and their efforts to organize parents to improve the school. Another purpose of the contacts at home is to learn what the parent concerns are and to encourage parents to become active in the school improvement activities. The home visitors gather information on parent complaints about education and the school, as well as facts about the family, their economic situation, and any social needs they might have. The canvasser also discusses the importance of parent involvement and asks about when the parents might be able to come to the school to volunteer or assist.

The Education Coordinator works with the Visitation Committee to organize the home visitation program and train the volunteers who will be making the visits. Often parents team up with teachers to make calls; community leaders, church members, and business men and women also volunteer to help.

In addition to the home visits, the volunteers also organize telephone banks to inform parents about ACT meetings and school events, and encourage them to attend.

Parent Discussion Sessions

During the home visit, the parents are personally invited to a discussion session, to meet with other parents in the neighborhood and brainstorm about the problems of the school and what might be done about them. Many of the parents agree to attend the session partly because they are angry and this provides them with an opportunity to express their feelings. Their child may be failing in school and they have no ideas about what to do about that. It is very helpful for them to hear the same complaints and hostilities from other parents, and to begin to realize that they may be able to join together to take action. A facilitator presides over these meetings; usually school personnel are not present.

Parent Visitation Day

A day is set aside each Fall for parents to go to the school, meet with their child's team of teachers, visit the classrooms, and have parent/teacher conferences. The number of parents taking advantage of this opportunity has been increasing; in Fall 1992, 350 parents attended the Parent Visitation Day.

Parent Volunteers

In addition to serving on the teams to make home visits to other parents, parents, grandparents, and other citizens are provided with many diverse opportunities to volunteer in the school. They help out in the library, the cafeteria, the playground, and the office. Parents come to the school to help monitor the halls, during and between classes. Parents also help with safety for children walking to and from school by providing "safe houses," marked so that the children can knock on the door for assistance if necessary.

Parent Education Program

Once a month a parent meeting is scheduled on such topics as parenting skills, how to interpret grades, preparing the child for the TAAS (Texas Assessment of Academic Skills) test, how to work on obtaining a GED, volunteer programs in the school, how to be supportive of children, suggestions for visiting the classroom and the school, and how to become active and empowered.

Parent Action Committees

These committees are composed of parents and teachers, and serve as advisory groups to the School-Based Management Committee. The three current School Action Committees address concerns related to communications, safety, and academic issues. The Safety Committee has been very active in trying to make the neighborhood around the school safer for those children who walk to school. They were successful in convincing the school district to have gates to an apartment complex near the school closed so that fewer outsiders came on school property. They also lobbied for crosswalks in front of the school to promote safer crossing areas.

School-Based Management Committee

This group, made up of four teachers, three parents selected by the PTA, one community leader, and the principal of the school, is responsible for many of the policy decisions needed to govern the school.

Recognition Program

The ACT Education Committee works with church members to provide encouragement to every child in the school. Their position is that any child can and should be recognized for some achievement or some progress. The focus is on low-achieving students because they typically do not receive praise or positive reinforcement. Morningside students are asked to take their report cards to a committee member at their church; if the report card indicates that the student has made any improvement since the last marking period, he or she is given special recognition.

Parent Involvement in Planning, Operating, and Monitoring

The community leaders and educators from the school had to rethink the traditional concepts of parent involvement and design a program which would be effective with parents of at-risk students. They believe that parents *do* care about their children and want them to have a good education, but they also realize that parents need some assistance to learn how to be involved in an effective way. Parents have much to contribute to the education of their children: they can read, count, shop at the store, go to the library, read the newspaper, watch television and movies. All of these activities can form the basis of education for their children, if parents become aware of these opportunities.

Many parents are very angry with the schools, and it is a challenge to transform the energy behind the anger into constructive action to improve the school. It is difficult to convince those who are so critical about education to accept responsibility for the quality of the school. It is easier to blame someone else for the problems, but this leaves parents with a negative attitude toward the schools. It is the organizers and volunteer leaders who change those negative attitudes into positive energy, and empower parents to take the actions needed for change.

Prior to Operation PUT, the PTA was not a very strong or active organization in the school. It was primarily involved in fund-raising activities and did not attract many parents.

When ACT first began to organize in Morningside Middle School, some PTA supporters felt threatened and worried that their organization would be supplanted by the ACT efforts. This has not happened; instead, the PTA leaders are now working with ACT, attending training sessions and other activities. The PTA has become stronger and is attracting more members. Their role in selecting parents to serve on the School-Based Management Committee has strengthened the organization.

Strengths and Weaknesses

The organizing efforts of ACT have been very successful—both the home visits and the larger community meetings they have sponsored. When the superintendent came to speak at the school, 800 parents attended.

One of the lessons learned during the years this project has been in operation is that building and maintaining parent involvement is a slow, gradual process. It is unrealistic to expect parents to be willing to take responsibility for the schools after many years of experience when they did not feel welcome at the school.

An important purpose of the project is to build a process to attain the goals and to bring about the changes parents want to see in the school. The process strives to develop commitment from the parents to spend time and energy on activities needed for school improvement. Through this, the project hopes to empower parents and encourage them to take ownership of their children's school, and to aid parents to motivate their children in the educational process.

The Parenting Program has been successful in promoting self-confidence among the parents and giving them a sense of empowerment. The message for parents is that Morningside is your school, you must learn to take some responsibility for it. Parents who have less formal education and low-paying jobs may tend to place all of the responsibility (and blame) on the school personnel who are the professionals with a high level of education. ACT and Operation PUT emphasizes that the contribution of all parents is necessary in order for the school to improve and the quality of education for the children to be enhanced. Parents must learn to take risks in order to become informed and involved.

Staff development efforts have been needed to change some of the attitudes and behavior of the teachers at the school. When parents visit the school, teachers need to know how to make them feel welcome. Some of the school staff are reluctant to have inexperienced parents working in the school. Some of the teachers are considered as "uppity" by parents in the neighborhood; parents and teachers must develop mutual respect for each other in order to build a partnership.

Outcomes and Evaluation

No formal evaluation of the parent involvement program has been completed, although much data is being collected from the parents during the home visits. Each year new questions are being added to the data sheet filled in by the home visitors, to determine whether parent attitudes are changing and whether they notice changes in the behavior, attitudes, and performance of their children. Many parents are reporting that their children have a better attitude toward school and are learning more. The number of fights at the school between classes has been greatly reduced.

Many of the parents who expressed harsh criticisms toward the school when the project began have changed their attitudes to be more positive and constructive. They are willing to come to meetings, participate in the brainstorming sessions, visit the school, and cooperate with efforts to bring about change. This project represents an unusual level of cooperation between school, parents, community, and churches. Teachers, too, have begun to change their attitudes toward parents and are willing to increase their interactions and relationships with parents.

Budget and Funding

The ACT budget for their education activities has grown from $65,000 in 1987 to $90,000 in 1992. This pays for the salary of the Education Coordinator and office expenses, supplies, and materials needed for the project. Grants from three foundations are used to pay the expenses of this project.

For Further Information Contact

Mrs. Odessa Raven, Principal
Reverend Nehemiah Davis, Chairman of ACT

Morningside Middle School	Allied Communities of Tarrant
2751 Mississippi	1801 Evans Ave.
Ft. Worth, TX 76104	Ft. Worth, TX 76104
(817) 922–6686	(817) 927–2463

Chapter 5

Programs in High Schools

Conventional wisdom has it that parent-family involvement in schools declines as the student moves from elementary to middle school and that by the time of high school it has all but disappeared. Conventional wisdom in this case is nearly right. Involvement has not disappeared but it is hard to find. It is hard to find commitment and high quality operating programs.

In some ways this is a puzzle—hard to understand. Certainly the challenges of adolescence continue and intensify, but so does the need for guidance, nurturing encouragement, and adult "presence." The student is now even closer to the time of careful planning for education and life after high school. The questions of college and the job world become more insistent. The pressures of daily life for high school students demand maturity and toughness in dealing with drugs, AIDS, weapons, and a long list of other pressures their parents did not face. Still, parents and family contain the strongest potential for influence and provision of a safe-haven and advice. The parent or guardian who takes the position that the high school student needs them less and that they are now on their own is making a costly mistake.

The project descriptions that follow underscore how much our world has changed. These schools have undergone vast changes in outlook and activity. By implication and specifics, they exemplify the reality that unless they attend in significant ways to the needs of the parents, they will not succeed as much or at all with the students. There is much that is exciting, admirable, and encouraging about these efforts. To those who believe that the more things change, the more they stay the same, you are about to learn that this motto does not hold true for the many serious efforts high schools are making to connect with parents.

The critics of public schools often contend that there are few risk-takers among those who run the schools and teach the children. The risk-takers may not be large enough in number to suit the critics, but the number is growing and it is a source of optimism about the future. Take a look.

PROGRAMS IN HIGH SCHOOLS

Baldwin Park Unified School District, Baldwin Park, California

Love, Leadership, & Literacy

C.F.A.H.S. (Colorado's Finest Alternative High School), Englewood, Colorado

Manual High School, Denver, Colorado

We Can!

Northrop High School, Ft. Wayne, Indiana

Parent/Teacher/Student Association

Paul Robeson High School, Chicago, Illinois

Super Parents Program

SUMMARY OF PROGRAM CHARACTERISTICS
High School Programs

Name of Program	Population Served	Components	Beginnings	Special Features
Baldwin Park USD Baldwin Park, CA Love, Leadership, and Literacy	Grades 7-12 130 Students 92% Latino 100% low-income	Basic Skiills Computer Assisted Instruction Staff training	Funded by federal grant from FIRST program—for at-risk students	Student Success Handbook Magic Circle Student empowerment
Colorado-s Finest Alternative High School (C.F.A.H.S.) Englewood, CO	Grades 9-12 Enrollment—525 80% Whites 20% Latinos 25% low-income	Counseling of Students Discipline Appeals Board School Advisory Team	School opened in 1980 to serve at-risk students	Student Portfolio, including Resume Dropout Rate 3% Community Service Required
Manual High School Denver, CO We Can!—Parent Involvement Program	Grades 9-12 Enrollment—1,000 Ninth grade—345 32% African-Amer. 50% White 10% Asian-Amer. 8% Latino 20% low-income	Parent Involvement Requirements Orientation Workshops Parents spend one day at school Incentives for parent involvment	Principal and parents started Program in 1987	Employers give paid time off Parent Empowerment Extra credit to students for parent involvement

(continued)

SUMMARY OF PROGRAM CHARACTERISTICS
High School Programs *(continued)*

Name of Program	Population Served	Components	Beginnings	Special Features
Northrop High School Fort Wayne, IN Northrop PTSA	Grades 9–12 Enrollment—2,000 75% White 23% African-Amer.	HIV/AIDS Education Alcohol/Drug Abuse Program Academic Excellence Program Feeder Fair	PTSA very active in organizing and promoting parent involvement	On Your Turf— Inner-city meeting Inclusiveness Rock, Roll and Remember Night
Paul Robeson High School Chicago, IL Super Parents Program	Grades 9–12 Enrollment—1,400 99% African-Amer. Low-income area	Annual Retreat Adult Learning Mentoring Program Local School Council Super Parents Group	Program started by principal, teachers, and parents in 1989	Bus Tours—Chicago Proposal writing by parents School-Based Management Team

LOVE, LEADERSHIP, & LITERACY
Baldwin Park Unified School District
Baldwin Park, CA

Major Components:
Basic skills
Computer Assisted Instruction
Special instructional materials
Staff development and training

Special Features:
Student Success Handbook
Magic Circle
Student Empowerment

Profile of Program, School, and School District:

Number of students enrolled in school district	15,000
% from Latino families	80%
% from families on public assistance	34%
Number of students enrolled in program	130
100 from Sierra Vista High School	
30 from Sierra Vista Middle School	
Number of families participating	80
% from Latino families	92%
% from African-American families	4%
% from Asian-American families	2%
% from White families	2%
% low-income families	100%

The **goals** of the program are:

- To develop a collaborative partnership between teachers, students, and families, based on **love** and caring;
- To increase the involvement of families of disadvantaged youth in grades 7–12, to improve their achievement;
- To improve the educational achievement of disadvantaged youth through a framework of instruction based on empowerment pedagogy (**literacy**, writing skills, cooperative learning) and new educational technology (computers and instructional television).

BACKGROUND

This program was started as a result of a Family-School Partnership Grant from the U.S. Department of Education, under the Fund for the Improvement and Reform of Schools (FIRST). The purpose of FIRST grants is "to seek, encourage, and reward innovative projects and reforms designed to improve the educational achievement of America's elementary and secondary school students."

The proposal was based on a successful Title VII project, implemented from 1980–1984, which focused on parent involvement. The successful components were later identified as Love, Literacy, and Leadership. The intention is to utilize these concepts with disadvantaged youth, so that their education will improve and they will stay in school rather than dropping out before graduation from high school.

The Baldwin Park School District serves a suburban area, predominantly filled with single-family dwellings. Many of the residents work in Los Angeles. It is estimated that 50% of the students in the district are considered at-risk. About one-third of the families with students in the schools are on public assistance. The median level of education completed by the parents in the district is 5th grade.

DESCRIPTION OF THE PROGRAM

Love, Leadership, and Literacy was originally housed in a Family Learning Center, located in a portable classroom at Sierra Vista High School, adjacent to the Middle School. A decline in available funding resulted in moving the program from the trailer into the high school.

Students are selected to participate in the program, on the basis of several criteria:

- They are failing two or more subjects.

- They have failed two or more minimum proficiency tests.

- Their total reading and math CTBS scores places them 2 years below grade level.

- Their absentee rate is 10% or more (18 or more days).

- Their school behavior indicates social and learning problems (pattern of disciplinary referrals and suspensions).

- Lack of parental involvement in or support of the student's education.

The staff for the program includes four teachers, four aides, and one home liaison aide who makes home visits. There is one regular teacher for each of four classes—English, Math, Science, and Social Studies. No more than 25 students are enrolled in each class. They all move at a different pace and receive much individual attention. The aides are bilingual and sensitive to the needs of at-risk students; they are typically college students, on teaching or professional career tracks, who can serve as positive ethnic role models for the students.

Before a student enters the program, both the parents and child sign a contract agreeing to the regulations and expectations of the program. If a parent does not call within the first half hour of the school day to inform the school of the child's absence, the classroom aide calls home. Following the second unreported absence, a parent-teacher conference is required. The third step requires that the parent come to the school and accompany their child through his/her classes. Parents are also asked to do this when there are serious discipline problems.

Components of the Program

Basic Skills

The instructional component strives for a higher level of learning and educational attainment for students in the project, and attempts to improve their ability to handle the more complex and technical concepts of language of grade levels 7–12. Basic and core academic skills are reinforced through the use of mainstream English, while stressing higher level thinking skills and social/emotional development. Cooperative techniques are encouraged; a theme-based curriculum is offered, including organization skills, communication, motivation, goal setting, and responsibility as themes.

Computer Assisted Instruction

This activity provides assistance to the students in all of the academic subjects. Computers are used in all phases of the writing process, as well as with other basic skills.

Special Instructional Materials

In addition to the computers, laser printers, and software, several special guides were developed for the project. The *Student Handbook* contains information and practical suggestions on such topics as study skills, homework survival, goal setting, motivation, self-esteem, communication, relationships, and sharing and caring.

A curriculum guide is based on nine monthly themes, including organization skills and time management; homework; sharing, caring, and giving; communication skills; relationships within the family; motivation (in school, at home, in the community); responsibility (being, acting, showing); and goal setting (short- and long-term).

Staff Development and Training

Staff are trained in new teaching theory, methodologies, and use of computer technology and software, materials and procedures. Staff training on student advocacy issues is supported through project efforts and school district inservice efforts.

Parent Involvement Component

Ongoing training seminars and workshops for parents are offered to develop a strong home-school partnership, assisting parents in how to help their children succeed in school. Topics include family communication, "Homework without Tears," and parents as partners in the learning process. The Magic Circle program emphasizes the circle of love and parent and student self-esteem. A 3-day Parent Workshop was offered to give parents skills as advocates, decision makers, teachers, and providers of encouragement; the parents received training in leadership, decision making and problem solving. A parent advisory committee provides opportunities for parents to participate in organizing the program and planning additional parent education workshops.

Additional Services for Students

Students are assisted in scheduling visits to college campuses, counselors work with students on career planning issues, and many outside speakers from the business community are invited to address the student group.

Parent Involvement in Planning, Operating, and Monitoring

Parents were consulted when the FIRST grant was awarded, to learn their views on the best approach to improve the education of their children. Parents are invited to the monthly meetings of the Bilingual Parent Advisory Council, where the various aspects of the program are discussed.

This project tries to focus on the family and their needs. In the past, the educators were most concerned about the students; as an afterthought they would contact the families. A better approach is to start with the family as a whole, and provide needed services to everyone. The staff has realized that there are many cultural and language factors which are related to students who are having difficulty with the schools. These must be addressed for the student and his/her family in any effort to prevent dropouts.

The home liaison aide provides "mentoring" to the parents by listening to their concerns and suggesting steps to take to solve their problems. The aides refer parents to adult basic education classes and social service agencies, as appropriate.

At a multicultural fair, sponsored by the district, the parents prepared an exhibit from FIRST. They also raised money to use for education appreciation: a reception and awards for the teachers in the program, and recognition for the students with outstanding performance.

Strengths and Weaknesses

The most successful aspect of the program has been the effectiveness in raising the consciousness and awareness of the teachers and administrators toward the family/school partnership concept. This process has motivated the students toward higher achievement, has helped to raise their self-esteem and to become more positive about their own expectations.

It is the philosophy of the program that if the home and school get together and collaborate in a loving and caring way, the students will benefit, and the instruction from teachers will improve.

Lack of time, funding, and personnel have been frustrations to those implementing the project. It is unrealistic to achieve success in this type of program in the 2 years of funding provided by the FIRST grant; at least 5 years are needed to have any lasting impact. Additional staff would greatly assist the project, but funds are not available to provide for that. It has been difficult to find bilingual people from the community to serve as role models to the students, with the time and the sensitivity to provide the support and assistance needed.

Outcomes and Evaluation

The teachers in this program approach the parents in a very positive way, and they are successful in motivating the students toward higher achievement. The principals are very cooperative in supporting and encouraging more parent involvement. The school district has a strong policy on parent involvement and continues to emphasize it. Parents are constructively involved in their children's education, and see greater opportunities for success and the possibility that they will graduate from high school.

Dr. Ira Nelken, a consultant with Ira Nelken & Associates, has completed an evaluation report for the 1991–1992 school year and will continue his assessment during the 1992–1993 year. Nelken gathered data from the students in the 8th grade, on seven instructional objectives: five related to reading, writing, and math, one about study skills performance, and one on student attitude and self-image. He found small gains in reading and written language performance, but they were not statistically significant. However, the gains in math performance were found to be statistically and educationally significant.

The performance on the minimum proficiency standards tests was more successful. In reading and language, 53.3% of the grade 8 participants were successful in passing minimum proficiency standards tests, compared to 36.8% in reading and 14.5% in language during the previous year. In math, 26.7% passed the proficiency standard compared to 11.8% in the year before.

Anecdotal records from program participants indicate that, in addition to increased performance in basic academic areas, students learned many technical skills, such as how to use a computer. They also learned about getting along with others, how to take responsibility, and that "you can make something out of your life."

The impact of the program on the lives of students and their families can be demonstrated by these examples:

- A student from the high school, who had been put out of five foster homes because of his behavior and attitudes, won second place in a national essay contest through NABE (National Association of Bilingual Education) and a $1,000 scholarship.

- A female high school student, who had left home upset that her father had deserted the family, caused family concern. Her brother was able to express his feelings about the situation by writing a piece at the computer center. In it he expressed his support and caring for their mother; the staff shared the writing with the mother. The mother was moved by her son's concern, and used his support to urge her daughter to return home.

Budget and Funding

A total of $175,000 annually, for school years 1991–1992 and 1992–1993, was available for this program. The funding is from the U.S. Department of Education.

For Further Information Contact

Ana Perez, Coordinator for Bilingual Programs
Love, Leadership, & Literacy
Baldwin Park Unified School District
3699 N. Holly Avenue
Baldwin Park, CA 91706
(818) 962–3311

COLORADO'S FINEST ALTERNATIVE HIGH SCHOOL (C.F.A.H.S.)
Englewood, CO

Major Components:
> Counseling of students
> Discipline Policy
> Appeals Board
> School Advisory Team

Special Features:
> Student Portfolio, including Resumé
> Dropout Rate only 3%
> Community Service requirement
> Classes scheduled 8 a.m. until 9:30 p.m.

Profile of Program and School:

	Day School	Night School
Number of students enrolled	325	200
% from White families	90%	60%
% from Latino families	10%	40%
% from low-income families	25%	

The **goals** of the program are:

- To create an environment for students who are not successful in the regular schools;
- To make sure all students graduate from high school and are prepared for college; and
- To require that all graduates from the school have attained competency equivalent to the 11th grade in reading, math, and writing.

BACKGROUND

This high school was opened in 1980, to serve the needs of at-risk high school students, who were having difficulty succeeding in the regular high schools. It is formally part of the Englewood, CO, school district, but is open for enrollment from students throughout the state. The name of the school was chosen by its students in 1980.

DESCRIPTION OF THE PROGRAM

Colorado's Finest Alternative High School (C.F.A.H.S.) has an enrollment of 525 students in grades 9–12. The student body is geographically diverse, with students from almost all of the metro area public and private high schools, with a few from other areas of the state. If there are no openings at the time a student applies, he/she is placed on a waiting list and provided the opportunity to enroll on a first come first served basis. Prior to admission, both the student and a parent must participate in an interview with the principal. In addition, prospective students are interviewed by a member of the student body. Students outside the Englewood School District must pay a $40 registration fee; all students must provide their own transportation to and from school.

The following characteristics of the Alternative High School were written by a parent:

- Offers each student the opportunity to work under little pressure.

- Lets students set the pace to coincide with their every day way of life.

- Gives each student the opportunity to work with peer groups who come from all walks of life but have one common goal, the chance to be accepted, the opportunity to succeed, the motivation to proceed.

- The staff emphasizes family unity and self-esteem.

- The staff is continually called upon to help pick up "broken pieces," nurture the will to learn, suppress the urge to quit, and always react joyously to bits of achievement.

- These students DO NOT need special education, but, rather, they need to be specially educated. The faculty and staff must be compensated and encouraged to remain with these schools, as continuity is the one ingredient that brings the Alternative High School together.

- Not a final alternative, but the best alternative.

The school is open from 8 a.m. until 9:30 p.m. It offers a night school for students who are at least 16 years old and hold full-time or part-time jobs. About half of the night students are not living with their parents, but are out on their own. Night school students begin school after 4 p.m. Students are required to complete their classes in one block of time, and are not allowed to take some day and some night courses at the same time. There are 260–270 students at the school at any one time.

Components of the Program

Counseling of Students

C.F.A.H.S. believes that the best counselor is a teacher that students know, trust, and respect. All teachers have a family unit of 20–25 students. The family unit leader assumes the counseling responsibilities for those students. They get to know the student as a person and as someone trying to gain academic knowledge. These family unit leaders are the liaison between the home and the school, and communicate regularly with the parents concerning the student's progress.

Discipline

C.F.A.H.S. has four basic rules which students must follow in order to attend the school:

- Students must earn 90% of the possible points in every class during each 6 week grading session.

- Students must not visit other school campuses during business hours.

- No antisocial behavior (intimidation, fighting, etc.).

- No drug usage or possession on campus.

Appeals Board

The appeals board is designed to help students resolve problems in the school. The board consists of three students and two teachers. Every member of the board has an equal vote. Their decision is final and cannot be overruled by the administration.

School Advisory Team

This is the policy board for the school, reviewing goals and objectives, monitoring the program, and overseeing evaluation. It also serves the functions of the state-mandated School Accountability Team. The team includes 25 persons: two students, one teacher, one business leader, one representative from the support staff, and 20 parent members.

Parent Activities

In addition to service on the School Accountability Team, parents support the school in many diverse ways. One parent, who works for U.S. West, arranged a full-day in-service for teachers, administrators, students, and parents on Total Quality Management through a U.S. West expert on TQM. He assisted them in defining goals and objectives, and in articulating the desired outcomes of the school.

Parents represent the school at state and national conferences on at-risk students. The parents sponsor an Annual Teacher Appreciation Day. Parents and students also plan and conduct a fashion show, with students choosing what clothes the parents and staff will model.

Annual Banquet

At this event, parents often tell those present about how grateful they are to the school for helping their children through some difficult times. Parents are very supportive of the school, and this enthusiasm serves to raise the morale of the teachers at the school.

Parent Involvement in Planning, Operating, and Monitoring

Since C.F.A.H.S. is a school of choice for students and their parents, there is much involvement and support from the parents. Parents chose the alternative school after seeing their sons and daughters have difficulty with the regular high school and talk about dropping out of school. Most of the parents are appreciative of the existence of a school such as this one and for its providing a caring and stimulating environment in which their children can learn and succeed.

When the school first opened there was very little parent involvement. The parents of many of the students who enrolled at this school felt they were not treated with respect at the regular high school their child had first attended. After experiencing negative interaction with school personnel at the traditional high schools, parents were pleased and appreciative to be treated with respect. Teachers and administrators began to recognize the many talents of parents of those at the school and started to encourage them to come to the school.

Parents took the lead in reviewing graduation requirements for the school, and insisted that academic standards should be strengthened for the students at C.F.A.H.S. They took the position that students graduating from this school should have attained at least the level of the 11th grade in math, reading, and writing. Also required for graduation are the following:

- 20 hours of community service;

- An oral exit interview with at least 3 teachers, to demonstrate an understanding of all academic areas;

- An *original investigation* documenting proficiency in using the scientific method;

- A career plan to include a financial plan for further schooling at a 2-year or 4-year college;

- A term paper;

- Training for first aid and CPR;

- Obtaining a voter's registration card if 18 years of age; and

- A portfolio of the student's academic career, including a résumé.

Parents have participated in the interviewing of teachers and other staff members for the school, and have been involved in the development of policies related to discipline and attendance. They are preparing their own list of proposals for school improvement which will be incorporated in the School Accountability plan.

Strengths and Weaknesses

The staff at C.F.A.H.S. strive to be nonjudgmental about the life styles and personal appearances of the students who attend the school. They accept skinheads, teenagers into "Heavy Metal"—any and all of the various costumes which young people wear. The school emphasizes respect for students, and the belief that all students can be successful in their studies and in attaining their high school diploma. The staff and parents have high expectations for the students at the school; the students understand what is expected of them and accept the fact that they will have to work hard to achieve it.

The turnover at the school is very low. Only one or two students each year decide to leave C.F.A.H.S. and return to the regular high school. It is estimated that the rate for completion of high school is 91%, with only a 3% annual dropout rate.

Over the last 10 years, 70% of the students who attended the school have graduated.

Three parent/teacher conferences are scheduled during the school year. In many cases, the student attends the conference along with the teacher and parent. Ninety-two percent of the parents generally attend the first conference of the year; 75% are present at the last one.

There is no athletic program at C.F.A.H.S. Many of the students disliked the competitiveness required to be involved in sports in the regular high schools. Those who choose to may participate in sports activities at their home school or at Englewood High School.

College level classes through Arapaho Community College are offered during the school day. Students are also provided with the opportunity to take a class on the Arapaho Community College Campus. During the winter semester of 1992, three courses were offered: college algebra or U.S. history for day students and sociology in the evening. The credit from these classes can be applied both to the graduation requirements at the high school and as college courses. Many students think they will not succeed in college; the opportunity to take college level courses results in their realizing that they can do well and encourages them to consider higher education after high school graduation. Seventy percent of the graduates from C.F.A.H.S. continue their education in 2-year or 4-year colleges.

The school experiences few discipline problems. No fights have occurred over the last year and a half. Each year, four or five students are dismissed from school for drug offenses.

Outcomes and Evaluation

In December 1991, and again in December 1992, the Colorado State Board of Education recognized C.F.A.H.S. as a school of excellence, one of three high schools in the state to receive that honor in 1991 and the only high school honored in 1992. The school was among a dozen schools that contracted with the State Department of Education to improve or sustain the high performance of their students over a 2-year period.

The school has also been recognized as one of the Governor's Creativity Schools.

For Further Information Contact

> Dr. Tom Synott, Principal
> Colorado's Finest Alternative High School
> 2323 W. Baker
> Englewood, CO 80110
> (303) 934–5786

WE CAN!—PARENT INVOLVEMENT PROGRAM
Manual High School
Denver, CO

Major Components:
Parent Involvement Requirements
Orientation
Parenting Workshops
Parents spend one day in school
Incentives to encourage parent involvement

Special Features:
Employers give parents paid time off
Parent Empowerment
Extra credit to students for parent involvement

Profile of Program and School:

Number of students enrolled in Manual High School	1,000
Number of students in the ninth grade	345
% from African-American families	32%
% from Latino families	8%
% from White families	50%
% from Asian and other families	10%
% from low-income families	20%

The **goals** of the We Can! Parent Involvement Program are:

- To increase parent involvement;
- To improve student achievement, especially for those who are performing below grade level;
- To empower parents; and
- To establish networks and form alliances among the parents of 9th graders at the school.

BACKGROUND

In 1987, a coalition of Denver schools, businesses, and organizations sponsored a 3-day visit from Dr. George McKenna, then principal of George Washington Preparatory Academy, and currently superintendent of the Inglewood, CA School District. He had been successful in promoting parent involvement at his school. The principal of Manual High School was very impressed with his presentation and his ideas. A Manual High School parent was similarly excited by the speaker; she talked with the principal about what could be done to carry out some of the ideas presented by McKenna. After 2 months of planning and promoting the program was begun.

DESCRIPTION OF THE PROGRAM

This program was initiated because of a strong belief that parent involvement is necessary to increase student achievement, and the improvement of student achievement, especially for those who are performing below grade level, is the primary mission of Manual High School. The We Can! activities serve to empower parents and establish networks and alliances among the parents of 9th graders in the school.

We Can! is specifically intended for the parents of the 345 9th grade students at Manual High School. It is designed to do more than invite parent involvement in the school; the plan is to "require" three commitments from parents of students entering the high school.

Components of the Program

Parent Involvement Requirements

A letter, dated August 1 and signed by the principal, is sent by first class mail to every parent who will have a 9th grader entering Manual High School. This letter details what the parents are "required" to do during the school year:

- Attend an Orientation Meeting with their son or daughter before school opens;

- Come to school one full day during the year to attend all the classes of their son or daughter; and

- Participate in one parenting workshop during the year.

Several workshops are offered during the year, some in the evening and others on the weekend. They cover such topics as the transition from middle school to high school, helping parents live with adolescents, parents' role in homework, how to communicate with teenagers, and how to help children succeed in school. One of the workshops is planned for both the parents and students. Workshops are conducted by parents and feature guest speakers, such as psychologists, counselors, and educators. A special effort is made to provide racially representative presenters.

Incentives to Encourage Parent Involvement

One of the most effective and creative inducements for parents to meet the requirement of attending school for one full day during the year is linked to their employment. The principal of the school prepares and distributes to each parent a letter addressed to the companies and organizations which employ the parents of the incoming 9th graders. She requests that they allow their employees who are parents to take a day off with pay to visit the school, attend classes with their son or daughter, and meet the teachers. Almost all of the employers have willingly complied with this request. During the past 5 years, only one employer has complained to the school about the request. The employers are asked to honor the absence as they would jury duty or court subpoenas.

All teachers give the students extra credit if their parents attend the "required" events. Another incentive to encourage attendance at the parenting workshops is the raffling of a prize near the end of the year. Refreshments are served and buttons reading *We Can!* are given out to identify 9th grade parents who have been involved.

Parent Leadership

A parent team of husband and wife led the parent involvement program for 3 years, while they had a child enrolled at Manual High School. During their last year they actively recruited other parents to take over and manage the program. Frequent phone calls were made to parents to encourage their participation.

Parent Involvement in Planning, Operating, and Monitoring

This program is planned and directed by parents, with the assistance and support of the principal and school administration. Since the program is designed for only one class of parents (those with students in the 9th grade) it is a challenge to find a parent of a 9th grader who will be responsible for the program for more than 1 year.

One strength of this program is the timing: parents are contacted before school starts with the hope that they will realize the importance of their involvement, not only in helping with the transition to high school, but also being informed about their child's school schedule and parenting issues related to the teenage years. The orientation and parenting workshops also serve as a method for getting parents to meet other parents and perhaps set up support networks. It is hoped that parents will feel empowered to play a major role in their children's high school education as a result of these "required" activities.

Parent attendance and participation in the PTSA has increased, perhaps as a result of the early and positive contact between home and school through the We Can! program. More parents work in the school as volunteers where they are impressed with the quality of the education provided. Greater parent support of Manual High School has been demonstrated as a result of this program.

Strengths and Weaknesses

The principal has been very satisfied with all aspects of the program. The teachers' responses have been positive; they have welcomed the parents who come to visit their classrooms. The attitudes of the students have shifted from "Please don't come" to "When are you coming?" Parents have been impressed that their employers would give them time off to attend school functions.

One disappointment has been that the We Can! program does not attain 100% parent involvement. Typically, between one-third and one-half of the parents of the 9th graders attend the orientation session, visit the school, and attend the parent workshops.

Any parent involvement program must work to build up a sense of trust between home and school. This has to be done year after year, as a new cohort of students enters the school. There are always feelings of distrust and skepticism on the part of some parents and some teachers; the attitudes of students in early adolescence do not encourage parent involvement in the schools.

Outcomes and Evaluation

The principal is keeping track of attendance, grades, and test scores, but no formal, statistical research study has been done on the effectiveness and outcome of the program. Parents have become more supportive of the high school and feel more comfortable in visiting and communicating with school officials.

Budget and Funding

Initially all expenses were paid for by the school. Now most of the expenses for the mailings, materials, and refreshments are paid for by a grant from KIDS (Keep Involved in Denver Schools), a local foundation. The raffle prize is usually donated by a local business. The PTSA also contributes money to take care of some of the expenses.

For Further Information Contact

Linda Bates Transou, Principal
Manual High School
1700 E. Twenty-Eighth Ave.
Denver, CO 80205
(303) 391–6300

NORTHROP PTSA
Northrop High School
Fort Wayne, IN

Major Components:
HIV/AIDS Education Program
Alcohol/Drug Abuse Program
Academic Excellence Program
Feeder Fair

Special Features:
On Your Turf—Inner-city PTA meeting
Inclusiveness
Rock, Roll and Remember Night

Profile of Program, School District, and School:

Number of students in Fort Wayne Community Schools	36,000
Number of schools in district	53
Elementary schools	36
Middle schools	11
High schools	6
Number of students enrolled in Northrop High School	2,000
% from African-American families	23%
% from Asian-American families	1%
% from White families	75%

The **goals** of the program are:

- To encourage parents to become more involved in their children's education;
- To build a closer relationship between school and parents; and
- To reach parents who are not active in the PTSA.

BACKGROUND

The PTSA (Parent-Teacher-Student Association) was organized at Northrop High School in 1971. The program is very active at the present time, because of the parent leadership and the support of the principal of the school, who provides continuing, positive support for an organization where parents, teachers, and students work together.

The current leadership of the PTSA has given much thought to the challenge of encouraging parent involvement at the high school level, where, typically, the amount of parent participation declines drastically. Parents often think that their children should be on their own by the time they are in high school and that there is no clear need for parent involvement. Mothers often reenter the workforce as their children become older, and, therefore, are not available for volunteer work at the school. High school students may indicate to their parents that they want to be independent and autonomous and do not welcome their parents' involvement at the school.

DESCRIPTION OF THE PROGRAM

The Northrop High School serves an area of the city covering 10 square miles, including inner-city neighborhoods and farm lands in the area surrounding the city. The enrollment consists of students from families of diverse backgrounds, including inner-city, rural, and urban families; children with disabilities; and low- to high-achieving students from all income levels. The programs and services of the PTSA are designed to inspire every student, to assist teachers and parents in making informed decisions for their students, and to provide them the opportunity to become involved at Northrop.

The PTSA is directed by a Board representative of the school population (African-American, Asian, Anglo, fathers, mothers, aunts, students, and administrators). Members of the Board include the President, Vice President, Secretary, Treasurer, a school administrator, a custodian (representing the school office and support staff), three teachers, and the Student Council President. Chairpersons from the Committees formed to implement the programs also sit on the PTSA Board.

The parents and teachers who carry out the programs are all volunteers. The emphasis is to offer a variety of artistic, multicultural, and academic programs to appeal to the broad and diverse range of backgrounds of Northrop students and their families.

Components of the Program

Communication and Social Events

The PTSA sponsors many successful events designed to attract all students and parents. The New Student Picnic greets and serves over 130 family members; approximately 500 parents and students attend orientations to meet administrators and PTSA officers and hear about policies and programs. Volunteer Participation Week and Teacher Appreciation Week provide opportunities for recognition of parent and teacher contributions. The Father/Student Breakfast and Senior Mothers' Tea are intended to reach additional parents and family members and bring them into the school. Rock, Roll and Remember Night brought together parents and teachers from Northrop and its feeder schools for a night of fun and socializing.

HIV/AIDS Education Program

A mailing containing brochures and other AIDS information was sent to 1,691 parents of Northrop students. A total of 160 freshman art students designed posters promoting abstinence from sex and IV drug use. All posters were judged and displayed throughout the school, and the winning posters were shown at the public library and the school's administrative center.

For the past 3 years, an AIDS awareness week has been held, featuring lectures, slide shows, dialogues, and rap sessions. The week culminates on Friday with each student completing an evaluation of the week and receiving brochures on free HIV testing and local support groups available for those affected by the virus. The media center has been presented with over 50 different brochures, articles, and newspaper clippings on HIV/AIDS.

In the spring of 1993, the topics for the awareness week were expanded to include not only HIV/AIDS education, but also topics related to nutrition, foods, anorexia, bulimia, building healthy relationships, and date rape.

Alcohol/Drug Abuse Program

Northrop High School was an active participant in Red Ribbon Week which emphasized the commitment of good citizenship by staying drug free. "Proud to be Drug Free" was the theme for Red Ribbon Week. The cafeteria, commons, and hall bulletin boards were decorated in patriotic themes. Red bows were provided for all school buses, red bookmarks were given to each student, and drug educational materials were distributed to staff and students, including a PTSA designed drug awareness brochure.

The PTSA provided volunteers and support for the drug testing program sponsored by BADD, "Bruins Against Drinking and Drugs." The program was voluntary, and 550 students participated in the drug testing. PTSA parents monitored the bathrooms during urine tests, registered students, and logged information for tests during registration. Students who test clean throughout the year receive special discounts and privileges at stores and businesses throughout the city.

After Prom offered students a fun, safe, drug/alcohol free activity from 1:00–4:00 a.m. Over 400 students attended. The party may have prevented drunk driving, drug usage, sexual encounters, and may even have saved lives.

Members of the PTSA attended and spoke at a City Council hearing on the extension of liquor licenses and the open container ordinance in Ft. Wayne.

On Your Turf

One of the general PTSA meetings was held at the Old Fort Y building, in the inner-city neighborhood served by the school. Invited were all feeder PTAs, principals and inner-city families; 75 parents from this neighborhood attended the meeting. Many of the parents who attended expressed a desire for more meetings in their neighborhoods, since the distance to the school and lack of transportation are barriers to their being active at the school.

Academic Excellence Program

One PTSA Committee supports the Northrop teachers in their efforts to improve students' academic performance. During the 1991–1992 school year, more than 120 students raised their GPA by 1.0 or more. The PTSA invited the parents and students to a recognition breakfast where awards were given out.

Homework Help

Study tables are designated in the Media Center for an hour and a half after school is over for students who wish to do homework or to receive help from an available teacher.

Parent Involvement in Planning, Operating, and Monitoring

All of the activities sponsored by the PTSA are planned, designed, and carried out by volunteer parents and teachers. Parents play an active role as officers of the PTSA Board and as Committee Chairpersons overseeing the various programs.

The approach to parent involvement has been changing during recent years, primarily because of the changes in family demographics. The increase in single-parent families and the fact that many mothers return to the workforce, requires a new look at the scheduling of events for these family members. More programs are being planned at the breakfast hour, to catch mothers and fathers before they go to work. More evening meetings are necessary, although some activities are still scheduled during the day.

A Parent Advisory Board has been formed at Northrop to meet and discuss strengths and weaknesses of the school, to plan some activities which will result in positive recognition of the effective factors in the school, and to offer assistance to the principal wherever needed.

Strengths and Weaknesses

The large geographical area served by the school continues to result in problems of distance and lack of transportation which discourage parents from going to the school. Meetings held in neighborhood locations are one answer to this barrier. The one "On Your Turf" meeting was very successful and may be repeated in other areas of the district.

A challenge to the PTSA and others at Northrop High School is how to change the attitudes of the community toward the school. The Parent Advisory Board was formed to discuss the good and bad aspects of the school and then to act to bring about more positive recognition of the positive qualities of the school in the city. The Northrop PTSA prepares a display for the Feeder Fair in which they address the concerns of parents and inform families of the positive features of the school.

The PTSA feels that the media has not been as supportive of their efforts at Northrop High School as might be desired. There has also been criticism of the way in which the media tends to address difficult issues. Following one minor racial incident, many felt that the media exaggerated the event and may have caused it to become more of a problem than it was at the start.

Each year new programs are tried; those which are successful will be continued, those which interest parents less are dropped.

Outcomes and Evaluation

The Northrop PTSA has received recognition for its successful program at the state and national level. The PTSA was one of 12 programs throughout the state, to be selected as an honor unit for the Indiana Advocates Award, presented by the state PTA. The organization also received a National PTA Advocates for Children Award.

The attendance at the meetings sponsored by the PTSA is one indication of their success and effectiveness. Membership in the organization is rising: during the 1991–1992 year there were 765 adult members; the following year a total of 880 had joined.

The PTSA has observed and heard much support from the teachers for their efforts at parent involvement; they look forward to greater participation by the teachers in the programs and activities sponsored by the parents.

Following the AIDS education program at the school, a parent survey was sent out to learn parents' opinions of the value of the activities and the information disseminated. Students were asked to complete questionnaires at the school. Both groups expressed positive reactions to the activities and the materials; some reported that they learned a lot from the effort, while others said they were already informed and did not learn much.

Budget and Funding

The current PTSA program budget is about $3,500 for the year. This is provided by a number of sources: PTA membership dues, a few fund-raising activities, and a grant from the Indiana Department of Education from funds received from the Federal government. The PTSA also received award money from the National PTA for its AIDS Education Program.

For Further Information Contact

Deb Reichard, 1991–1992 PTSA President
Northrop High School
7001 Coldwater Rd.
Ft. Wayne, Indiana 46825
(219) 425–7560

SUPER PARENTS PROGRAM—"WHERE DREAMS BECOME REALITY"
Paul Robeson High School
Chicago, IL

Major Components:
> Annual Retreat
> Adult Learning
> Mentoring Program
> Local School Council
> Super Parents Group

Special Features:
> Bus Tours of Chicago
> Proposal Writing by Parents
> School-Based Management Team

Profile of Program and School:
> Enrollment at Paul Robeson High School
> (Grades 9–12)   1,400
>   % African-American   99%

The **goals** of the program are:

- To help parents understand their children as adolescents;
- To assist parents in their educational, vocational, and other interests; and
- To inform parents about education at the Paul Robeson High School.

BACKGROUND

The parent involvement program was started by the principal in 1989. Parent involvement activities had been tried previously, but had never been successful. The principal included teachers and parents in the design and implementation. The design of the current program is based on the results of a survey of parents, who were asked about their needs and concerns.

Paul Robeson High School is located in the Englewood section of Chicago, in a low-income neighborhood where most people live in multiple unit dwellings. The area is filled with abandoned buildings; some new single-family homes are being constructed in the neighborhood. The majority of the students come from the immediate area, though some are bused in from other parts of the city.

DESCRIPTION OF THE PROGRAM

On the letterhead stationery of Paul Robeson High School is the phrase "Where Dreams Become Reality." This vision not only applies to the students who are enrolled at the school, but also to the parents and families of those students. The main emphasis of parent involvement activities at Paul Robeson High School is a recognition of the parents not only as the mothers and fathers of teenage high school students, but as individuals with their own interests and futures apart from the lives of their children. Just as the high school students are searching for their individuality, independence, and are on the threshold of beginning careers, their parents are faced with similar issues and choices. Parents are welcome in the school, and the administrators and teachers do not feel threatened by their presence. They are given respect as human beings and their potential contribution to the school is recognized.

The parent involvement effort of the school is carried out by regular school staff, with no additional personnel employed. As many as 300 parents attend some of the meetings; 50 parents attend regularly and are known by the staff by name and face.

Components of the Program

Annual Retreat

Each year 30 parents are invited to join the staff in a 3-day retreat, where parent involvement activities for the coming year are planned and designed. Parents who have been to at least eight school meetings, and who have volunteered a minimum of three times during the year, are invited. Members of the Local School Council also attend. In past years, the retreat has been held at Indian Lakes, Nordic Hills, and other resorts.

Super Parents Group

A total of 20–25 parents are active in the Super Parents Group, which meets once a month, on Saturday morning, since many parents feel it is unsafe for them to attend night meetings.

School-Based Management Team

A School-Based Management Team (SBMT) has been formed by the principal, to monitor day-to-day operations of the school, to take responsibility for the building and grounds activities, and to initiate suggestions for school improvement. Teachers, paraprofessionals, parents, and students all are members of the SBMT; the teachers are elected by the faculty and the parents are selected by the Local School Council.

Adult Learning

This very important component of the parent involve-ment program includes many diverse projects, such as stress reduction classes, and the following activities:

- A group of parents wanted to learn how to write proposals so they could assist in seeking grants for school projects. The school offered a seminar to parents on proposal writing. As a result several parents actually wrote proposals and received awards for the school. This is a perfect example of the school investing time and energy in the parents, and benefiting from their efforts as a result.

- Another group of parents wanted to learn how to use the computer. The school arranged for classes in desktop publishing. The parents then decided to publish a newsletter. They were successful in getting a grant to fund the newsletter, and then wrote it, formatted it, and printed and distributed it.

- In response to a request from parents who feel isolated from others in the community and the city, the school arranges for a bus to take parents on tours of different neighborhoods in the city. The tours, scheduled for Saturday or Sunday, end with dinner at an inexpensive, ethnic restaurant in the community they are visiting. The principal often is present on the bus tour and at the dinners in order to become better acquainted with the parents. About 30–40 parents participate in this activity; the bus is provided at no cost to the parents, and they pay for their own dinners.

Mentoring Program

The mentors in this program are not persons outside the school but are active parents who become involved as surrogate parents for some of the students at the school and role models for other parents who are not as involved. They are viewed as extended family members, nurturing other parents and students alike. These parents reach out to other parents and encourage them to become active. They make sure that any new parents are greeted and welcomed at the school.

Local School Council

As is the case with all schools in the Chicago Public School System, this school is governed by a Local School Council, composed of 10 persons, including parents, school officials, and community leaders. The School Council members receive special training in order to learn about the educational issues they must decide and effective procedures for meetings and decision making. The Council has responsibility for preparing the school budget, evaluating the principal, and overseeing the curriculum of the school.

Parent Involvement in Planning, Operating, and Monitoring

The parents play an active role in many school-related events. They plan and conduct the orientation for incoming parents; they volunteer in the school; they write grants for funding of various school projects; they prepare and disseminate the school newsletter; they are responsible for planning and operating the Parents Group.

This group has also been active in Creating a New Approach to Learning (CANAL), a citywide program, created by federal funds, to improve the academic program in racially identifiable schools in Chicago.

Parents also play a major role in the Local School Council, which is the decision making body for the school. The Council reviews and revises school policies; makes budget decisions; and is responsible for hiring and evaluating staff. Parents are also active in the School Based Management Team.

Strengths and Weaknesses

The most successful aspect of this program has been the individual growth of many of the parents. They have learned how to greet and interact with other parents. They have taken responsibility for the Parent Group, and many have become active volunteers in the school. They have learned to use computers, have written plays, and put on slide presentations. Many have gone back to school; some have found better jobs.

However, there are still unmet needs among many of

the families whose children are in the school. The school attempts to help, but is not always able to improve every aspect of the family's life. The school officials would like to see greater numbers of parents taking part in the activities offered by the school.

The major barriers which have been identified are (1) the feelings of isolation which parents have in their role of raising children and (2) reluctance to come to night meetings because of safety issues. The program has tried to overcome these by scheduling more meetings during the day and on weekends, and by the bus tours of the city. The school administrators and teachers realize that adjustments to the parent involvement program will need to be made continually, as more is learned about what works and what parents want. The school conducts surveys on a regular basis to determine whether the activities and classes are meeting parents' needs, and what else can be done to improve their lives.

Outcomes and Evaluation

Many changes in attitudes and practices have been observed as a result of the parent involvement efforts. The teachers have become accustomed to and accepting of parents in the building, and have been treating them with respect. Teachers and parents are attempting to work together in a collaborative relationship, which diminishes the negative attitudes which school staff often have toward parents. The parents who are active in the school are accepted by the teachers as partners, feel comfortable in their role, and strive to help all students at the school, in addition to caring and advocacy for their own child.

The parents have been very supportive of the restructuring of the school governance procedures, which give the School Council much power and authority. Many principals throughout Chicago have not been supported by the School Councils, but at Paul Robeson High School, the principal enjoys wide community support, partly as a result of her efforts to meet the needs of parents whose children attend the school and to respect their involvement in all aspects of the school.

Budget and Funding

It is estimated that the parent involvement activities cost about $6,500 annually. This includes the expenses for the newsletter, the school being open one Saturday per month for the Parents Meetings, the retreat, and the bus tours of the city. The money is allocated from federal funds and grants from private foundations.

For Further Information Contact

Dr. Jackie Simmons, Principal
Super Parents Program
Paul Robeson High School
6835 So. Normal Blvd.
Chicago, IL 60621
(312) 723-1700

Chapter 6

Districtwide and Community Programs

One of the impressive developments in efforts to form new, more successful parent-family-school connections is the decision of some school districts to adopt policies that make efforts districtwide and direct significant funds for support of such efforts. It is one thing for a school with an energetic, imaginative principal to decide to reach out to parents as part of an overall strategy to increase student success and achievement. It is quite another to have a district move forward with plans for all schools in a district and/or community. The dynamics become different in important ways. The message is sent—this is important, we will all do it, and we will help with training and money. It now becomes a professional priority deserving of attention and respect by all.

The same is true of efforts that, while short of full district involvement, are committed to full involvement of communities with multiple schools. Under these circumstances, the professionals do not feel marooned or uncertain and the parents and families soon come to know that the schools have made them a priority and will be making special efforts in their behalf.

School districtwide and communitywide efforts also bring resources to bear that are not always available to an individual school. The creation of Parent Centers, access to leadership of community organizations and the programs of community organizations often encourage new ways of approaching and supporting parents and families. School districtwide efforts and smaller scale communitywide efforts are the fullest expression of the belief that parents and families are of unduplicated importance to students, and the success of students is linked to the degree of effort and success schools have in reaching and involving parents.

The school districts and communities described through the projects and programs that follow may well be pointing to the scope, commitment, and substance of parent-family involvement efforts needed for the future. They certainly represent out of the ordinary expressions of the importance of significant adults in the attitudes, motivations, and success levels of children in that irreplaceable place called school.

PROGRAMS IN SCHOOL DISTRICTS AND COMMUNITIES

Austin Independent School District, Austin, Texas

> IMAGE—International Multicultural and Global Education

Austin Independent School District, Austin, Texas

> MegaSkills Parent Involvement Program

Avance, San Antonio, Texas

> Family Support and Education Program

Bronx Educational Services, Bronx, New York

> Parent Organizing and Education Project

McAllen Independent School District, McAllen, Texas

> McAllen Parent Involvement Program

Natchez-Adams School District, Natchez, Mississippi

Natchez-Adams Chapter 1 Parent Center

Saint Paul School District, St. Paul, Minnesota

Frogtown Family Resource Center

San Diego City Schools, San Diego, California

Home-School Partnership

SUMMARY OF PROGRAM CHARACTERISTICS
District and Community Programs

Name of Program	Population Served	Components	Beginnings	Special Features
Austin ISD Austin, TX IMAGE— International Multicultural and Global Education	Enrollment—678 # elementary—245 # middle—333 # high school—100 50% Latinos 42% Whites 6% African-Amers. 70% low-income	Multi-grade classrooms Interdisciplinary, thematic curric. Team teaching Active learning HIPPY preschool	New approach for 3 schools; vertical team of teachers working together Began in 1989	Vertical Team approach Learning core and satellites Performance-based assessment
Austin ISD Austin, TX MegaSkills Parent Involvement Program	Enrollment—70,000 # schools—91 36% Latinos 19% African-Amers. 45% White	MegaSkills Workshops Family Calendar "Recipes" for educational activities at home	Introduced by A+ Coalition to reduce dropout rate. Funded by IBM, Chamber of Commerce	Pilot program for middle & high schools Parent volunteers trained as leaders
Avance San Antonio, TX Family Support and Education Programs	# served—3,000 98% Latino	Even Start Parent-Child Educ. Child Development Padres a la escuela Family Resource Ctr.	Organization started in 1973, focusing on family-centered services	Intervention for hard to reach families Toy Making Fatherhood Program

Program	Demographics	Activities	Background	Goals
Bronx Educational Services Bronx, NY Parent Organizing and Education Project	Enrollment—6,000 # schools—7 70% Latinos 25% African-Amers. 85% low-income	Outreach activities Local meetings Leadership Dev. Adult education Parents organizing	Started organizing parents' union in 1991, to work collectively for better schools	Parent Empowerment Political action
McAllen ISD McAllen, TX McAllen Parent Involvement Program	# students—21,000 # schools—31 87% Latinos 12% Whites 63% low-income	Adopt-a-School Evening Study Centers Parent Education	Evolved from migrant program, Chapter 1 to all parents	Transition to Middle School Keys for a Better Life All staff bilingual
Natchez-Adams School District Natchez, MS Natchez-Adams Chapter 1 Parent Center	# students—6,200 # schools—8 70% African-Amers. 75% low-income	Teacher referrals Workshops Computer program Literacy class Tutorial Program Leaning Labs on Wheels	Center opened in 1987; moved to central location in 1989	"Prescriptions" for Chapter 1 children Positive Parent-Teacher Conferences Orientation for transition to middle school

(continued)

SUMMARY OF PROGRAM CHARACTERISTICS
District and Community Programs (continued)

Name of Program	Population Served	Components	Beginnings	Special Features
Frogtown Family Resource Center St. Paul, MN	# families – 400 24% African-Amers. 33% Asian-Amers. 20% Native-Amers. 95% low-income	Home visits Drop-in Center Parent Education Family literacy	Funded by grants from State Early Childhood and Family Education	Prenatal support Parent empowerment
San Diego City Schools San Diego, CA Home-School Partnership	Enrollment – 126,000 # schools – 145 29% Latino 17% Asian-Amers. 35% White	Mobile Parent Resource Center Parent Involvement Task Force School Development Project Parent Involvement Incentive Grants	Implemented to carry out school board policy passed in 1989	District policy on Parent Involvement Parent Involvement Conference Diverse, multi-cultural, multi-language population

IMAGE—INTERNATIONAL, MULTICULTURAL AND GLOBAL EDUCATION
Austin Independent School District
Austin, TX

Major Components:
> Multigrade classrooms
> Interdisciplinary, thematic curriculum
> Team teaching
> Active learning
> Performance-based assessment
> HIPPY Preschool Program

Special Features:
> International, multicultural, and global awareness
> Vertical Team approach
> Learning core and satellites

Profile of Program and Schools in Project:

	IMAGE Program	Entire School
Student Enrollment	678	2,900
Number of students at elementary school	245	685
Number of students at middle school	333	1,000
Number of students at high school	100	1,200
% from African-American families	6%	
% from Latino families	50%	
% from White families	42%	
% from low-income families	70%	

The **goals** of the program are:

- To approach teaching and learning in a way that is comprehensive and philosophically different from tradition, conventional education;
- To help students to construct and create new information, in order to be successful in the information age.

BACKGROUND

The IMAGE program developed as a result of two separate efforts. The first began in the fall of 1989, with a workshop, "Teachers as Agents of Change," sponsored by St. Edward's University, assisted by a grant from Southwestern Bell. Pat Hays, President of St. Edward's, personally invited teachers from three schools—Travis Heights Elementary, Fulmore Middle School, and Travis High School—to participate. They formed the original "Vertical Team," an effort to look at some basic issues affecting pre-K through 12th grade education.

The second effort began in March 1991, with a school attendance boundary issue, which served as a catalyst to bring parents together to influence the decision of the school board. Public hearings on the school board proposals to shift school boundaries were held in the spring of 1991. Parents and community members joined with the faculties of the three schools involved in the Vertical Team and eight central Austin elementary schools to form the Inner City Coalition for Equitable Education (ICCEE).

The ICCEE took the position that the proposed boundary changes would lead to even more inequities in the educational system than existed previously. The new configuration would put an undue burden on certain schools, which would be assigned a high proportion of low-income populations who have substantial social and educational needs. Some schools would become more Anglo and affluent, while others would experience an increase in children from Latino families and children eligible for free lunch. The ICCEE had some influence on the school board. The boundaries were changed, but not as drastically as originally proposed.

The result of the efforts devoted to the boundary issue was a collaboration between parents and community leaders and the teachers and principals of the vertical team schools. This collaboration led to the design of the IMAGE proposal, which was presented to the school board in May 1991.

In the fall of 1991 the three schools represented on the vertical team were selected by the NEA's National Center for Innovation to become the sixth site in the nation for the Mastery in Learning Consortium. The IMAGE proposal expanded the "Vertical Team" to include the staffs, parents, and students of the elementary, middle, and high schools, and consultants from the NEA. An IMAGE Steering Committee was formed, including members from St. Edward's University and parent and/or community representatives from all three schools.

DESCRIPTION OF THE PROGRAM

This is not considered a "program" by those who are involved in planning, designing, and implementing it. It is a new way for three schools to approach teaching and learning. The approach is comprehensive and philosophically different from traditional, conventional education. Students, teachers, parents, business people, and others from the community work together as active participants in planning curriculum for educating students for the 21st Century. The emphasis is away from the traditional model of students receiving information from the teacher and then memorizing it.

During Phase I of the project, from September 1991 to August 1992, many events and activities occurred in support of the further development and refinement of IMAGE, including:

- IMAGE Potlucks, to involve parents and community in learning about the new project;

- Formation of an IMAGE Steering Committee and participation of the Committee in a retreat where the goals of IMAGE were prepared and adopted; and

- Collaboration among teachers to develop interdisciplinary units, multiage groupings, and increased exchanges between teachers and students of the vertical team schools.

IMAGE—Phase II, involves implementing certain aspects of the program for all of the students at each school, while creating a more involved "development project" for a limited number of teachers and students at the school. (This format was chosen because not all of the teachers were ready to change and commit to all aspects of the IMAGE concept at the beginning of the 1992–93 school year.)

In order to recruit students for the developmental project, a letter was sent, during the summer of 1992, to the parents of all of the children at the elementary school, asking if they would like their child to be enrolled in the IMAGE program. The response was very positive, and resulted in a heterogeneous group of students. A total of 36 faculty members, pre-K through 9th grade, were involved directly during the 1992–1993 school year. In Fall 1993, the 10th graders will be added to the cohort, as well as a new set of entering pre-K students.

The entire faculty at each school will be asked to be involved in the evaluation of the project. Evaluation will be in the spirit of constructive feedback and collaboration, keeping in mind the eventual implementation of a more finely tuned plan for all the students and teachers at all three campuses the following year.

Components of the Program

IMAGE's Essential Characteristics

Essential characteristics of the IMAGE project include:

- A thematic, interdisciplinary approach to the curriculum;

- Flexible use of time;

- Active learning;

- Team teaching;

- Multiage groupings at the elementary level;

- Performance-based assessment; and

- Expanded inclusion of parents and other community members.

IMAGE Steering Committee

About 30 persons comprise the Steering Committee, including four teachers from each of the three schools, the three principals, the area superintendent, six parents or community leaders, and three people from St. Edward's University. Two parents or community leaders are chosen to represent each school by being nominated and voted upon by all parents. The intention is for the Steering Committee membership to be a demographic reflection of the population of the school; Latino and Anglo parents are represented on the committee.

Learning Core and Satellites

The IMAGE learning community includes students from pre-K through 12th grade in multiage core groups facilitated by a teaching team. Learning in the Core involves the student actively. Assessments are outcome based and the goal is mastery. Essential to the Core are second language acquisition, information literacy, technological competency, and physical health. Instruction is characterized more by coaching than by traditional front of the classroom teaching. Roger Taylor's "not a sage on the stage but a guide on the side" is a very important concept to the teachers. Students are expected to be active, involved in their own learning, generators of activity.

The concept of "satellites" focuses on extending students' interests, exploring new ones, and deepening skills and knowledge within those interests. Satellites will also offer accelerated programs to help those students who have fallen behind in the basic skills. Several satellite programs are planned, one for communications, one for the Fine Arts, and another for Health and Human Services.

Learning in the Satellite includes opportunities for direct instruction as well as project creation, often similar to apprenticeship programs or internships. Satellites are not necessarily a place, but can occur in many locations. They are intended to be a part of the regular school day, and will be staffed by people from the IMAGE community, including parents, professionals, and retired people. Students will spend increasing amounts of time in the Satellite as they mature and become more independent in their learning. It is likely that high schoolers will be involved up to 2 days a week, and elementary students as much as 1 day per week.

During the 1992–1993 school year, the communications satellite program started, with participation and guidance from a local TV station, a local advertising agency, a newspaper, and the local Chamber of Commerce. Eight student representatives from the three schools and several adults attend meetings of the Editorial Board which is responsible for a weekly TV news franchise. Students are encouraged to propose ideas for stories for the news, and will be involved in producing and directing segments for local broadcast.

The Health and Human Services satellite project has been established at the elementary school level, and involves the students in efforts to make sure they and their families have adequate medical and dental services. In addition, the nurse and other health professionals emphasize teaching the students about health issues while they are receiving services.

Another satellite which is being planned involves having children create a store. One business which is very active as an "adopter" of the school is a toy store, which specializes in books and learning games. The proposal is for the students to learn how to order inventory for the store, how to market or advertise the products, and also how to work as salespeople in the store.

HIPPY (Home Instruction Program for Preschool Youngsters)

Twenty-five families with 3- and 4-year old children participate in the HIPPY program. Parent paraprofessionals meet with parents in their homes to teach them lessons that they later teach to their child. Parents meet a second time at the school to hear presenters on topics such as health, nutrition, child development, and discipline, or to learn arts and crafts activities to do with their children. Parents are employed by the HIPPY program as Parent Educators and to fill the professional jobs in the program.

Communities in Schools

CIS is an organization operating in the schools, assisted by volunteers who are parents, community, or business leaders. CIS is responsible for a number of activities, including referrals to counseling services and arranging for parent and community volunteers in the schools. Many volunteers work in the schools, in the classrooms or other areas of the school, as mentors, tutors, and counselors.

Adopt-a-School

This is a parent-coordinated effort, which arranges for businesses to provide funds and services to the school. A total of 28 businesses work on projects in the Travis Heights Elementary School, providing such services as mentors and tutors, in-kind contributions to meet the needs of the school, dental and health services, and plans for landscaping. One law firm pays a parent to run a before-school child care program.

Open Forum

These evening meetings are scheduled for parents who have expressed a desire to meet regularly and frequently to talk about issues related to the school. The agenda is set by parents who also run the meetings. This gives all parents an opportunity to express their views on a number of issues, such as the format of the new report card which was not readily accepted by a number of parents.

Permanent Guest Teachers

It has been a challenge to find a time for teachers to get together with other team members to plan programs, discuss successes, and revise programs to address failures. One technique is to use parents, who have the appropriate qualifications, as Permanent Guest Teachers to enable teachers to have time to meet to compare notes, evaluate programs, and make plans.

Parent Involvement in Planning, Operating, and Monitoring

The parents who were active in the boundary issue in 1991 became major participants in the planning of IMAGE.

They have served on the Vertical Team, the Steering Committee, and the Budget Committee. Parents are involved in developing a new report card, needed to reflect the new performance-based assessment for IMAGE students.

One of the many drafts prepared during the process of initiating IMAGE presents a School-Parents Continuum, from "Parent as Visitor" on one end, to "Parent as Partner" on the other. Some of the roles included for parents as partners include:

- SBI (School-Based Improvement) involvement

- Classroom participants

- PTSA/boosters

- Fund raisers

- Serve in teaching role

- Volunteer tutors and mentors

- Legislative lobbyists

- Guest speakers

- Publishers

- Parents as students

Parents have attended many activities, workshops, discussions, and social events related to the establishment of IMAGE. The presentations on authentic assessment and multiage classrooms were followed by small discussion groups, where parents met with their children's teachers to talk about the implications of the new concepts for that particular classroom and grade. It is crucial that parents be involved from the beginning in understanding and accepting the new vision, so that they will enthusiastically choose to have their children participate in the IMAGE program in the three schools.

Parents are invited to serve on all of the committees active in the school. Sometimes there is reluctance on the part of some parents to take on leadership roles; many would prefer to volunteer frequently at the school, rather than donate their time to committee meetings.

The PTA at the elementary school has evolved as a result of the establishment of the IMAGE program. It is more active in school board affairs, has established a School Board Watchdog Committee which tapes every meeting, testifies when needed, and sends letters to the members.

Strengths and Weaknesses

The initiation of the IMAGE program and the publicity surrounding it were beneficial, particularly to the middle school and high schools, whose images were negative. Many parents and community leaders believed rumors about gang activities; their participation in the school has begun to change those perceptions.

Although the Developmental Project may be described as functioning as a school-within-a-school, there is not the conflict and hostility which often occur in this kind of situation. All personnel emphasize the importance of communication, and the development project students are not segregated from the others at the school. It is expected that by the fall of 1993 most of the teachers will be participating in the program so there will be no division within the schools.

One problem experienced by the IMAGE program is the large numbers of visitors from all over the country who wish to visit the school and observe the program firsthand. It is very exciting to be the center of attention, but so many outsiders in the school may be distracting to teachers and students. The school district is considering limiting visitor days to once a month and asking visitors to pay for the privilege of visiting and observing the IMAGE program.

Evaluation and Outcomes

A survey form has been developed to gather baseline evaluation data from IMAGE staff members and others concerning the effectiveness of the IMAGE project. It includes three sections, questions on the individual teacher, questions about the school, and questions about the IMAGE project.

During the fall of 1993, the three schools in the IMAGE program will be host to the Rapporteur Team, a team of educational professionals formed by NEA. The Team comes to the school to interview teachers, administrators, and parents, to allow them to view their progress through a new pair of eyes.

The New Report Card promises to provide much information which can be used to evaluate the IMAGE program. Two separate forms have been designed: one consists of open-ended, narrative questions, and the other includes a checklist of items to determine the students' progress on developmentally appropriate tasks. The first form will be utilized for marking periods 1, 3, and 5, and the other for periods 2, 4, and 6. Included in both forms are sections for open-ended student assessment and for parent assessment. This should provide teachers with feedback of the reactions and opinions of both the students and the parents.

Budget and Funding

The major expenses for this program are devoted to teacher training and time for planning the program. IMAGE received $50,000 from the School District for the 1991–1992 school year, and $100,000 for the 1992–1993 year. No funds are expected for future years. Additional funding is being sought to pay for Teacher Apprentices (Student Teachers) from St. Edward's University.

The National Education Association (NEA) provides money to pay a consultant to serve as liaison for the Mastery in Learning Consortium, to pay the expenses for the liaison and others to attend conferences, and to pay for the Rapporteur Team which will evaluate the IMAGE program during the fall of 1993.

Additional funding for special projects, such as the Early Bird Program (child care before school), is donated by the various companies active in the Adopt-a-School program.

For Further Information Contact

Kris Asthalter
IMAGE—International Multicultural and Global
Education

Travis Heights Elementary School
2010 Alameda
Austin, TX 78704
(512) 442-5121

Fulmore Middle School
201 E. Mary Street
Austin, TX 78704
(512) 442-6411

Travis High School
1211 E. Oltorf Street
Austin, TX 78704
(512) 440-5001

MEGASKILLS PARENT INVOLVEMENT PROGRAM
Austin Independent School District
Austin, TX

Major Components:
MegaSkills Workshops
Family Calendar—Working and Playing Together
"Recipes" for educational activities at home
Parent Outreach

Special Features:
Pilot program for middle schools and high schools
Parent volunteers trained as workshop leaders

Profile of Program and School District:

Number of students enrolled in the district	70,000
% from African-American families	19%
% from Latino families	36%
% from White families	45%
Number of schools in the district	91
Elementary schools	66
Middle schools	14
High schools	11

The **goal** of the MegaSkills Program is to develop the 10 attributes associated with school success:

- Motivation
- Effort
- Initiative
- Caring
- Teamwork
- Confidence
- Responsibility
- Perseverance
- Common Sense
- Problem Solving

BACKGROUND

The MegaSkills Program was created and developed by a former teacher, Dr. Dorothy Rich, Director of the Home and School Institute in Washington, DC. Since its first demonstration year in 1989, with developmental funding from the Mac-Arthur Foundation, over 1,700 workshop leaders from 34 states have been trained. These leaders, selected by schools, agencies, and businesses, receive materials and training to enable them to provide parent workshops in their organization or their community. More than 48,000 parents have participated nationwide in the workshop sessions, during the 3-year period, 1989–1992.

MegaSkills was introduced to Austin in 1990 by the A + Coalition, a partnership between businesses and the Austin Independent School District (ISD), which was looking for a parent program to help reduce Austin's 25% dropout rate. A study done by the Coalition showed that the most important ingredient in a child's success in staying in school is the parent. Research of available programs led them to choose MegaSkills as a program to increase parent participation in the schools and help address the needs of the students. IBM, a founding member of the A + Coalition, sponsored one of its employees, Kathy Monte, to serve for 2 years as a program coordinator.

The Austin program started in the 1990–1991 school year. Funded by contributions from IBM and the Southwest Area Council of the Greater Austin Chamber of Commerce, 81 volunteers were trained to present workshops for parents, with 65 of them assigned to 38 Austin elementary schools. The first schools targeted for the program were those with large numbers of low-income families. The workshops were also conducted in Spanish in those schools with large Latino populations. In January 1991, the Austin School District hired Jo Ann Farrell to be the MegaSkills Facilitator for the district. Each year the program has expanded, offered in 53 elementary schools in the 1991–1992 school year, and all but two of the 66 schools at the elementary level in 1992–1993.

DESCRIPTION OF THE PROGRAM

The MegaSkills program consists of a series of five to eight parenting workshops, offered on a regular basis, which last from 1–1½ hours each, and focus on MegaSkills—the basic values, attitudes, and behaviors that determine a child's achievement and ability to make informed life decisions in a drug free environment. Parents of all socioeconomic groups are encouraged to participate.

The workshops are conducted by MegaSkills Leaders, volunteers who receive 2 days of training from AISD/Project A+ personnel who have been certified by the Home and School Institute. Workshops are usually conducted at a school or business site. Churches and libraries have also been used. It generally works out best when there is convenient space for providing child care for attending parents.

A total of 280 MegaSkills volunteer leaders have been trained to work in Austin schools, neighboring districts, local businesses, and city agencies. These include parents, principals, teachers, counselors, and community leaders.

Components of the Program

MegaSkills Workshops

The initial parent workshop includes an overview of the MegaSkills series, with experiential exercises, such as having participants identify their child's special traits, group discussion on realistic expectations of schools, and the educational responsibilities of parents. In every workshop there is active discussion, role playing, and demonstration.

Continuing workshops focus on the 10 specific Mega-Skills:

- Confidence—feeling able to do it

- Motivation—wanting to do it

- Effort—being willing to work hard

- Responsibility—doing what's right

- Initiative—moving into action

- Perseverance—completing what you start

- Caring—showing concern for others

- Teamwork — working with others

- Common Sense — using good judgment

- Problem Solving — putting what you know and
  what you can do into action

Each workshop includes information sharing, large and small group discussions, and demonstrations or hands-on activities which can then be reproduced at home with children. Specific parent concerns, such as how to handle TV watching, how to use free time, how to teach the 3R's at home, how to work effectively as partners with the school, are integrated into the program. "Recipes" for additional inexpensive home learning activities are also provided.

Five to eight workshops are offered in each school; only one series is typically made available during the school year, but some schools offer the program twice. Attendance at the workshops ranges from 7–40 parents. Parents who attend at least five workshops are presented with a certificate at the end of the session.

MegaSkills in the Secondary Schools

A committee has been formed to adapt the MegaSkills program for implementation at the middle schools and the high schools. During the 1992–1993 school year a pilot program is being tested in two middle schools. The format of the workshops is similar to that used in the elementary schools, but different materials are distributed, addressing issues of particular importance to early adolescence.

Family Calendar

An attractive, useful Family Calendar, available in English and Spanish, has been published and distributed. Entitled "Working and Playing Together," the calendar features one of the MegaSkills for each month of the year, illustrated by a drawing from a student in the schools. A task or activity is suggested for each day of the month, to support the MegaSkill of the Month. Two new topics have been added to the 10:

Family Time—Working and Playing Together and Goal Planning—Making Choices. The calendar sells for $2.50 and the proceeds will be used to prepare next year's calendar.

Parent Outreach

A pamphlet has been prepared and distributed to suggest ways in which leaders and/or schools can publicize the MegaSkills Program to groups of parents who are not strongly involved in education. It addresses issues related to techniques for contacting parents and how to adapt the workshop outline to be responsive to parents from different cultural, linguistic, and economic backgrounds. It also includes ideas for follow-up activities after the workshops are completed, and suggestions for home visits and face-to-face personal contacts with parents.

Additional Materials

The MegaSkills Program from the Home and School Institute includes materials to be distributed to parents on home learning activities, recipes, and "thoughts to take home." The Austin program has supplemented these materials with 75 additional pages which are given to all of the leaders in the fall. These supplementary materials are collected from a number of sources, including leaders and parents. The leaders can decide which materials they wish to incorporate into their workshop design.

MegaSkills Leaders

The MegaSkills Facilitator is always looking for new people to become trainers, since some of those who have done it in the past may not be available to continue. The goal of the program is to have a base of four leaders at each school, including one person on the staff of the school. Potential leaders are often identified from parents attending the workshop. Principals are asked to recommend parents to be trained as leaders, and to consider school adopters who might want to participate.

The following principles articulated by the Home and School Institute serve as a philosophical foundation for the program:

- Every family has strengths.

- Parent involvement in education is a basic, legitimate education service.

- Parent involvement programs are needed throughout the age and grade spectrum.

- Families need and want practical help in helping their children learn.

- Family activities need to be practical, easy-to-do, and linked to skills and attitudes needed for student success.

- Schools today need programs that reach culturally diverse audiences.

- The total community needs to be involved in support of children's education.

In addition to learning how to present material, conduct a workshop, and facilitate group discussions, the leaders are also responsible for meeting with the school principal to agree on how they will handle administrative questions such as:

- How will materials for distribution be duplicated?

- What incentives will be offered (*e.g.*, gift certificates, drawing for prizes at the end of each meeting)?

- Who will provide food, recommended as essential for every meeting?

- How will baby-sitting be provided? By whom?

Parent Involvement in Planning, Operating, and Monitoring

Many of the leaders and presenters of the MegaSkills program are parents. The MegaSkills Facilitator for the district is in regular contact with parent-leaders, and welcomes suggestions and feedback from their experiences. One of the concerns of the program is that those who attend the workshops are parents who are already involved in their children's education; that the parents who could benefit most are reluctant or unable to attend. Efforts need to be made to make all of the teachers and school personnel aware of the value of the MegaSkills program, so that they will encourage parents to attend.

Strengths and Weaknesses

The major strength of the MegaSkills program is the atmosphere of positive communication which is evident at the workshops. Parents can come to the workshops, be treated with respect, and not be talked down to. Many parents disliked their own school experience; many parents do not know what to do about their own children who are having difficulty in school. Acting as facilitators rather than as teachers or experts, the leaders provide parents with an opportunity to enhance their abilities to work effectively with their children in developing skills which will lead to success in school and in life.

Parents appreciate the program because it provides them with a nonthreatening, nonjudgmental situation where they can explore topics of mutual concern and learn from each other. Their most frequent comment is "I had no idea so many other people shared my problems." Parents often establish long-term networks and develop a more comfortable supportive relationship with the school.

The lack of administrative support from some of the schools has been one barrier to the program's effectiveness. The program will be more successful in a school if the team presenting the workshops includes parent-leaders and staff from the school. Although all of the trained MegaSkills leaders are volunteers, the principal's support of the program is very critical. It will determine whether the teachers and counselors will be given time off of their regular duties to conduct the MegaSkills workshops. It will affect whether the principal will use some of his/her discretionary fund for the MegaSkills program, for copying of materials, incentives, food, or other expenses. Administrative support ensures that the program will be taken seriously by faculty, parents, and school community leaders.

The leaders are supposed to follow the outline and format they have learned in their training sessions, but they have some autonomy in their approach to the workshops. The district facilitator has had only one complaint about the content of the workshop, where the leader read from the Bible during one of the school sessions. Having the workshops presented by a team of two or three trained leaders, one of whom is a teacher or counselor from the school, helps to ensure that the appropriate content is being discussed.

The MegaSkills program in Austin has received much local and national publicity. As a result, many other organizations, businesses, and schools outside of the district want to participate in the program. Arrangements have been made for persons from local organizations and neighboring communities to be trained as MegaSkills leaders. They attend the regular training sessions and pay an agreed upon fee for the training, so that they can offer the workshops to their employees as a company benefit.

Outcomes and Evaluation

Evaluation of a program for parents that is expected to help children is, by definition, very difficult to quantify. The MegaSkills Facilitator is working closely with the Austin Independent School District (AISD) Office of Research and Evaluation (ORE) to design survey forms which will help to document program success, track student absentee rates, discipline problems, and grade improvements. Most of the evidence about the program's success thus far, has been collected from conversations with parents, leaders, and principals, and through various kinds of anecdotal material.

During the 1991–1992 school year, ORE tracked 1,196 students, from preschool through grade 6, whose families participated in the MegaSkills program. The following are some of their research findings:

Student Performance Findings

- In comparing students' 1992 scores on the Iowa Test of Basic Skills and the Norm-Referenced Assessment Program for Texas with their 1991 baseline scores, MegaSkills students exceeded predicted gains at statistically significant levels on two comparisons, achieved predicted gains on 11 comparisons, and were below predicted levels on no comparisons.

- The rate of discipline incidents for MegaSkills students in 1991–1992 was lower at a statistically significant level when compared to their rate for the 1990–1991 baseline year, and was lower than for elementary students districtwide.

- The attendance rate for MegaSkills students was higher than that of elementary students districtwide.

- The percentage of MegaSkills students not promoted was lower than that for elementary students districtwide.

Principals' Perceptions of the Program

- 74% reported fewer or much fewer behavior problems.

- 74% reported better or much better attitudes.

- 69% reported improved academic work.

The principals also reported that the training increased parents' involvement in their children's education (86%) and increased or improved communication between parents and teachers (67%).

Parent Perceptions of the Program

A tally of the feedback from 1,666 parents from more than 30 different schools indicated:

- 80% said the workshops helped increase their understanding of their role in their children's education.

- 71% agreed that the workshops helped them understand the skills and behaviors that children need in school.

- 67% reported that the workshop lessons helped improve communication between them and their children.

- 49% reported that since attending the workshops they have increased their involvement at their children's school.

Budget and Funding

The main costs of the MegaSkills Program are the training of the leaders, the salary for the Facilitator, and the materials, incentives, and food for the workshops at the local schools. Funds are available through AISD's Drug Free and Chapter 1 program grants, and from the contributions of the A + Coalition and local businesses, including IBM, Motorola, the Southwest Area Council of the Greater Austin Chamber of Commerce, and Southwestern Bell.

For Further Information Contact

Jo Ann Farrell, MegaSkills Facilitator
Austin Independent School District
1111 West 6th Street
Austin, TX 78703
(512) 499–1700, Ext. 4580

FAMILY SUPPORT AND EDUCATION PROGRAMS
Avance
San Antonio, TX

Major Components:
>   Even Start
>   Parent-Child Education
>   Early Childhood Program
>   Literacy and Continuing Education Classes
>   Child Development Program
>   Padres a la escuela
>   Family Resource Center

Special Features:
>   Intervention program for hard to reach families
>   Toy Making
>   Fatherhood Program

Profile of Program and Population Served by AVANCE Programs:

Number of adults and children served by Avance	3,000
% of Latino families	98%

Avance's **mission** is:

- To strengthen the family unit;
- To enhance parenting skills which nurture the optimal development of children;
- To promote educational success; and
- To foster the personal and economic success of parents.

BACKGROUND

Avance is a private, non-profit community organization. Its focus is community-based intervention which is family-centered, preventive, comprehensive, and continuous through integration and collaboration of services. By providing support and education services to low-income families, Avance fulfills its main purpose which is to strengthen and support families. Avance was created in 1973 with seed money from the Zale Foundation. Avance is a Spanish word meaning to advance. Avance has many success stories about "parents who have made a commitment to improve and advance forward, to be responsible and to attain a higher quality of life, for themselves and their children." Avance has been nationally recognized for establishing a successful family intervention program for hard to reach families, with special emphasis on serving Latino families.

Many of the current programs were designed from information and data gathered from a survey conducted by Avance in 1980. The survey found that parents were lacking in basic knowledge about children's developmental needs, how to acquire job skills, how to sustain hope in the face of long-term adversity, how to build a sense of control over one's life, and how to overcome social isolation. A high incidence of abuse and neglect of children among young parents was detected in this survey.

The staff has used the survey to focus its program, emphasizing the parents' own development, building self-esteem and perception of opportunity, improving decision making skills, and providing specific knowledge of child development.

DESCRIPTION OF THE PROGRAM

The Avance Family Support and Education Program serves more than 3,000 predominantly low-income Latino adults and children each year. These individuals and families are characterized by:

- Several generations of living in poverty;

- An 80% high school dropout rate among the parents;

- A high degree of stress and isolation;

- Lack of knowledge of child growth and development;

- Significantly high potential for child abuse and neglect; and

- Lack of salable job skills.

The Avance Service Area includes low-income, predominantly Latino neighborhoods in San Antonio and Houston, Texas. The Avance intervention model begins with families with infants and young children. Services provided are comprehensive in scope, community-based, preventive in nature and provided in a sequential manner to children and parents. The Avance program is offered in the home, school, and in centers, some of which are located in public housing projects.

Components of the Program

Even Start

The Avance Even Start Program was started in San Antonio in 1989. The initial grant was for 4 years. The Program serves 426 families To be eligible, they must include a child under 7 years of age, and the parents may not have completed high school. Most of the families (98%) in the program are Latino; 100% are low-income.

The Program serves nine schools located in three school districts in San Antonio. All schools are in low-income, high-crime areas; some are in middle class communities. Three K-5 schools in the South San Antonio School District were selected for the Even Start program because their children have the lowest test scores in the district. Many of the parents are recent immigrants from Mexico. They see the U.S. as the land of opportunity, and are looking for the opportunity to help their children survive and do better in school. Four schools in the

Edgewood School District were selected, based on the needs of the families in those neighborhoods, and two of the schools are in the San Antonio Independent School District.

The goals of the Even Start program are:

- To increase the education of the parents;

- To prepare children for school; and

- To provide parenting and life skills to the parents.

Even Start is a 12-month program, divided into two tracks: a 9-month program featuring a parenting track and a 3-month track of life skills and parental involvement in schools. The second track is a literacy track, including adult education, preparation for the GED, job training, and college preparation for the parents.

The parenting segment concentrates on children from birth to 3 years of age, and emphasizes the key concepts of parenting, how children learn, what parents can do at home to help their children learn, the importance of being involved in the school, how to build self-esteem and be a good role model. These classes are held once a week for 2 hours at all of the nine schools in the Even Start program.

The Even Start program has a staff of nine, including one coordinator, two parent educators, and six paraprofessionals who serve as assistants in the program, providing child care, making materials, and performing other needed tasks.

Parent-Child Education Program

This is a 9-month intensive parent education program for low-income parents and their children under 3 years of age. Each class meets for 3 hours once a week: the first hour consists of parent education lessons; the second hour consists of a toy making class; the third hour features a special resource speaker who discusses such topics as nutrition or talks about community programs and support services. During this time, the children are in child care at the center. Transportation is provided to enable the families to attend the classes.

The toy making portion of the class emphasizes the

importance of learning through play. Mothers make approximately 30 toys (books, puzzles, dolls, puppets) out of inexpensive materials, to stimulate the child's learning environment. Using the toy as a teaching tool, Avance helps the parents acquire the skill of teaching. In addition, the toy making hour provides the mothers a therapeutic outlet to release tension and an informal opportunity to talk and share experiences with other mothers.

Every family is visited at home once a month by a staff member of the program. The child is observed playing with a toy that was made in class. The lessons for the classes and the home visits are drawn from the Avance curriculum, developed by parents and others who grew up in the same kinds of neighborhoods and are familiar with the issues facing the families.

At the end of the 9 months a graduation ceremony is held at a local college or university for those families who have participated in the classes and met certain criteria. A parenting certificate is presented to the mother or father, and the child under 3 years of age, dressed in a cap and gown, receives a reading book.

Early Childhood Program

Children ages 3–5 and their parents attend this program once a week: parent classes are held while the children learn and play together; joint parent and child activities are also scheduled. The program emphasizes language development, social skills, and academic preparation.

Literacy and Continuing Education Classes

These are held once a week for 2 hours in two of the elementary schools in the program. They include a wide range of topics and activities: preparing for the GED, preparing for and applying to college, life skills, and leadership training. The parents are also referred to other agencies for additional needs, such as financial assistance, emergency food needs, housing, educational advocacy, and translation of school materials.

Comprehensive Child Development Program

Avance was one of 24 grantees to receive funds from the federal Head Start Bureau to implement a 5-year national demonstration project, designed to provide indepth services to families in order to enable the family to become self-sufficient. It is targeted toward families where the mother is pregnant or has a child below the age of 1. A case manager is assigned to the family and designs a service plan to identify any and all services the family needs, including health, education, job training, and job placement.

Avance-Hasbro National Family Resource Center

Funded by the Hasbro Children's Foundation, the Center provides Avance material, curriculum, training, and field assistance to individuals throughout the country, interested in addressing social and educational problems among high-risk families with young children.

Padres a la escuela (P.A.E.)

This program, cosponsored by Avance and the National Committee for Citizens in Education, Washington, DC, was started in October 1991. It serves all parents in four of the schools, providing them with information about the school and encouraging them to become involved. About 20–25 parents attend the P.A.E. workshops which are scheduled once a month during the day.

P.A.E. is advocacy oriented and teaches parents how to communicate with the school and how to work to improve their child's education. Workshops have been presented on parent involvement, parent/teacher conferences, corporal punishment, suspension, how to appeal school actions, and many other topics. The session on corporal punishment created a lively debate between parents and staff. Many of the older parents, with a "spare the rod and spoil the child" frame of mind, were not opposed to corporal punishment and did not feel the need for this workshop.

Fatherhood Program

By working closely with the fathers of children in schools served by Avance programs, Avance underscores its commitment to preserving the family unit and attempts to help the father grow personally, educationally, and economically. The program teaches the fathers parenting skills and encourages the fathers' involvement with their children.

Parent Involvement in Planning, Operating, and Monitoring

Many of the parents who have been active in Even Start or P.A.E. have become active in the schools, as volunteers, as PTA members and leaders, with COPS (Communities Organized for Public Service), and running an after-school computer program. The skills which they learned and the self-confidence and self-esteem developed as a result of their participation in the parenting programs have enabled them to become role models and assume leadership roles in education groups and community organizations.

One of the lessons learned by Avance staff is that many parents are reluctant, or even afraid, to be involved in the schools. They may feel inferior to the well-educated teachers and administrators, and do not have the confidence to visit the school or talk with the teachers. The Avance program, through the parent education classes and programs such as Padres a la escuela, seeks to provide the parents with strong support for starting to become involved in their children's education.

As indicated earlier, the Avance curriculum used in the parent education classes is designed and developed by people who grew up in the neighborhood. They are aware of the issues parents wish to learn about and discuss, both those related to education and the schools and others concerning family needs and community resources.

Strengths and Weaknesses

The most successful aspect of the program has been the progress made by many parents in reaching their educational and employment goals. Many are learning English, have obtained better jobs, have taken on roles they were previously afraid of, completed their GED certification, and entered college.

Changes can be seen in their children as well: many who have gone through the early childhood program are now on the Honor Roll. Teachers have observed that the younger siblings of children enrolled in Even Start are far ahead of their older brothers and sisters in terms of self-control and following directions. Many of the younger children seem to be learning English with greater facility. One boy who only spoke Spanish when he began the program now is fluent in both languages; he wrote a poem, in English and Spanish, which received districtwide recognition.

There is a need to work with some parents to help them examine their values. They may feel that since they are poor they can steal to obtain what they need. They try to take advantage of the system wherever they can. Avance staff is attempting to address this issue in the parenting and adult education classes.

The programs sponsored by Avance are more effective when they are school-based, rather than center-based. Avance has developed a comprehensive framework and models for the components of the programs, and their experience has shown that it has been easier to reach parents through the schools. However, the process of being accepted by the administration of the school districts and the schools has often presented a barrier.

Outcomes and Evaluation

Changed Attitudes and Practices on the Part of School Personnel

Many principals and teachers have tracked children in the Even Start program and have commented that they show great progress. They observe that these children are better prepared for school when they enter kindergarten. School librarians have commented that the literacy levels have improved as a result of these programs. Many principals have included the Even Start goals as part of the school goals, and view the program as an integral and important part of the total school program.

Changed Parent Attitudes

Parents are more confident and independent, better informed, more involved in the schools, better educated, and more honest. Values have been clarified, a more positive attitude is being displayed by parents, and they are no longer trying to manipulate the system for their benefit.

Reformed School and District Policies

As a result of the Padres a la escuela program, many schools have become more open and welcoming to parents. However, some school staff members have become more cautious, unsure of how parents will handle all of the new information they are receiving. In one school, P.A.E.'s activities convinced the principal to put up a welcome sign for parents and to begin an open door policy for parents at the school.

Increased Parent/Community Support

A local market donates fruits and vegetables on a weekly basis to the program. Pepsi-Cola sponsored a back-to-school party for the children and provided free backpacks. USAA Insurance Company provides Christmas gifts for more than 300 students. A local girl scout troop has provided a Thanksgiving dinner to one of their most needy families. A local restaurant hosts a dinner for over 400 families.

Improved Student Achievement

The Avance Even Start staff sees a strengthening of the family in support of education. They keep family profiles with records of report cards, certificates, and other performance measures. The first children who went through the program are now in first and second grade. The majority of these students are on the Honor Roll, and are speaking English very well.

In 1991, the Avance 18th Year Reunion was held; the family support and education program's first group of mothers were contacted to learn of their progress and celebrate their successes. Among the 31 original families which participated in classes between 1973–1975, a total of 21 were located. Of these 21, only two had high school diplomas when they enrolled in Avance. Since then, 11 have earned a GED. A total of six mothers have gone to college.

The "Avance babies" were about 17 or 18 years old when contacted in 1991. Of the 23 children located, all but one had graduated from high school or were still completing school. Of those who had graduated 50% were in college and one had joined the military.

University of Houston Evaluation

In 1987, the Carnegie Corporation provided a grant to conduct a comprehensive evaluation of the Avance Family Support and Education Programs. Dr. Dale Johnson, from the University of Houston, was asked to design and conduct the evaluation. His study gathered and analyzed the attitudes, knowledge, and behavior of the parents served by the Avance programs, and found that:

- Parents who went through the program were more likely to see themselves as teachers of their children. They were less likely to have strict, punitive attitudes about discipline. They felt warmer about their children and were less likely to feel aggravated.

- Parents completing the classes had an increased knowledge of child growth and development. They provided a more stimulating home environment, as documented by videotapes taken of the mother and child interacting.

- Mothers in the program talked to their children more frequently and had more developmentally appropriate communication with them than did parents not in the program. They were also more likely to encourage their children to speak with them. The mothers were more likely to use toys in an educational way, and used more praise with their children. They had a more positive affect when interacting and were more likely to provide structure and mediation to the child's environment. And they generally felt more positive about parenting and also had an increased knowledge of community resources.

An analysis done of the parents who enrolled in the literacy and continuing education classes indicated that 60% of the parents who had completed the first year of Avance's program enrolled in the second year. This proportion was twice as high as the 30% of the comparison (control) group who reenrolled in adult education classes.

Budget and Funding

The cost of the Even Start program is about $200,000 a year. The first 4 years of funding was from the U.S. Department of Education; the Texas Education Agency is providing money for the program during its fifth year of operation.

Avance receives grants from a number of foundations, corporations, and government programs, including United Way, Carnegie Corporation, Brown Foundation, Southwestern Bell, Tenneco Corporation, the Texas Department of Human Services, and the City of San Antonio.

For Further Information Contact

Gloria Rodriguez, Chief Executive Officer
Elizabeth Lopez, Even Start Director

Avance   Even Start Office
301 South Frio, Suite 310   435 San Dario
San Antonio, TX 78207   San Antonio, TX 78237
(512) 270–4630   (512) 431–6616

PARENT ORGANIZING AND EDUCATION PROJECT
Bronx Educational Services
Bronx, NY

Major Components:
- Outreach activities
- Local meetings
- Leadership development
- Adult education
- Parents Organizing

Special Features:
- Parent empowerment
- Political action

Profile of Program and School District:

Number of schools in School District #8	29
Elementary schools	20
Junior high schools	9
Number of schools targeted in Project	7
Elementary schools	5
Junior high schools	2
Number of students enrolled in 7 schools	6,000
Ethnic Composition of 7 Schools in Project	
% African-American	25%
% Latino	70%
% Other	5%
% of families with limited English	40%
% of low-income families	85%
% of children from homeless or formerly homeless families	30%

The **goals** of the Parent Organizing and Education Project are:

- To organize and build a parents' union and plan a strategy for bringing about changes in the schools;
- To help parents see what they can do collectively to bring about change; and
- To bring about major changes in the schools, including improved facilities, better supplies, and respect for parents and children.

BACKGROUND

Bronx Educational Services, a private nonprofit organization, has offered basic education and literacy classes for adults since 1973. About 180 adults are enrolled in classes each term. The organization has always believed that the acquisition of literacy and language skills cannot be separated from people's day-to-day lives and, therefore, has always integrated community issues into program curriculum. One topic which is always of great interest to the adults in the classes is education; the students are aware of the shortcomings of their own education and are deeply committed to their children's education.

One of the readings distributed in class in the fall of 1991, was a survey from the *New York Times* which reported on reading levels in the public schools in New York City. As the adults in the literacy class studied the results of the survey, they noted that the schools in the South Bronx, in the vicinity of Bronx Educational Services, ranked near the bottom of the city in reading scores. They realized that their children were attending the schools with the lowest reading levels. Some of the parents had attended the same schools themselves and began to wonder if their lack of literacy skills was a result of poor education at the time they were enrolled.

The adults in the class wanted to explore the issue of literacy in the schools further, and proposed to visit some of the schools to talk to them particularly about the reading curriculum. Seven or eight persons visited a nearby local school; they made an appointment with the principal and requested that they be allowed to observe one of the classrooms. The principal arranged for them to visit a 4th grade classroom; the class was large, with 40 children in it, but the teacher had many years of teaching experience in the New York public schools.

The visitors were shocked by what they observed. The teacher made remarks to them which demonstrated a lack of respect for his students and for the adults from the literacy class. The teacher talked to the visitors about the children being stupid and lazy. He remarked to the students, "Listen to these people because you don't want to grow up like your parents and go on welfare." These comments were made in a demeaning manner which was embarrassing to the adults observing the class.

After leaving the school, the literacy students discussed what they had seen and heard, and came to the conclusion that they should be talking with the parents of these children about what is going on in the classroom. They considered selecting one of the schools in the neighborhood, and concentrating their efforts on school improvement there. They surveyed the adults in the classes at Bronx Educational Services to determine whether their children were clustered in one school, but found that they attended many schools in the area.

The parents began to contact existing organizations active in public education issues, such as Save Our Schools which mobilized to oppose budget cuts in education. They met other parents in the district who were upset about the schools and ready to organize for action.

In January 1992, the Parents Organizing and Education Project was formed, in conjunction with the parents and some staff of one elementary school. It has grown to include parents from all elementary and junior high schools in the southernmost part of Community School District #8.

DESCRIPTION OF THE PROGRAM

District #8 is very large: it spreads from the South Bronx into Throggs Neck and Pelham Bay. There are vast economic and ethnic differences between these two sections of the Bronx. Six of the schools in the South Bronx, all within 2 miles of each other are among the most overcrowded, least effective schools in New York City. At least three of them serve a large number of homeless and formerly homeless children, all have among the lowest reading scores in the city, the highest rates of probationary staff, equipment that is broken or antiquated, serious security problems, bathrooms without doors on the stalls, water fountains with no water, and inadequate supplies and materials.

Many of the parents are insecure in English, some have their own literacy problems, and many did not finish school themselves. All too often, when their children are not learning they blame the children themselves or their own shortcomings as parents. This further alienates them from participation in the schools.

The group uses a variety of tactics, including direct action. Sometimes confrontation is necessary to bring attention to unjust situations that have been allowed to exist for many years. For instance, 50 parents had to take over the district office before school board members and district staff would take their concerns seriously. The hope is that following the confrontations, the parents involved will be able to move to a more collaborative effort with the school personnel.

The vision of the program comes from the strong belief in organizing as a way to affect change in education. Organizing includes not only political activity, but also suggests people involved in the process of gathering data, considering alternatives, and drawing conclusions. The organizers of this project realize that most people care about their children's schooling but don't know how to have an impact. They do not think they have the ability or the right to affect change, so they do not speak out.

Parents from seven schools are currently active in the organization. The activities shift in response to events in the individual schools. In the fall of 1992, much emphasis was placed on school improvement in one of the junior high schools with a reputation for weapons, violence, and very little academic activity. There is much dissatisfaction among the parents, and the Principal appears to be supportive of some change. Parents who are active in the Project will be proposing that major restructuring of the school take place, with the formation of schools-within-schools, smaller classes, and major efforts made to improve school climate and school safety.

There are two co-coordinators, four community organizers, three of whom are VISTA volunteers, and one part-time teacher, who serve as the main staff on the project.

Components of the Program

Outreach Activities

These include door-to-door organizing, distribution of literature in front of the schools, or petition drives. Between January and the end of the summer of 1992, nearly 500 parents with children in South Bronx public schools were contacted.

Project staff go to where the parents are. When staff talk to people in their own living rooms, the parents and citizens are freer to discuss their concerns, their fears, and their ideas. They are made to feel like someone cares enough to hear what they have to say, to come to their home. This is an important first step to reaching parents who normally are not active on their own. After the first contact, staff or parent leaders stay in touch with any parent that expressed interest. They are kept posted, invited to meetings and actions, and asked for their input.

Local Meetings

Many meetings are held for parents in each school, but some are for all parents in the South Bronx end of the school district. They are held at the Bronx Educational Services offices, community centers, people's homes—the closer to the parents' homes the better. As many as 35–40 people attend each meeting. In addition to gathering information, they work on proposals for change. Initially, parents spent time brainstorming on changes they would like to see in their schools. As a result of their work, they put together a proposal for change that lays out the issues common to all seven schools. Additionally, parents from each school have added their specific concerns.

Central Planning Meeting

Representatives from each of the school communities, organizations in the area, and staff from the project meet whenever necessary, to share information and plan future strategies. The organization is in the process of putting together a Project Board for this purpose.

Workshops in Leadership Development

These are designed and sponsored by the Project in order to assist parents in gaining skills needed to be effective in their efforts to improve the schools through collective action. They discuss what their vision of effective schools includes, read about and visit schools that are working, learn about curriculum controversies, bilingual education, special education, budgets, and plan strategies for educational change.

Adult Education

Parents are welcome at the literacy classes and the ESL classes offered by Bronx Educational Services. Some of the parents became connected with the project through the classes, and others learn about the classes through the project.

Speak Out

The first "Speak Out" was held in July 1992, with about 100 parents in attendance. This was the first time a group of parents had come together to publicly present their concerns to the local school board. Their hope was that their issues would be heard and could begin to be addressed before schools opened in September. All of the nine school board members had been invited and three were expected to attend.

Not one appeared at the meeting, which was a major disappointment to the organizers. When no school board member showed up, parent leaders did not hesitate to take 50 parents to the school district office. After a 3 hour takeover, district staff and school board members were forced to take the group and its concerns seriously. Because of this and the media coverage of the event, the parents felt their collective strength for the first time on that day. It was an important moment in the growth of the organization.

It was because of that takeover that almost all of the invited officials came to the next rally/speak out held by the parents group on October 21, 1992. This included seven out of the nine school board members, as well as five of the principals of the schools in the area and a number of persons from the district staff and the superintendent's office. Proposals on nine issues were presented to the school board members; the school board was asked to consider the changes proposed and respond to the group in a timely way.

School Improvement Proposals

The nine issues of concern which were presented to the Community School Board #8 on October 21, 1992, were:

- Reading scores and abilities

- After school programs

- Genuine parent involvement in decision making—requesting a clear written policy statement; encouraging principals to meet with all parent groups

- Security

- Conditions of school buildings

- Lack of nurses

- Definition of family—support of a curriculum that teaches tolerance and respect for all people

- Encouraging parents to participate in Community School Board meetings—structuring the meetings in a manner that supports participation rather than hinders it

- Selection of principals

Attending School Board Meetings

The parents in the project have learned that they must become informed, not only about educational issues affecting their children's schools, but also be aware of the policies and decisions made by the school board. They are now regular participants at school board meetings, and can monitor progress on their many concerns. Their mere presence forces a different kind of accountability.

School Board Elections

The parent group realizes that the changes they support are more likely to occur if the members of the school board believe in quality education for South Bronx children. They have had the opportunity to observe the school board and assess the political positions of its members. The parents expect to become active in school board elections, locating new candidates to run, conducting registration drives among the parents, and sponsoring voter education efforts.

Many parents favor the replacement of the district superintendent with a new person who would be more responsive to the parents and the community. They realize that they will have to change the school board membership in order to be able to choose a new superintendent of the district.

School Choice

All parents in the New York City school system are allowed to enroll their children in any school in the city as of September 1993. In order for it to have any meaning to children in the South Bronx, more schools in that area have to be quality schools. The organizers in this project realize that choice will not affect the parents in the South Bronx, because there will be no funds for transportation and the few good schools will be filled immediately. They are trying to inform parents about choice, and gather support for alternative schools in the neighborhood or schools-within-schools, so that there will be a choice between schools of differing structures and philosophies.

Parent Involvement in Planning, Operating, and Monitoring

The parents are active in every aspect of this project. They are becoming better informed about the issues and the political process which can either bring about change or maintain the status quo. They are asking questions, not only at the project meetings, but also at their children's schools. Parents are now beginning to view themselves as "agents of change," to feel empowered to speak out and expect to be listened to.

The decisions concerning activities and policies governing this project are made in parent meetings, both small meetings that each school may have, and larger meetings where parents from all the schools come together. A project board is currently being developed to provide a more organized and systematic approach to the collaboration.

The school's approach to parent involvement is to bring parents in to give approval routinely to the policies and practices of the school. Often it is necessary for the school to have parents involved to meet federal mandates, state requirements, or local policy. From the parents' perspective, the school simply wants them to sign off and agree to what has already been decided, rather than being consulted before the decision is made.

Often parent involvement programs are set up in a way that supports the agenda of the administration. Whether intentional or not, usually only a small group of parents are brought in, coddled, nurtured, made to feel important. These few parents are never given the training necessary to (1) represent other parents by seeking their genuine input, (2) make informed decisions on the issues, (3) participate as equals with teaching and administrative staff. They are expected to participate in difficult decisions, but have no independent support. Teachers and administrators in New York City have strong unions, and receive constant training and access to resources. Parents are dependent on their districts for the minimal support they receive.

The PA, or Parent Association, which exists in every school in New York City, is viewed as an organization run by the principal who puts on pressure to approve everything proposed by the school. The PA officers are not trained in ways of involving other parents, in budget or curriculum issues, or in hiring criteria. PAs are perceived by many parents as too tied to the administration and not at all interested in soliciting other points of view.

The PA meetings are structured so as to encourage parents *not* to think, whereas the organizing effort of this project places emphasis on questioning and challenging. In some of the schools in this district, the Parent Project will be able to work with the PA of the school; in others they are in conflict with the PA and will not rely on them for support. In some of the schools, the principal will not meet with parents, but only with representatives from the Parent Association.

The project recognizes that there are many reasons why a majority of parents do not get actively involved in their children's schools. It is, however, committed to identifying the obstacles, addressing them, and strengthening the decision making capacity of parents.

Strengths and Weaknesses

The parent organizing effort has focused attention on the fact that the parents and the community are dissatisfied with the schools. They want to be more involved and they want to see changes made in the school. The project has attracted many parents, who were not previously involved, but are now becoming active. The teachers and administrators are starting to respond, and some progress has been observed with such issues as building repairs, painting, and replacement or repair of furniture.

The project has tried to organize parents from families living in homeless shelters, but their participation is minimal. These families experience a high degree of mobility, and are under stress from the challenge of everyday survival. However, some of the parents in formerly homeless families have become strong leaders in the Parent Organizing and Education Project.

Schools have been allowed to deteriorate for many years and those who have been in positions of authority during that time are largely responsible. The initial attention focusing on these seven schools was threatening to many administrators and staff. At first they tried to discredit the organization, then they tried blaming each other. Finally, begrudgingly, plans are being made to implement some changes.

Outcomes and Evaluation

Many positive outcomes have been achieved through the work of this parents group. They have been meeting with school board members and principals of individual schools to express their concerns and discuss proposed changes. The

District Superintendent visited the junior high school targeted by the Parents Organizing Project, which he had never done during his 18 years in that job. The President of the School Board devoted an issue of his monthly report on the schools in South Bronx; they are typically never mentioned in this report.

Some staff and principals are actively supporting the efforts of the Project. Others are still resistant. In two schools, parents active in the Project are definitely being kept outside of school decision making. In most other schools, parents are more welcome and invited in. With the exception of two Parent Associations, all are working more and more closely with the Parent Organizing and Education Project. South Bronx schools have a very high percentage of new teachers whose jobs are not secure. Many of them, while recognizing the inequities, are hesitant to speak out.

The project has resulted in much support from community and neighborhood groups; many parents are actively involved. Small changes are happening in the schools. The process of organizing parents for collective action for change is successful.

Budget and Funding

The budget for this project is between $95,000 and $125,000 per year. Funds come from grants from the Edna McConnell Clark Foundation and the Aaron Diamond Foundation.

For Further Information Contact

Barbara Gross
Mili Bonilla
Parent Organizing and Education Project/Mothers on
    the Move (MOM)
Bronx Educational Services
965 Longwood Ave., Room 309
Bronx, NY 10459
(718) 991–7310

MCALLEN PARENT INVOLVEMENT PROGRAM
McAllen Independent School District
McAllen, TX

Major Components:
Partners in Excellence Adopt-a-School Program
Evening Study Centers for parents and students
Parent Education

Special Features:
Follow the Yellow Brick Road—transition to middle school
Keys for a Better Life
All staff are bilingual

Profile of Program and School District:

Population of McAllen	97,000
Number of students enrolled in district	21,500
% from Latino families	87%
% from White families	12%
% who have limited English	32%
% from low-income families	63%
Number of students eligible for Chapter 1	6,200
Number of families in migrant program	400
Number of schools in the district	31
Elementary schools	19
Middle schools	6
High schools	3
Alternative schools	3

The **goals** of the program are:

- To provide effective and positive communication between schools, home, and community;
- To promote parent and community involvement so that parents and community members become effective partners in the improvement of McAllen schools; and
- To provide parent education, awareness, and training programs and activities that are beneficial for parents and their children.

BACKGROUND

The first parent involvement effort in this district began in 1958, with a program for migrant worker families. About 10 years later, the Southwest Educational Development Laboratory was instrumental in providing support and technical assistance in the planning and implementation of the parent involvement program. In 1979, it was expanded and redesigned as a regular Chapter 1 program. About 6 years later, under the leadership of a new superintendent, the program was augmented from serving only Chapter 1 students to including all students and families.

The design and objectives of the program have been influenced in part by the parent involvement goals adopted by the state in 1989, and in part by the federal government guidelines for parent involvement in the Chapter 1 regular and migrant programs. The state goals are:

- To encourage parental participation in all facets of the school program;

- To increase interaction between school personnel and parents regarding the development and performance of students;

- To provide educational programs that strengthen parenting skills; and

- To expand adult literacy program, to help parents provide educational assistance to their children.

DESCRIPTION OF THE PROGRAM

McAllen, Texas, is located 7 miles from the Rio Grande River, the boundary between Texas and Mexico. Each year a large number of families arrive from Mexico, with limited English proficiency. A total of 87.12% of the families with children in the McAllen schools are Hispanic; about one-third of the students in the school have limited proficiency in English. All parents in the district are eligible to participate in some component of the Parental Involvement Program.

The Parent Involvement Program is headquartered at the central administration building, and is under the direction of the Administrator for Specially Funded Programs. The staff includes five Parent Coordinators and five paraprofessional community aides, all of whom are bilingual. Each of the Parent Coordinators is assigned to work with 5–7 schools at both the elementary and secondary levels.

The majority of program activities take place in neighborhood schools, using available classroom space and school libraries. Other events are held in community buildings and participants' homes.

Components of the Program

Partners in Excellence (P.I.E.) — Adopt-a-School Program

More than 300 local businesses, churches, and individuals have been recruited as partners with the schools to provide direct financial help and in-kind contributions for school activities. Some of the partners serve as tutors, mentors, and volunteers.

Parent/Student Community Evening Study Centers

Centers are located on four different school campuses; each has its own director and teaching staff who work closely with the building principal and teachers of each participating school. In order to be eligible for participation in the program, students must qualify for Chapter 1, have limited English proficiency, come from migrant families, have been retained in a grade at school, or be recommended by a teacher or principal.

Classes are held twice a week, from 6–8 p.m. on Tuesday and Thursday evenings. Both parents and children must attend. Educational assistance in all subjects is available for children from prekindergarten through the 5th grade. Activities for children include help with homework, reinforcement of material learned in the classroom, computer assisted instruction, and enrichment activities such as art and drama. Activities for parents focus on learning English as a second language, parenting skills, basic literacy, and computer assisted instruction.

Parent Education Programs

These programs are designed sequentially so that parents can move from one level to another and cover a variety of topics related to the range of children's ages and stages. Parents attend once a week for 1½ hours for a series of 6-9 classes, depending on the program. The following parenting programs are used:

- Early Childhood STEP—for infants, birth to 5

- STEP (Systematic Training for Effective Parenting)—in English and Spanish (PECES—Padres Eficaces con Entrenamiento Sistemático)

- STEP TEEN—for parents of adolescents

- THE NEXT STEP—follow-up program for groups which have completed STEP and STEP TEEN

- Reflections for Living—values clarification

- Responsive Parenting—ages and stages of child growth and development; positive discipline, self-esteem.

Follow the Yellow Brick Road

A series of six presentations for 5th grade students and their parents, developed by a McAllen I.S.D. parent involvement coordinator, Mrs. Norma Woolsey. It provides students with information on middle schools and an opportunity to discuss many issues associated with the transition. A map of the school is distributed; report cards and progress report procedures are discussed; male and female Physical Education coaches talk about the sports programs; principals and counselors discuss school policies and answer questions from students. After the series has been completed with the students, parents are invited to participate and receive the same information.

Keys for a Better Life

This six-session course, developed by a McAllen I.S.D. parent involvement coordinator, Mrs. Raquel Garcia, is designed to help parents increase positive family communication and strengthen relationships. The seven "keys" are faith, enthusiasm, self-confidence, imagination, communication, determination, and love.

Dropout Prevention Program

Helps parents to have a better understanding of the causes of dropping out and steps they can take to help their children stay in school.

Other Programs

The parent involvement staff is constantly looking for and utilizing new programs that are available and suitable for this parent population. Other activities include:

- Parents of prekindergarten through 5th grade children are provided with educational activities appropriate to be used with their children at home.

- TAAS (Texas Assessment of Academic Skills) Tips for Parents are provided in order to help prepare their children to take this test, required in Texas for graduation from high school.

- D.A.R.E. – Drug Assistance Resistance Education

Radio Talk Show

"Discusiones Escolares" consists of a series of 10 minute radio programs, broadcast over five radio stations in the city, about topics related to education. The parent involvement coordinators serve as moderators, and answer questions from parents who call in. Tapes of the shows are available to parents.

Parent Involvement in Governance

Parent representation on decision making groups include:

- District Advisory Council for Chapter 1 regular and migrant programs. Federal guidelines require parent participation on the district-level advisory council, with parent representatives providing the parents' perspective and taking the information and decisions from the district level back to the local school.

- Chapter 1 Parent Advisory Council (PAC). A PAC, composed of parents, is required at every school. Two representatives from each school PAC go to the District PAC Meeting, to provide input from local parents and serve as communicator from the district level back to the local school.

- The school district is moving toward school-based management; parents serve on many committees, including Drug Education Committee, Discipline Management Committee, and Sex Education Committee.

- P.T.A. and P.T.S.A.

McAllen Volunteer Program

Parents are encouraged to sign up to work in the library, office, classroom—wherever there is a need.

Parent Involvement in Planning, Operating, and Monitoring

Parents are involved in the programs not only as participants, but also as members of the local Parent Advisory Committees, the district advisory committees, and the school-based management committees. Every year the approach to parent involvement is reviewed and revised according to community needs. The community is growing rapidly, and the programs must be flexible to meet needs of new families.

Some of the focus has been shifting away from parenting skills toward academic and curriculum concerns, since an increase in student achievement and improvement of the schools are primary goals of any parent involvement program. More effort is being made to involve parents in their children's day-to-day learning; workshops are being conducted for parents on how to work with their children at home in support of the school curriculum.

Strengths and Weaknesses

The instructional activities and parenting programs have been very successful, and continue to be well attended. It is estimated that 75%-80% of the parents participate in at least one of the activities in this program. The Evening Study Centers have also been well received; approximately 450 students are being served and 300 parents are participating during the school year.

The community is actively involved in many of the school activities. There are more than 300 business partners participating in the Partners in Excellence project. Experts from community organizations and agencies provide workshops, speak at conferences, and participate in in-service training for teachers and parents. Some of the topics covered include gangs and stages of growth and development.

The challenge is to reach the reluctant parents, those who may need the information and the support most. It is not a question of language, since the staff is bilingual. The community aides are diligent in their approach to these families: home visits, picking them up for meetings, and telephone calls. More could be done if there were additional staff to make continuing personal contacts with hesitant parents. Efforts continue to be made to add much needed additional staff to address the following needs:

- Additional study centers (elementary and secondary levels)

- Baby-sitting services

- Transportation services

- Take-home videos and computers

Outcomes and Evaluation

An annual report of the parent involvement activities is prepared each year, with some efforts to assess the successes and weaknesses, but no formal evaluation has been undertaken. Dr. Larry Koehler, McAllen I.S.D. Director of Research and Evaluation, is beginning work on the design for a formal evaluation of the program. The McAllen program was chosen by the Association of Supervision and Curriculum Development as a model parent involvement program; ASCD has prepared a video on the McAllen program which is being distributed nationally.

Many changes in attitudes and practices have been observed as a result of the parent involvement efforts. Teachers are beginning to feel positive about parent involvement and are more welcoming to them in the classroom. Parents are becoming more active in the education of their children, both at home with homework activities and in volunteering at the school. Parents and teachers both express positive attitudes about the improvement in student achievement, partly as a result of the emphasis on parent/school partnerships.

Budget and Funding

The annual budget for the program is $469,491. Several sources provide funding for the program, including federal Chapter 1 and Chapter 2 monies, state grants for compensatory programs, and local funding from the district.

For Further Information Contact

Norma Woolsey, Parent Involvement Coordinator
McAllen Parent Involvement Program
McAllen Independent School District
2000 No. Twenty-third Street
McAllen, TX 78501
(512) 632–8737/8738/8739

NATCHEZ-ADAMS CHAPTER 1
PARENT CENTER
Natchez-Adams School District
Natchez, MS

Major Components:
>   Teacher referrals to Parent Center
>   Parent Center Program
>   Workshops for Parents and Teachers
>   Take Home Computer Program
>   Educational Materials for Home Use
>   Adult Literacy Class
>   Tutorial Program
>   Learning Labs on Wheels

Special Features:
>   Individualized "prescriptions" for Chapter 1 children
>   Positive Parent-Teacher Conferences
>   Orientation Program for Transition to Middle School

Profile of Program and School District:

Population of County	35,000
Number of students enrolled in public schools	6,200
Number of Schools	8
Primary Schools (K-1)	2
Elementary Schools (Grades 2–6)	2
Middle School (Grades 7–8)	1
High School	1
Parochial Schools	2
% of population African-American	70%
% on free/reduced lunch	75%

The **goals** of the program are:

- To help parents increase their child's academic achievement;
- To teach parenting skills; and
- To assists parent to raise their own educational level.

BACKGROUND

In 1987, a pilot program began in one of the district's more disadvantaged neighborhood schools. The first 2 years were spent making activity packets, contacting parents for conferences, making home visits, and informing teachers about the Parent Center. Because the Center was located in a neighborhood school, it was viewed as serving only that population.

The Parent Center was moved to the Central Office in 1989. This move was precipitated by court-ordered school closings for desegregation purposes, and to comply with new guidelines from the federal government requiring parent involvement in all aspects of the Chapter 1 program. The school district felt that the Parent Center could and should serve the entire school system. By locating the Center in the Central Offices, they were able to build a districtwide service concept, encouraging much broader participation by means of a neighborhood neutral location.

DESCRIPTION OF THE PROGRAM

The Natchez-Adams Parent Center is staffed by the Parent Coordinator and two teacher assistants. It serves about 3,500 children from 1,700 families; children from the six public schools and two parochial schools are eligible for services. The Center is open from 8 a.m.-4 p.m. on weekdays, 12 months of the year.

Parents are referred to the Center through word-of-mouth personal contacts with other parents, from teachers who refer them at the parent-teacher conference at the school, from the Judge at the Youth Court who will refer parents for parenting skills classes, and from the welfare department to encourage parents to improve their own education.

Components of the Program

Teacher Referrals to Parent Center

Most parents' introduction to the Parent Center is a result of parent-teacher conferences. Teachers complete a "prescription" form indicating skills in which a child appears to be deficient or may need additional work.

Parent Center Program

The parent takes the written referral form to the Center, where the staff puts together materials for the parent to take home to work with the child on the skill that has been identified. This is a voluntary program for parents who choose to participate.

If the parent does not stop by the Center, the Chapter 1 staff make a home visit to check on what is happening and to try to encourage the parent to become more active in helping the child do better in school.

Workshops

Workshops are offered for both the teachers and the parents. One of the first workshops of the year is for teachers, since it is critical that they are aware of what the Center can do to support them. As teachers accept the need for parent involvement and Parent Center support, the teacher referral rate climbs. They are also provided with a session on Positive Parent-Teacher Conferences, along with a printed sheet on tips for a more successful conference.

Workshops for parents include "Parent to Parent—A Drug Awareness Program," parenting skills, assertive discipline for parents, the single parent (how to survive), and "How To" sessions on such topics as reading, self-esteem, math, behavior, and motivation.

Take Home Computer Program

The Parent Center has 40 Apple computers available for use by the parents and students. Parents are given a 1 hour orientation on the use of the computer, and can then borrow the computer for a period of 6 weeks. Computer software and workbooks appropriate for the child's educational needs are provided for the parents to use. A computerized "prescription" in reading and math is included, containing directions for correlating the computer material and workbook.

Educational Materials for Home Use

Parents check educational materials out for 2 weeks, much like a library. These materials include activity packets, learning games, videos, computer software, cassette tapes, workbooks, and recreational reading materials.

Adult Literacy Class

A day and night class to help parents who are beginning to read is offered at the Parent Center. Two daytime GED classes are available, one with child care. A preschool teacher works with the children while the parents work on their education. One night GED class is also offered.

Tutorial Program

A tutorial program for students has been established in three housing projects; one teacher and one assistant are available to help students on Tuesdays and Thursdays from 5 p.m.-7 p.m. Funding for this activity is provided by the Beer Institute Fund and the school district. The purpose of the program is to promote literacy and to prevent substance abuse. Parents of students attending the tutoring program must agree to go to a monthly workshop on drug awareness. A special newsletter is distributed for those in the housing project, with news on educational activities and tips for parents on home-work, etc.

Chapter 1 Learning Labs on Wheels

The Chapter 1 program serves both public and parochial schools. During the summer, when the parochial schools are closed, the Parent Center uses the parochial school vans, which are equipped with computers, educational software, and learning areas. The Chapter 1 Learning Labs on Wheels travel between four housing projects, providing opportunities for the children to use the computers.

Parent of the Month

Every month, the center chooses five parents of the month, one from each of the five public elementary schools, in recognition of their work with their children. They are given T-shirts and their pictures are posted on the bulletin boards in every school and in the newsletter.

Orientation Program for Parents

The Chapter 1 program provides an orientation session for parents with children in grades K-7. It is especially important for parents of students in the 6th grade who need a great deal of information—on attendance policies, dress code, adolescent adjustment problems—to be prepared to go into the 7th grade at the middle school.

Parent-Teacher Conferences

Parent-Teacher Conferences for the Chapter 1 children are held either at the school or at the Parent Center. Teachers are given release time to enable them to schedule the Parent/Teacher conferences there. After the parent meets with the teacher, the Parent Center staff can work with the parent, not only on educational issues but on other needs as well, including social services, housing, employment, and health.

Newsletter

This is prepared and distributed to parents once a month. It includes tips for parents on how to work with their children and information on the adult literacy or GED programs. Whenever a parent successfully completes the GED program or their literacy goals, they are featured in the newsletter.

Parent Involvement in Planning, Operating, and Monitoring

Each school has a parent advisory committee made up of teachers, administrators, and parents. It meets twice a year to review and monitor the program and make suggestions for improvements. A parent survey is conducted to identify parent needs and assist in planning future programs.

The Parent Center places emphasis on parents' helping their children with academics through the materials provided by the Parent Center, as well as encouraging parents to become more active in the PTA. In order for the parents to be successful in helping their children with education at home, the teachers also have to be informed about the activities, services, and resources of the Parent Center, so they can refer parents to the Center for assistance.

Strengths and Weaknesses

Suggesting that parents stop by the Parent Center for materials for home learning for their children has been a very successful strategy. Parents are also asked to go to the Parent Center if their child fails a course at school. All parents are expected to work with their children at home, and are given special materials and assistance to do so. Another program which has proved effective is the computer program.

The central location of the Parent Center is one of the keys to its success. Originally, the Center was located in a school building, and parents perceived of the services as available only for that school. The full-time Parent Coordinator has also been an important factor in the Center's success.

Many of the parents eligible to participate in the Parent Center programs have a low level of education themselves, and lack the self-esteem and confidence to become involved. Through working with these parents individually and providing them with positive reinforcement for their efforts, staff at the Parent Center are attempting to overcome the parents' feelings of inferiority.

Adult education has emerged as a key to many aspects of parent involvement. Parents are less likely to be able to help their own children unless they too are being assisted in improving their educational skills—learning to read, developing self-esteem, or preparing for the GED.

Outcomes and Evaluation

The staff at the Parent Center have observed and experienced many changes in attitudes and practices, though no formal evaluation has been completed. The teachers are cooperating with the efforts of the Parent Center by referring parents to them for services, materials, and assistance. The referral process helps to establish a spirit of partnership between parents and teachers. The teachers appear to be more sensitive to the need to tell parents positive things about their children in addition to the problems and weaknesses.

Parent attitudes have drastically changed: they are more aware that they are needed and that they must be involved in order for their children to be successful. Parents used to think of Chapter 1 as a "dumping ground" for children who couldn't succeed in the regular classroom; now they feel positive about it and look on it as a constructive program to make sure their children succeed. About 1,200 parents attended a recent Parent Rally.

The number of parents visiting and using the Parent Center has shown marked increases since it opened. A total of 120 parents were served in the 1987–1988 school year. Five years later, this number increased to approximately 2,000 for the 1991–1992 school year. Indications are that student achievement has improved, though it is difficult to determine if the activities of the Parent Center are directly responsible.

The Natchez-Adams Parent Center has been awarded a Certificate of Merit from the U.S. Department of Education for Outstanding Progress in Compensatory Education Programs.

Budget and Funding

The Parent Center requires about $100,000 per year to operate. This money is made available through the Chapter 1 allocation to the Natchez Adams School District.

For Further Information Contact

Millicent Mayo, Parent Coordinator
Judy H. Sturdivant, Chapter 1 Coordinator
Chapter 1 Parent Center
Natchez-Adams School District
P.O. Box 1188
Natchez, MS 39121
(601) 445–2897/2819

FROGTOWN FAMILY RESOURCE CENTER
St. Paul School District
St. Paul, MN

Major Components:
Home visits
Drop-in Center
Parent Education and Support Groups
Family literacy: adult basic education, early childhood education, and parent education

Special Features:
Prenatal support
Parent empowerment

Profile of Program and Frogtown Family Resource Center Participants:
Number of families participating in
program .... 400 per year
% African-American 24%
% Latino 2%
% Asian (mostly Hmongs) 33%
% White 21%
% Native American
(Lakota, Ojibwe) 20%
% Low-income 95%

The **goals** of the program are to support families in their pursuit of:

- Constructive parent/child relationships;
- School readiness;
- Forums for cultural expression and pride;
- Supportive social networks;
- Further adult education (ESL instruction, preparation for GED); and
- Individual and community action aimed at community betterment.

BACKGROUND

The Frogtown Family Resource Center was established in June 1990. It is sponsored by the St. Paul Public Schools and funded by two state grants from the Early Childhood and Family Education Program. Community leaders, state officials, and St. Paul school teachers and administrators were involved in the design and implementation of the program, as well as community residents and social service agencies.

The concept and design of the Resource Center were based on the research and studies of many educators, including Moncrieff Cochran, from the Family Matters Project at Cornell University, and Paulo Freire, the Brazilian educator, who developed and elaborated liberation pedagogy. The focus is to empower people to deal with oppression and power in order to take responsibility for their lives. In the GED classes the adults not only learn adult basic education skills, but also read about and discuss themes that affect their daily lives: violence, political issues, oppression. The students become better able to take control of their lives. The home visitors from the program try to assist the parents to decide what their goals are and how to work toward them. *Everyone becomes both teacher and learner.*

DESCRIPTION OF THE PROGRAM

The Frogtown Family Resource Center is located in a store front building, in an economically disadvantaged neighborhood in St. Paul. Partners in the project include: St. Paul Public Schools, Community Education, Model Cities Health Center, Ramsey County Public Health, St. Paul-Ramsey Nutrition Program, St. Paul American Indian Center, Women's Employment and Resource Center, and Loaves and Fishes Too.

Thirteen people staff the Frogtown Center, including: one project manager, four paraprofessional home visitors, two parent educators, one adult basic education specialist, one early education teacher, two teaching assistants, one community outreach worker, and one van driver. The staff is chosen to reflect the diverse characteristics of the population served: four African-Americans, three Asian-Americans, two Native Americans, and four European-Americans.

The focus of the Center is on families with children prenatally through kindergarten. About 400 families a year participate in the activities of the Center. Most of the referrals are from public health nurses and other community organizations. Many participants come through "word of mouth" or off the street because of the Center's location.

Components of the Program

Home Visits

The four paraprofessionals on the staff work with 25 families each. The focus ranges from prenatal support and child development information to crisis intervention. The home visits are made weekly to monthly, depending on the situation and circumstances. The home visitor may bring a tote bag of toys and books for families to use during the hour she is in the home.

Drop-In Center

Parents and their children are invited to attend the Drop-In Center, open from 11 a.m. until 3 p.m. Mondays through Thursdays. The Center's van is used to provide transportation to families who wish to go to the Center. The activities at the Center are informal: there is a play group for the children, and casual, social interaction for the parents.

Parent Education and Support Groups

Once a week, a more formal program is offered, with a planned parent-child activity for one-half hour, and a parenting class for 1½ hours. Groups are formed to respond to the needs of the families: a Native American Women's Support Group, a kindergarten readiness group, a Dad's group, and a young parents group. The Native American Group often begins each meeting with speakers on issues specifically of concern to the Native American community, and may include activities such as beadwork, sewing dancing costumes, and participating in ritual ceremonies.

Family Literacy

Three different classes are offered: one for basic skills, one for GED preparation, and one for English as a Second Language. Each class meets twice a week for 3 hours; all include parent education and early childhood education as part of their curriculum.

Prenatal Support

The home visitors provide the pregnant women with information about nutrition, health maintenance, and medical services. They assist the parents in getting ready for the baby's birth. Also available is free pregnancy testing.

Parent Involvement in Planning, Operating, and Monitoring

Parents from each component of the program meet once a month as the Parent Advisory Council to discuss the activities, critique what is happening, and make suggestions for changes. Parents are also active in planning and carrying out other activities at the Center, such as cultural celebrations, writing for the newsletter and organizing a baby-sitting cooperative. The staff of the Center come from diverse backgrounds, ethnically, educationally, and economically, and represent both education and social service experiences. They are constantly redefining parent involvement. They are making the effort to move from the role of helpers to one of facilitators, so that parents will be empowered to speak for themselves. The guiding philosophy of their efforts is "If you've come here to help me, you are wasting your time, but if you've come because your liberation is bound up with mine, then let us work together."

An effort is being made to form clusters of parents who will address problems and issues as a group, rather than letting everything be handled as an individual effort. One of the home visitors learned that people in the neighborhood are afraid to call the police when there is a disturbance in the area; this problem was taken to a group of parents for some brain-storming and a possible solution. When there was a problem with a Head Start teacher, the Head Start director was asked to meet with a group of parents to clarify the issue and try to solve it.

Strengths and Weaknesses

A major strength of the program is its diversity. The parents who are served by the Center activities are from different ethnic and racial backgrounds and the staff is chosen to reflect the diversity in the population in the neighborhood. The program rejects the deficit model of the limitations of low-income minority families and, instead, builds on the strengths which result from the diversity.

Though the staff feels positive about their mission and about the successful integration of the many diverse segments of the population, they feel great frustration because of the dire circumstances facing those who live in this neighborhood. Racism and poverty are complex and powerful. A total of 16 parents have received their GED certificate as a result of the classes at Frogtown Center, but they still have difficulty lo-cating jobs which will pay enough to support their families. The Center staff also are concerned that the current funding is not stable and secure.

The Frogtown Resource Center is formally administered by the public schools, but no formal procedure has been developed to follow up on the performance of children whose parents have received services from Frogtown. Staff at the Resource Center provides much assistance to families whose children are ready to enter public school: they help families understand the school system, aid with translations of school material if needed, encourage parents to visit schools, and facilitate necessary appointments with school officials.

Outcomes and Evaluation

Many positive outcomes have been noticed as a result of the successful operation of the Frogtown Family Resource

Center. Staff attitudes have changed: they have moved from helper to learner, from teacher to facilitator, thus empowering parents to take a larger role. The home visitors have observed a change in the way the parents treat their children as a result of the home visits. They tend to be less harsh with them, more supportive, and feel more comfortable with the idea of being involved with their children's education.

An evaluation component is included as a part of the state grant for Frogtown Center. Data on the first year of the program, through September 30, 1991, was gathered and analyzed by the City of St. Paul's Department of Planning and Economic Development.

Evaluation of Home Visits

Surveys were completed via telephone or in person with parents who had received at least 6 months of home visits. Of the 38 parents contacted, 27 were reached and agreed to be interviewed. Overall, parents seem to be pleased with the services and assistance they receive.

- 71% of parents said the visits were a lot or some help.

- 93% said they would recommend their visitor to others.

- More than 40% said they liked most the fact that their children learned basic skills and information, and that the children had activities that kept them busy.

- Over 50% of the parents reported that the most important thing they got from the visits was parenting skills information.

- About 40% said they saw changes in their families as a result of the visits.

Evaluation of Drop-In Center

Surveys were completed via telephone or in person with people who had visited the Center at least 5 times. Of the

46 people contacted, 25 agreed to be interviewed. Overall, parents seem to find the Drop-In Center helpful and are satisfied with the services they receive.

- 80% said the Center was a lot or some help.

- 96% said they would recommend the Center to others.

- When asked what they liked most about the Center, parents most commonly reported liking the activities for children.

- More than 25% of parents said the most important things they got from the Center are the socializing opportunities for parents and the help teaching kids basic skills and information.

Status of Goals

The Family Center has met or exceeded all of its goals, providing parenting support and skills and basic education to 119 families through home visits and to 287 families through the drop-in Center. In addition, the Center helped 35 adults acquire basic skills through ESL and literacy classes, and provided educational services to 103 families.

The data demonstrates that the Center is successful in serving the ethnic and racial minorities:

	Number of families participating		
	Home visits	Classes	Drop-In Center
African-American	16%	33%	34%
Latino	2%	4%	4%
Asian	50%	38%	26%
Native American	29%	16%	13%
White	3%	9%	21%

This indicates that the African-American and Latino families are well-represented in the classes and drop-in center; the Asians and Native Americans receive a higher frequency of home visits and participate less in the classes and drop-in center.

Budget and Funding

The annual budget for the Frogtown Family Resource Center is $250,000; the funding is from the state of Minnesota, through the Early Childhood and Family Education Program.

For Further Information Contact

Ann Lovrien, Project Manager
Frogtown Family Resource Center
377 University Ave.
St. Paul, MN 55103
(612) 290-8376

HOME-SCHOOL PARTNERSHIP
San Diego City Schools
San Diego, CA 92103

Major Components:
Mobile Parent Resource Center
Parent Involvement Task Force
School Development Project
Parent Involvement Incentive Grants

Special Features:
District Policy on Parent Involvement
Parent Involvement Conference
Diverse, multicultural, multilanguage population

Profile of Program and School District:
Eighth largest district in the U.S.

Total Enrollment	126,000
Total Number of schools	145
Elementary schools	109
Middle schools	21
High schools	15

Racial/ethnic composition of student body

% White	35%
% Latino	29%
% Asian-American and Indo-Chinese	17%
% African-American	16%
% Other	3%

60 languages are spoken by families in the district
Families are from a wide range of socioeconomic
levels

The primary **goals** for the parent involvement program in the San Diego City School District are:

- To support and encourage collaborative partnerships between schools and parents; and
- To ensure school success and academic achievement of all students.

BACKGROUND

The event which marked the beginning of this impressive school district parent involvement effort was the August 1988 approval by the board of education of a formal Parent Involvement Policy. The policy provides direction and leadership to the district and makes it clear that parent involvement is to be a priority in the years to come. The Parent Involvement Policy reads as follows:

> The Board of Education recognizes the necessity and value of parent involvement to support student success and academic achievement. In order to assure collaborative partnerships between parents and schools, the board, working through the administration is committed to:
>
> a. involving parents as partners in school governance including shared decision making.
>
> b. establishing effective two-way communication with all parents, respecting the diversity and differing needs of families.
>
> c. developing strategies and programmatic structures at schools to enable parents to participate actively in their children's education.
>
> d. providing support and coordination for school staff and parents to implement and sustain appropriate parent involvement from kindergarten through grade twelve.
>
> e. utilizing schools to connect students and families with community resources that provide educational enrichment and support.

The board was influenced by the work of Janet Chrispeels, with the San Diego County Department of Education, and by the active dropout prevention efforts in the City, which concluded that greater parent involvement might be a key element to effective program designs. The research findings of Anne Henderson at the National Committee for Citizens in

Education and Joyce Epstein at Johns Hopkins University also served as an important influence.

The district formed a Parent Involvement Task Force composed of parents, community leaders, and district staff. The responsibility for implementing parent involvement programs throughout the district was assigned to the Parent Involvement and Support Unit within the School Services Division. The Parent Involvement and Support Unit has a coordinator, 2½ resource teachers, and persons to translate material into many different languages. They are responsible for providing coordination for district level efforts in parent involvement and for providing technical assistance to schools as they develop their parent involvement programs.

DESCRIPTION OF THE PROGRAM

All parent involvement programs at the school and district level are to follow a general framework that includes a vision statement and three supportive components:

(1) Building staff capacity to work effectively with parents;

(2) Planning and implementing comprehensive parent involvement programs at schools; and

(3) Follow-up and support to sustain ongoing parent involvement.

In response to the ethnic and language diversity of the population, the Home-School Partnership staff maintains regular and continuing relationships with many community groups, including the Parent Institute for Quality Education, which serves Latino families; the Center for Parent Involvement in Education, primarily an African-American organization; and the Union of Pan Asian Communities, whose members are Asian and Pacific Islanders. The staff knows that outreach strategies must be modified for the diverse ethnic groups.

Components of the Program

Mobile Parent Resource Center

One of the first items for which funding was sought was a Parent Center. The proposal was rejected; instead the district provided a bus. The staff decided that the bus could serve as the parent center, and they became very creative in their efforts to convert it. They sent the bus to Donovan State Prison, where it was renovated and redesigned. The bus is equipped with books on parenting, books for children, educational games and other materials that parents can check out for home use.

This Mobile Parent Resource Center is available to go to schools, neighborhoods, and other locations where they are invited. The bus is staffed with a part-time resource teacher and an aide. The Mobile Parent Resource Center began operation in July 1992, visits 3–4 schools each week, and intends to meet with each school three times during the school year.

A series of workshops for parents is offered through the Mobile Center, featuring topics which parents have selected. Topics have included:

- How to have a successful parent-teacher conference

- Homework without tears

- How to communicate with your child

- Building self-esteem in your child

- Organizational and study skills

- How to help your child be successful in school

- Improving your child's reading skills

The parent involvement staff meets with the school staff prior to the arrival of the Mobile Parent Resource Center. They provide the school with fliers about the activities to take place in the bus as part of a recruitment kit, in order to assist with outreach.

Parent Involvement Task Force

A major component of the Home-School Partnership is the Task Force, formed by the district to advise the school board about what parents need, to monitor and evaluate district efforts, and to propose new directions for the district to consider. The Task Force is made up of 45 members: approximately 30 are parents and community leaders and 15 are district and school staff members. They are selected on the basis of their activism and commitment toward parent involvement, and to ensure a balance of diverse ethnic and racial representation.

The Task Force meets eight times a year and serves as an advisory group to the district, provides ongoing assistance and guidance for districtwide activities, and performs a monitoring and oversight role related to parent involvement programs in the district schools. The Task Force also has the responsibility for screening proposals and making recommendations to the superintendent and school board concerning which schools will receive Parent Involvement Incentive Grants.

The Task Force has been active since 1988, but, according to one community member, its actions tend to be reactive rather than proactive. Its strength is that it works with all of the power groups in the district—it is a slow process to come to consensus when dealing with so many disparate viewpoints. The members of the Task Force often feel they are not fully recognized by the district or consulted over all issues related to parent involvement.

Participation in School Development Project

Four schools in the San Diego School District are implementing the Comer Process as part of the School Development Project. The success of this effort is heavily dependent on staff and parent relationships. Indications are that the new and improved structure of the schools in the School Development Program is resulting in significant increases in student test scores.

Parent Involvement Incentive Grant Awards

Starting with the 1990–1991 school year, the district has budgeted $100,000 to provide funding to schools with innovative parent involvement programs. Grants of up to $10,000 have been given to 18–20 schools each year. The purpose of the grants is to encourage schools to develop promising practices and innovative programs that move beyond traditional parent involvement activities and incorporate strategies to promote collaborative partnerships with parents.

In their proposals, schools must select one or more priority areas under the three priority components: capacity building, partnership development, and follow-up and support. The Parent Involvement Task Force reviews the proposals and makes recommendations concerning who will receive the awards.

Activities funded by the grants include the following:

- The purchase of a voice mail communication system;

- Publication of a handbook for parents of incoming 9th graders, to be prepared by parents;

- Establishment of a bilingual homework hotline;

- Parenting workshops; leadership training for parents;

- Computer lending program;

- Hiring a bilingual parent advocate;

- Establishing an Office of Parent Advocacy;

- Family literacy program;

- Translation of materials into other languages;

- Opening a parent room with multicultural, multilingual parenting materials; and

- Establishing a community resource center.

Staff Development

There are four major programs to provide training to staff so that they will be effective partners with parents:

(1) Parents Growing Together—includes information on parenting, child development ages and stages, discipline at home and in the school, and parent/school interaction;

(2) Family Reading—teaching staff to work with parents to improve children's reading skills;

(3) Family Kindergarten—training kindergarten teachers to establish a strong relationship with parents from the very beginning;

(4) Training for planning parent involvement programs.

Staff development is not mandated or required by the district; each school decides through its governance team what they wish to do for staff training and how to utilize the in-service days. Since parent involvement is a major goal of the district schools, many schools schedule staff development on this topic.

Leadership Training for Parents

The Parent Involvement Task Force works with staff to design a training program for parents who are serving on governance teams, required at each school. The training includes such topics as information and data gathering, role playing, and strategies for bringing about change.

Parent Involvement Conference

The Home-School Partnership Program has sponsored a successful annual parent involvement conference every year since 1988, "Home/School/Community Working Together for Student Success." This is a 1-day conference; of the 1,000 persons attending, 60%-70% are parents. The low registration fee of $15 per person includes child care, breakfast, and lunch.

There are about 80 workshops, many in both English and Spanish, some in other languages common in the San Diego area. This is an opportunity for parents to get together, celebrate what they are doing in their own schools, and be inspired by speakers and workshops to go back to their communities and continue their good work.

Parent Involvement in Planning, Operating, and Monitoring

The Parent Involvement Task Force, described earlier, is the key structure on which the Home-School Partnership Program depends. The Task Force is the oversight group for the establishment of the parent involvement policy by the school board. It is considered to the factor responsible for the success of the whole project. In addition to the tasks and activities listed, the Task Force is constantly reviewing and redefining parent involvement. The concept of parent involvement is often very limited; there is a need to encourage parents and staff to rethink what parent involvement can be, to look at it in a much broader way. They take the five roles of parents developed by Janet Chrispeels very seriously, but are constantly refining the definitions and components of those types. The complementary or mutual roles played by parents and staff are always under scrutiny, with efforts to strengthen and enhance them in order to build a sounder and more potent collaboration.

Strengths and Weaknesses

All of the programs and activities described above are considered successful. The major weakness identified is "not being able to measure the impact as much as we would like." Parent involvement is difficult to evaluate, and no data is as yet available in this district to substantiate the conviction that students are doing better in school.

Those leading the program have observed noticeable prejudice on the part of educators against certain groups of parents. This is one of the barriers to successful implementation of the program. Many teachers and administrators are resistant to the emphasis placed on parent involvement; they do not share the enthusiasm of the district leaders that this is an appropriate strategy to which they must devote time and energy. There has been an effort to alter and shift staff attitudes through extensive training and to help people rethink what parent involvement is. A special newsletter, *The Vital Connection*, published quarterly by the Parent Involvement & Support Unit, is directed toward staff. It includes brief reports about research information on the value and benefit of parent involvement, lists of resources, and announcements of upcoming events.

Outcomes and Evaluation

There has not yet been an outside evaluation conducted to assess the effectiveness of the various components of the Home-School Partnership Program. The staff is working with the Evaluation Department within the school district to develop a method to evaluate the impact of the Parent Mobile Resource Center and the Parent Involvement Incentive Grants. Participants are asked to assess the Parent Involvement Conference each year and the evaluations are extremely favorable.

Those involved in the administration of the program see some improvement in teacher attitudes and changed teacher practices in the case of those receiving grants from the district. Parent attitudes and practices have shown some change, measurable at the local school level. Major progress has been observed in reformed school and district policies.

The attendance at the Parent Involvement Conference has risen during the 5 years it has been scheduled. The sponsors no longer have to beg people to come; many in the community attend every year and keep coming back. More and more teachers and other staff members attend. Parents and others in the community have come to expect it, and eagerly await it.

Budget and Funding

It is estimated that the Mobile Parent Resource Center costs about $30,000 a year. The grant program supporting parent involvement innovations in individual schools has been budgeted for $100,000. No estimates are available about other costs. Funding for the Home-School Partnership Program is from district general funds, Chapter 1 monies, and funds allocated for integration purposes.

For Further Information Contact

> Jeana Preston
> Home-School Partnership
> San Diego City Schools
> Rm. 2121, 4100 Normal St.
> San Diego, CA 92103
> (619) 293-8560

Chapter 7

Common Characteristics

The programs selected for this publication represent considerable diversity. This result was planned and purposeful, since we attempted to learn about programs at all levels of schooling, in many geographic locations, which serve children from families with diverse cultural, language, economic, and social backgrounds. We expect that the reader will find value in seeing and understanding the diversity of program elements and the populations served.

These programs do not represent a randomly selected sample; this volume cannot be characterized as controlled research. Therefore, it would be inappropriate to attempt to identify a list of characteristics from these programs which might be considered as necessary in order to design an effective parent-family involvement program. However, as we became increasingly familiar with the elements of each program we began to see factors common to many of the programs. In this chapter we present our conclusions about common program elements that range from how the programs began to the many roles parents can play with regard to their children's education.

HOW THE PROGRAMS CAME INTO BEING

Charismatic Leader

We were impressed with the fact that, with few exceptions, program beginnings were associated with a "spark plug," an energetic, committed individual who appears to possess extraordinary convictions that "this" must be done, and done in the best possible way. These charismatic leaders energize others and form staffs who want to be trained, work hard, and serve families. In some ways this seems trite, an "of course" item, but, in fact, there is much involved, including a substantial potential danger to the health and continuance of these programs. There are generalizable lessons involved.

Programs are unlikely to have successful beginnings (and later success as well) if the leadership is cautious, has low energy, and is ambivalent about potential outcomes. A substantial drive, vision, and optimism are required. On the other hand, we discovered repeatedly that many programs recommended to us no longer existed or were of such questionable quality that they did not meet our requirements for inclusion in the book. More often than not, we discovered that the founding leader was gone, burned out, transferred, promoted, or removed for a variety of other reasons, including financial.

The reason for the charismatic leader's no longer being involved is not of primary importance. What is important is that once the leader is gone the programs faltered, ran less successfully, or disappeared. There is an obvious lesson. Always, from the beginning, build and train second level staff strength, staff who will be in a position to move into program leadership whenever the day arrives. Blindness or inattention to this point will have the highest cost for families and children when program quality suffers or in the worst of circumstances the program is terminated.

External Model

Federal programs, such as Head Start and Even Start, impose certain requirements on the schools or organizations who receive the grant money. Program models, such as HIPPY, MegaSkills, QEP (Quality Education Project), and TIPS (Teachers Involve Parents in Schoolwork), provide schools with specific guidelines for the design and implementation of the parent involvement program.

In many cases, the ingredients of the successful program have been developed by the principal, teachers, and parents in the local school. We are impressed with the wealth of creative and effective components in these local programs. We conclude that both external models and internal program design can result in successful parent involvement projects.

Sources of Funding

Availability of funding is obviously of importance to any program's beginning. However, our experience in carefully analyzing over 50 programs made it clear that the source of the funding has no overriding influence on start-up success, pace, or quality. While federal and state funds may have an advantage in terms of outreach and encouragement to small groups, it is also true that local policies, private nonprofit organizations, parent-teacher groups, and community initiatives can and do have success in motivating and encouraging similar efforts. The more important "common" point is that funds to begin successful programs come from a full range of possibilities and are not limited to federal and state tax resources.

A second striking conclusion is that many of the most active programs have been initiated and continue to thrive with no outside grant money and a minimal operating budget. The resources most often identified as responsible for the success of these programs include time and energy from administrators, teachers, and parents and support from community agencies and local businesses.

REJECTION OF A DEFICIT MODEL OUTLOOK

For many years, the professional approach to the learning problems of low-income and minority children was that the child and the family had problems that had to be "fixed." This led to a widespread and intense commitment to remediation programs, materials, and teacher training, all of which revolved around the deficits and/or problems that were supposed to exist in the child. Hundreds of millions of dollars have been expended in pursuit of this form of "help" for children. The results have been mixed at best. True, some improvements have been tied to this approach, but there has always been a dissatisfaction and doubt among many that the outcome matched the effort.

In recent years, the work of Henry Levin, creator of the Accelerated Schools model, Stanley Pogrow, who developed the HOTS (Higher Order Thinking Skills) program, and others raised different questions and possibilities, and created alternative approaches and materials. It is possible, they contend, that remediation freezes the child, the teacher, and the parents into a mind set that insidiously works against improvement or progress. An integral part of the new approach holds that reaching for potential by challenging and accelerating expectations will have better results. Slowly, but in important ways, this new approach to children is spreading into school systems and schools. It is too early to call it a large scale movement, but the importance of its differences from the deficit model are gaining attention and breaking the stranglehold of remediation in more and more places.

Prior to the close examination of a large number of successful programs, we did not know if the attitude about parents and families would also be prisoner to old stereotypes or whether we would find examples of stepping away from the constraints of the deficit model toward approaches that build on strength and potential. One of the more exciting conclusions about the programs in this book is the fact that program leadership and staff firmly reject deficit models and have proceeded to design and implement programs that are directed to developing the potential in families. This approach may be a factor in the kinds and levels of success achieved.

In all of the programs described in this book, we found positive attitudes on the part of school personnel toward parents and an appreciation of *both* the difficulties and problems many families experience in daily life *and* the strength of their commitment and contribution to the education of their children.

DEVELOPING PARENTS' EDUCATIONAL, EMPLOYMENT, LANGUAGE, AND SOCIAL SKILLS

Most traditional parent-family involvement programs focus on the ways to involve parents that are directly connected to what *the student* needs to succeed in school and what *the school* needs of the parents to achieve the same goal. That seems to be logical and make sense. Unfortunately, however, it is only logical and sensible for another era—one that is past.

It is common to the successful programs we selected that they take a much broader view of the way to become involved with families. The broader view embraces the reality that children's success in school is tied to factors that in the past were not addressed by schools and remain unaddressed by the majority of schools today. The child's view of himself/herself is greatly influenced by the things that are going well or poorly in his home. If his parents are unemployed, underemployed, poorly educated, and socially isolated, the self-esteem, motivation, and optimism of the student about school and the future are affected. Successful parent-family programs address these issues in a variety of ways that are new and different, such as providing parents with the opportunity to obtain their GED, to learn computer skills, and to gain work experience through volunteering at the school.

We have included in this book descriptions of programs in schools representing a wide variety of demographics: urban and rural, low-income and middle class, and those with enrollment from Latino families, families of migrant workers, Asian-American families, and Native American families. Effective programs recognize that many parents have limited English proficiency and include literacy and language classes to encourage parents to learn English. They also provide staff to communicate with parents in their primary language and invite parents from other cultures to share their experiences in the school curriculum.

EMPHASIS ON EARLY CHILDHOOD

The importance of beginning to work with children and families at the earliest possible age is common to the program elements of all of the preschool programs and some of the elementary school programs selected. Dedication to the belief that quality efforts at an early age will yield the largest gains in the future, stands out in all of the programs. There are, in addition, strong similarities in how program staff reach out to parents in unconventional ways through extensive schedules of home visits, structured parent-child activities in settings outside the home, and monitored home activities that encourage interactions between the young child and parents and/or other important adults in the home.

PARENTING EDUCATION

The overwhelming majority of parents want to be "good" parents, supporting their children's physical and mental development and hoping for a future better than their own. However, the uncertainties parents have about their efforts to be good parents is a mine field that can easily involve unintended slights or outright disrespect if not carefully considered by those in a position to organize programs that could address parental concerns. The best situation is to pick up on signals or indicators that the parents themselves give or clearly express. Next best is a staff with excellent fingertips for laying out a wide array of options for parents who are privately and quietly concerned about how "good" a parent they might be and how they might take advantage of training and materials that would make them stronger, more nurturing and supportive parents.

The programs we selected have successfully walked the line of respecting the initial insecurities of parents about their parenting skills, but proceeded to diplomatically offer specific routes to improvement and greater confidence. All programs included here exhibit the critical necessity not to patronize or unintentionally demean, and to take program actions that lead to involving parents in ways that result in parenting practices that are more confident, more contributing, and more active than had been true before their participation in the program.

PARENTS IN THE SCHOOLS

How much parents should be in the schools is a long-standing, unresolved question in public education. Many educators, if they were to be utterly candid, might say that parents as volunteers in classes, running fund-raising events, and participating in American Education Week, would be a full and sufficient list. Some parents would assert that the traditional line-up should be extended to full membership and voting equity on policy setting committees and/or school-based management councils.

What we have found in the programs we selected is that the "parent in the schools" process is beginning to open up. Volunteering in schools is certainly evident in these schools, but even that is changing to include jobs in the school that provide training and experience for outside employment or provide first experiences in activities that previously would have been off limits to parents, such as proposal writing to secure needed funds for school or parent programs. The opening up and extension of new roles is also evident in the form of parents trained to make home visits on behalf of the school; parents teaching and working with other parents in workshop settings on curriculum and school success, as well as parents trained to be "teacher for the day" substitutes when called upon by the principal.

EXPANDING ROLES FOR STUDENTS

Our own definition of parent-family involvement expanded as we gathered more and more examples of innovative programs. We did not expect to find instances of students being involved in systematic ways, although the word family incorporates the possibility of student participation. While it may stretch the ordinary meaning of "common" to include this development in a common characteristics summation, we feel that the existence of fledgling efforts to involve students deserves attention.

We believe it is noteworthy that we found secondary schools (and a few elementary schools) where students:

- Are regularly involved in parent-teacher conferences;

- Sign contracts concerning goals and expectations;

- Serve on school advisory committees;
- Are encouraged to become knowledgeable and involved in local and national political activities; and
- Serve on the policy and appeals board of a large alternative high school.

The quality and interest in secondary school education could be helped in important ways if we see a continuing expansion of student roles.

PARENTS INVOLVED IN GOVERNANCE

While it is not yet a major educational reform measure, there is increasing interest in programs that bring parents into the governance area. They vary in type and level of involvement in decision making, but the important point to be made is that all the parent and family involvement programs included in this book are increasingly involving parents in school governance and assessment issues that were previously the exclusive domain of boards of education and school administrators.

Only a few years ago it was considered radical to involve parents in policy and governance issues of school operations, but now we find movement toward this form of parent-family involvement to be common. Parents are gaining a sense of ownership and a sense of reasonable control over the quality of education their children are receiving in school by a greater participation in committees and councils making decisions about education.

CONCLUSION

The common characteristics identified in the innovative projects selected for this book attest to the new forms of parent-family involvement needed in the future. If schools are to have important help from parents and families in improving the quality of schools and assisting students to have greater opportunities to succeed in school, then the need to restructure parent-family involvement is as serious as the pressing need to restructure schools themselves.

School personnel should take leadership in this effort because they are increasingly beleaguered in a society where nationwide only 25% of the households have children in public schools. There is undeniable logic to the proposition that those adults most important to children should have respected roles in the school lives of their children. The innovative programs in this book recognize the changing nature of the schools and society that surrounds them. They contain common viewpoints, connections, and program elements to enlist and develop the strengths of the diversities they confront. Their examples should serve to encourage and give direction to others.

Chapter 8

Program-Based Evaluation

In the 1993 book *Families and Schools in a Pluralistic Society*, Nancy Feyl Chavkin, editor, states in her "Introduction:"

> The reader will observe one noticeable omission . . . —the lack of strong evaluation data. Parent-involvement programs have not yet been funded well enough or long enough for practitioners to undertake the extensive evaluation that these successful programs deserve. . . .

Before we started interviewing educators, parents, and community leaders about parent involvement programs, we had decided to include in this book only those programs which have been in existence long enough to be considered established and ongoing, and have a solid evaluation design for assessing program effectiveness and achievement of stated goals. Most of the included programs have stated goals and objectives, carefully designed methods and activities for reaching those goals, but, as yet, have not collected or analyzed data to determine whether the desired outcomes are being achieved. The "Outcomes and Evaluation" section in each program description includes much anecdotal material and some data on such factors as parent attendance at activities or hours of volunteer work in the school. Many of the local programs also distribute and collect evaluation forms from participants at various activities and programs; these results are used to revise and improve the operation of the component.

Educators with a strong research background might argue that it is unrealistic to expect a school or a community organization to conduct a rigorous evaluation of their program. In order to do so they need a trained researcher and a control or comparison group, longitudinal data, and carefully articulated research hypotheses relating input variables with outcomes. Such evaluation plans require much effort, resources, and a long period of time to complete. In some cases, particularly with those programs sponsored by national organizations, a national or regional evaluation may be underway, to collect and analyze data from sites where the program is being implemented. Often their findings reach the education journals and national conferences, but may not be reconnected to the local program where the findings might be used to revise and improve the program.

Most of the programs we examined do not have staff with research backgrounds to conduct this type of study. However, we continue to firmly believe that the design and implementation of local programs should include an evaluation piece, with an effort to establish baseline data and gather subsequent information to determine whether the components and activities of the program have been successful and effective in achieving the desired outcomes.

During the process of collecting information for this book, we reviewed several documents which discuss evaluation processes and techniques that are less academic and theoretical and more practical and potentially helpful to those who are directly involved in parent involvement projects. We summarize these with the expectation that parents, community leaders, and educators may be able to learn from them some pragmatic approaches to gathering information about their parent involvement programs in order to identify strengths and weaknesses, and to utilize feedback to change and improve program processes and components.

We recognize that there are flaws in some of the evaluation methodologies, but we consider them honest efforts to examine and assess the effectiveness of the programs in achieving their goals of increased parent-family involvement and improved student achievement and behavior. Those in the process of designing programs may be able to include some of these strategies and techniques in their planning.

Included in this chapter are descriptions of five evaluation efforts associated with parent involvement programs. The first two discussed are examples of evaluation processes and approaches: the first is Action Research, developed by the Institute for Responsive Education, Boston, Massachusetts, for use by the League of Schools Reaching Out; the second was developed by Dr. Beverly McConnell for the Parent Leadership Training Program sponsored by the Citizens Education Center, Seattle, Washington. Evaluations of two parent involvement models, MegaSkills and QEP (Quality Education Project), are then presented as examples of research efforts to assess the effectiveness of those two programs. Finally, we describe a new publication, *Taking Stock: The Inventory of Family, Community and School Support for Student Achievement*, which provides a methodology for surveying and strengthening school support of parent, family, and community involvement.

ACTION RESEARCH

The first example of evaluation activities initiated at the grassroots level has been developed by the League of Schools Reaching Out for use by the 15 schools participating in their multisite action research case study. An *Action Research Handbook* has been published to assist those schools gain more knowledge about what works best to improve student learning by reaching out to families and communities. In his "Introduction" to this handbook, Don Davies writes:

> Parent/teacher action research is parents and teachers studying their own problems and proposing actions

> to improve their own schools. . . . The purpose is to
> gain knowledge—not for the sake of knowledge but
> to act to improve schools and children's learning. . . .
> to move away from dispassionate, clinical research
> that investigates subjects in controlled settings and
> has researchers operate at arms length from the
> people and things being studied.

In order to prepare for this type of evaluation, it is suggested that the school appoint an Action Research Team or Committee composed of parents, teachers, administrators, students, and any other school staff involved in the parent involvement effort. The *Handbook* includes a detailed outline of the steps to take to study, and evaluate, a parent involvement project. These include:

- Choosing the project to study; specifying goals and objectives; identifying outcomes and indicators of change;

- How to study the project; gathering baseline data, documenting events, and progress of the project;

- Data collection strategies, including questionnaires, interviews, journals, focus groups, project logs, portfolios;

- Organizing and interpreting data; and

- Writing and sharing your findings.

The school described in this book, which is currently utilizing the *Action Research Handbook* for evaluating their program, is Atenville Elementary School, Harts, West Virginia. In addition to the more conventional data being collected on parent attendance at school events, number of parent volunteer hours in the school, and number of contacts made between home and school, they are using the Portfolio concept to collect and analyze data. *Student portfolios* are used in many school systems as a supplement to more conventional report cards. Atenville has extended the portfolio idea to families and the school: the *family portfolio* contains a record of the home visits, telephone calls to the parents, the attendance of the parents at school events, and copies of any correspondence between home and school. The *school portfolio* is a combination scrapbook and journal of the school's activities and accomplishments. It includes data on student achievement, the number of suspensions and other disciplinary actions, and the proportion of students promoted to the next grade.

EVALUATION OF THE PARENT LEADERSHIP TRAINING PROGRAM

Dr. Beverly B. McConnell is a consultant to the Citizens Education Center (CEC), Seattle, Washington, and is working on the evaluation of the Parent Leadership Training Program sponsored by CEC. A total of 12 school sites have participated in this program; they have sent teams to CEC for leadership training, and the teams have planned and implemented parent involvement programs at their schools. The evaluation is designed to gather information from the sites on how successful program strategies are in achieving program outcomes. The outcomes in the case of these programs might be defined as intermediate outcomes, in the sense that they relate primarily to participation of parents in the program, rather than to changes in student behavior or performance which might occur as a result of greater parent involvement.

Dr. McConnell begins by posing a number of evaluation questions, each related to an important variable in the design of the program:

- **Coverage.** "Are we reaching a high proportion of families in the school?"

- **Sustained Interest.** "Are we retaining the interest of parents so they are willing to come back?"

- **Economic Index.** "Are we reaching the low income families in proportion to their numbers in the school population?"

- **Language Index.** "Are we reaching the language minority families among our school families in proportion to their numbers of the school population?"

- **Ethnicity Index.** "Are we reaching minority parents in proportion to their numbers in the school population?"

- **Male Index.** "Are we reaching a reasonable proportion of fathers, as well as mothers (who have traditionally been more likely to participate in school events)?"

- **School Staff Index.** "Are we involving a high proportion of school staff, or are only a few participating?"

- **Community Index.** "What proportion of the people planning and carrying out these events are community members (rather than school staff, or parents)?"

- **Parent Provider Index.** "What proportion of the people planning and carrying out these school events are parents of the children enrolled in the school?"

- **School Change Index.** "What distinguishes sites which report implementing many school changes to make their schools more user friendly by families, or in response to parent/community voiced concerns, as opposed to those who made few or no school changes?"

Each of these questions forms the basis for the development of an index which can be used to measure effectiveness with regard to a particular variable. The indexes measure the level of participation in the program, but do not address the affects of parent involvement on student achievement or school behavior. The findings might assist the school in identifying factors to make the programs more attractive and appealing to parents, but do not address the larger questions of program effectiveness in achieving the overall goals and objectives.

Because she is working with 12 schools implementing similar programs, Dr. McConnell can use the numerical indexes to compare the performance of the schools participating in the program. However, it may be feasible for a school or an organization to use the index as a way of evaluating a single program; if data is gathered consistently over a period of several years, the indexes can be used to determine if the intended outcomes of the program are improving over a period of several years. The index concept can also be used to measure whether the program is reaching the parent population intended.

For instance, if 50% of the students at the school are Latino, and only 30% of the parents attending a particular event are from Hispanic families, one could conclude that this particular component of the program was not successful in achieving its goals of reaching all families. Likewise, if the proportion of students in the school from low-income families is 70%, and 90% of those attending the parent meetings are parents from these families, the program has succeeded in attracting this segment of the parent population.

In the McConnell evaluation plan, one member of the team responsible for the parent involvement activities is asked to keep data recording which parents attend and how often they come, which staff participate, and what participation there is from the community. In addition to the attendance records, staff also prepare descriptive notes on how the programs were run, how parents and others were recruited, and what happened at the meetings. These descriptions can be helpful to the team in identifying program practices related to effective outcomes based on actual practice rather than hypothetical goals.

The FOCUS program at Wapato Primary School in Wapato, Washington, described in this book, is one of the 12 schools which participate in the CEC evaluation effort. Included in the section on "Outcomes and Evaluation" is a discussion of how this school is utilizing Dr. McConnell's 10 indexes to assess the effectiveness of the program.

EVALUATION RESULTS OF QUALITY EDUCATION PROJECT

The Quality Education Project provides consulting services to schools and school districts for the purpose of increasing parent involvement in and support of their children's education. An evaluation of the program in schools for the 1990–1991 school year has been prepared; it measures parent involvement during a baseline year and compares it to parent participation in 1990–1991 following the introduction of the Quality Education Program into the schools.

Seven components are included in the first part of the evaluation study: back to school night, open house, parent pledge, parent/teacher conference, weekly folder, principal newsletter, and teacher newsletter. Parent participation increased in all of these categories following the establishment of QEP in the schools; the largest gain was for the weekly folder component, with an 82% increase, and the smallest was 30% percent for turnout for parent/teacher conferences. The Total Average Gain was calculated at 54.3%. The large increase in the participation in the Weekly Folder and the Parent Pledge components is not surprising, since these are activities that probably were not in the schools prior to the QEP project.

The researchers also evaluated changes in student achievement using a number of standardized tests — Stanford, SRA, CTBS, CAT, and ITBS. They converted the test scores in NCE (National Curve Equivalent) scores so that the data would be consistent. They compared the scores for the 1990–1991 school year with a baseline statistic, and concluded that students in QEP schools in California showed a significant average gain of +1.6 points. The QEP research report expresses the results this way:

> Students in QEP schools demonstrated a +1.6 average NCE score gain. This gain is considered significant using the treatment-no treatment system of analyzing scores. Students in the no treatment group would be expected to show no gain or loss relative to the national norm. The fact that QEP students demonstrated a gain is significant because QEP serves the lower socioeconomic group. This group generally demonstrates a decline in test scores yearly.

The same procedure was used in the Mississippi schools where QEP is implemented. Students in grades 3 and 5 were compared using baseline scores on the BSAP (Mississippi Basic

Skills Assessment Program). The total average gain in the seven districts was +4.8 points. The analysis also compared the scores of the students at QEP schools with those in control schools where a +0.3 point gain in BSAP scores was attained. For this same group, the statewide gain was +2.2 points. The researchers concluded that "QEP test score gains are better than the statewide scores and significantly better than matched control schools."

The third segment of the QEP evaluation consists of a survey of parents, staff, and students in the second and 5th grades of the Mississippi schools utilizing the QEP approach. Parents were asked questions concerning the child's behavior and attitudes about education and school. They were asked whether the child's grades have improved and whether the QEP program is helping the child. Again, the researchers received very positive responses from parents, with 85% reporting that their child's grades have improved and 88% responding that the QEP program is helping the child.

EVALUATION OF MEGASKILLS PROGRAM

The Office of Research and Evaluation of the Austin Independent School District evaluated several aspects of the MegaSkills program in the Austin schools. They gathered data on achievement, behavior, and attendance for the 1,196 elementary school students whose families had participated in the MegaSkills workshops. They made two different comparisons using this data. One comparison was between those students whose parents were in MegaSkills (experimental group) and the remainder of students in the same schools (control group) whose parents had not attended the MegaSkills workshops. The second part of the evaluation compared the control group on the same variables before and after their parents attended the MegaSkills program. The evaluation also included a survey of principals and one of parents to determine their perceptions and attitudes.

The researchers found that, in 1992, the students in the "experimental group" improved over their own 1990–1991 performance, and also outperformed their fellow elementary students on standardized tests, discipline, and attendance. The researchers compared the students whose parents had voluntarily attended the MegaSkills program with those in the same schools who had not been present. They used scores on the Iowa Test of Basic Skills (ITBS), the Norm-Referenced Assessment Program for Texas (NAPT), and the Texas Assessment of Academic Skills (TAAS). The researchers also examined discipline incidents, attendance rates, and promotion rates, and concluded that, in all of the areas studied, the MegaSkills students improved significantly.

A survey to ascertain the perceptions of principals and parents of the MegaSkills program revealed that 74% of the principals responding reported fewer behavioral problems and better attitudes from the MegaSkills students, and 69% reported improved academic work. Eighty-six percent of the principals reported that the training increased parents' involvement in their children's education, and 67% noticed improved communication between parents and teachers.

Parent perceptions of the program were also found to be positive, with 80% reporting that the workshops helped increase their understanding of their role in their children's education, and 49% reporting that they had increased their involvement at their children's school since attending the MegaSkills workshops.

"TAKING STOCK"

The publication, *Taking Stock: The Inventory of Family, Community and School Support for Student Achievement*, available from the National Committee for Citizens in Education, provides a systematic way to look at the school's relationship with families, a tool for self-evaluation to identify strengths and weaknesses, and a practical approach to increase parent involvement leading to improved achievement. It includes a questionnaire to be used to survey school personnel and family members about the effectiveness of the parent involvement activities of the school, and suggestions about preparing an Action Plan to improve family-school relationships.

The five areas included in the inventory are:

- **Reaching Out to Families:** What is the school doing to create effective two-way communications with families? How is the school extending itself to the community and inviting parents and citizens to share in the life of the school?

- **Welcoming Families to the School Building:** How does the school make family members feel comfortable when they come to school? What is being done to show parents that they really belong there?

- **Developing a Strong Relationship between Families and the School:** What is the school doing to build trust and collaboration among parents, teachers, other staff, and administrators? In which ways are they working together to improve student achievement?

- **Helping Parents Understand the School Curriculum:** What information do families receive about the school's educational program and what is taught in each grade? How are parents involved in setting goals for student achievement and in evaluating their progress?

- **Helping Parents Be More Effective as Parents and as Community Members:** Does the school collaborate with families to provide a parent education program? How does the school help provide connections to community services and organizations?

Taking Stock is a beginning, not an end. It is intended to introduce the components of an effective family-community-school partnership, help a school assess how well it is reaching out and working with its community, and show how to use the results to develop a detailed action plan for improvement.

The process of *Taking Stock* falls into three stages: (1) Conducting the survey or inventory, interpreting the results, and reporting to the school community; (2) developing an Action Plan; and (3) implementing the Action Plan. For each stage, it is recommended that a team be formed, composed of the principal, parent leaders, representatives of teachers and other staff, student representatives, and community leadership.

The questionnaire form included in *Taking Stock* can be used as is, or could be modified and adapted. The main purpose is to gather data on the opinions of school personnel and parents concerning how well the parent involvement program is working. Additional questions can be written which apply more directly to the specifics of the components of a particular program. In many cases, the school already has an Action Plan; the *Taking Stock* process would enable the principal to evaluate the various activities of the plan, and learn about the areas where additional effort is needed.

SUMMARY

As parent involvement programs evolve and mature, the efforts at evaluation and assessment will expand and improve. We suggest there is no one evaluation model appropriate for all programs designs. More effective evaluations will result from thoughtful efforts by staff and parents in each local program as they try to measure and analyze the link between specific program components and desired outcomes.

REFERENCES

Chavkin, Nancy Feyl, editor. *Families and Schools in a Pluralistic Society*. 1993. State University of New York Press, State University Plaza, Albany, NY 12246.

League of Schools Reaching Out. *Action Research Handbook for Fifteen Schools: A Multi-Site Action Research Case Study*. November, 1991. Center on Families, Communities, Schools and Children's Learning. Institute for Responsive Education, 605 Commonwealth Avenue, Boston, Massachusetts 02215.

Making Connections between Parents, School and Community: The Parent Leadership Training Program, Evaluation for 1991–1992. Prepared for the Citizens Education Center by Dr. Beverly B. McConnell.

"MegaSkills Students Improve School Performance: New Research Findings from the Home and School Institute."

Fall 1992. The Home and School Institute, MegaSkills Education Center, 1201 16th Street, N.W., Washington, DC 20036.

"QEP Evaluation 1990–1991," "MS-QEP Evaluation 1990–91," and "QEP P.E.P. Report." Quality Education Project, 639 W. Monterey Road, Corona, CA 91720.

Taking Stock: The Inventory of Family, Community and School Support for Student Achievement. 1993. National Committee for Citizens in Education, 900 Second Street, N.E., Suite 8, Washington, DC 20002.

Chapter 9

What Recent Research Says About Parent Involvement

The purpose of this chapter is to review the major research literature on the relationship between parent attitudes and activities and the behavior and academic achievement of children and the quality of education provided in their schools. The research selected and summarized here will present strong evidence of the positive benefits of parent involvement, with particular emphasis on school-family partnership programs.

This chapter begins with a brief look at the historical background of the relationship between parents and schools. The second section includes a discussion of literature reviews and bibliographies which themselves contain specific citations and annotations of many research efforts. The third section reviews recent research efforts which demonstrate the benefits of parent involvement, in terms of student achievement, impact on teachers, school climate, parent empowerment, and improved schools.

Next, we summarize articles and studies related to the role of low-income, minority parents. The fifth section includes a discussion of several programs implemented in the 1970s and 1980s (including James Comer, Moncrieff Cochran, and Joyce Epstein) which not only demonstrated the positive role parents can play in the education of their children, but also provided research data for statistical analysis. The last section cites reports which include descriptions of many types of parent involvement programs.

Taken together these six sections provide an important overview of the distance traveled from a few early and prominent studies to recent years with increasing numbers of researchers and studies. The response to repeated calls for more rigorous examination of cause and effect in parent/family involvement efforts should enhance the importance of establishing and improving such programs in the many endeavors made to improve schools and increase student success.

HISTORICAL BACKGROUND

James Coleman, sociologist at the University of Chicago, has traced the transformations that have occurred in the homes, schools, and society, from the early 1800s up to today, in a publication prepared for the Office of Educational Research and Improvement, *Parental Involvement in Education*, June 1991. Coleman points out that during the last 2 centuries society has been transformed from a set of communities where families were the central building blocks to a social system in which the central organizations are business firms, and families are at the periphery.

The first transformation occurred when household production was replaced by the employment of the man in a job outside the home, usually in the factory or office. Consequently, the role of the father and mother in providing an environment for the child to learn productive adult skills was no longer feasible. During this period, elementary and secondary schooling came into being to replace some of the educational functions which had gone on before in the home.

The second transformation, occurring during the 20th Century, entailed women leaving the household to enter the paid labor market. Coleman argues that this resulted in a further decline in the child rearing functions taking place in the home.

Coleman considers the school system as a "constructed" institution, designed to carry out educational functions not provided by other institutions such as the family. As the educational functions of the family have declined and the composition of the family has changed, the role of the school must change if it is to meet the needs of the diverse family population of today.

Frank Nardine, on the faculty of the University of Wisconsin at Milwaukee, looked at some of the historical background of parents and the public schools in his article "The Changing Role of Low-Income Minority Parents in Their Children's Schooling," published in the Winter 1990 issue of *New Directions for Adult and Continuing Education*. In colonial America, the rearing and educating of children were two separate activities: parents reared and teachers educated. Following the colonial period, emphasis was given in the public schools to the need for "acculturation" of immigrant parents to the American way of life. This was the beginning of the concept of the deficit model, focusing on the inadequacy of immigrant parents, and the need for "compensatory" education for the children from these families. It was not until the 1960s and 1970s when this set of assumptions began to be replaced by the notion that all parents have strengths and can be empowered to take a more active and positive role in their children's education.

The quantity and quality of parent involvement in the public schools during the period 1945–1985 has not been documented or studied extensively. In *New Directions in Parent Involvement*, authors Norm Fruchter, Anne Galletta, and J. Lynne White, characterize parent participation during this period as traditional and conventional, consisting primarily of PTA fund-raising organizations and parent volunteers. Parents were expected to monitor homework, attend parent/teacher conferences, and support classroom and school activities when invited. Those most active were middle class, suburban mothers who were not employed outside of the home.

Oliver Moles discusses the historical context of the relationships between public schools and ethnic, minority families in Chapter 1 of *Families and Schools in a Pluralistic*

Society. He describes the school efforts to educate and socialize children from immigrant families with practices and rules which tended to deter family-school connections. During the 1960s, minority groups became more activist in demanding that public school systems become more responsive to the needs of their children. During this decade and the next two, a number of federal laws were passed which recognized the importance of parents in their children's education.

The passage of the Elementary and Secondary Education Act in 1965 marked the beginning of a series of far-reaching federal laws related to education. Many of these included provisions for involvement of parents in the planning, monitoring, and evaluating of programs funded by federal dollars. These include Chapter 1, Education of Disadvantaged Children; Head Start and Follow Through Programs; Bilingual Education Act; P.L. 94–142, Education of Handicapped Children Act; and Even Start which integrates early childhood education with adult education.

EARLY LITERATURE REVIEWS ON PARENT INVOLVEMENT

Urie Bronfenbrenner was one of the first researchers to address the issue of the impact of parent involvement on children's learning. In his study *A Report on Longitudinal Evaluations of Preschool Programs, Vol. II: Is Early Intervention Effective?* (1974), he analyzed several intervention programs for preschool-aged disadvantaged children. Bronfenbrenner concluded that children participating in this type of program show higher and more durable gains if their mothers are actively involved in their learning. The most impressive, long-lasting gains were made in a 2-year program where tutors visited homes twice a week and demonstrated the use of toy kits to mothers and children.

In an article in *The Review of Educational Research*, Summer 1979, Richard Barth reported on his review of studies of teacher-parent collaboration to reinforce children's positive school behavior at home in order to improve their academic performance. Several systems were studied, including sending notes home from school, withholding privileges or allowances, and positive rewards; they all resulted in a beneficial effect on academic achievement or improved behavior.

"What Does Research Say About the Effects of Parent Involvement on Schooling?" is the title of a paper presented at the Annual Meeting of the Association for Supervision and Curriculum Development in 1978, by Ira Gordon, a Professor at the University of North Carolina, Chapel Hill. Gordon reviewed the research on parent involvement, and concluded that the more comprehensive and long-lasting the parent involvement, the more effective it is likely to be, not only on children's achievement but also on the quality of schools. He considered several models of parent involvement: the Parent Impact Model, which addresses the influence of parents and home on the child's learning behavior; the School Impact Model, which refers to parent involvement in the school in such roles as volunteer or committee member; and the Community Impact Model, including influences on education from home, family, and community.

In the 1981 and 1987 annotated bibliographies, *The Evidence Grows* and *The Evidence Continues to Grow*, Anne Henderson looked at research studies on various aspects of parent involvement and student achievement. About half of them focused on parents and their interactions with their children as critical variables in the child's success in school. The other half of the studies addressed the relationship between school and home and examined actual programs to strengthen communication and build partnerships between home and school. Her introduction to the 1987 publication states that "the evidence is beyond dispute: parent involvement improves student achievement. When parents are involved, children do better in school, and they go to better schools."

Diane Scott-Jones, a researcher currently at Temple University, published a comprehensive review of the literature entitled "Family Influences on Cognitive Development and School Achievement," in the 1984 *Review of Research in Education*. She suggests that no one broad theory can be used to conceptualize the relationship between the family and the child's cognitive development and school achievement. This is because of the many variables involved, including biological factors, health and nutrition, environmental factors, family structure, race, socioeconomic status, family processes, and parental expectations. The mother-as-teacher model is successful, especially in the case of young, middle class children. Scott-Jones also concludes that parents' beliefs and expectations are associated with high levels of performance on cognitive tasks.

Oliver Moles, a staff member of the Office of Educational Research and Improvement in the U.S. Department of Education, is the author of "Synthesis of Recent Research," published in *Educational Leadership*, November 1982. After reviewing and assessing a number of studies of parent involvement, Moles concluded that:

- The interest in parent participation is clear, strong, and specific from all sides;

- Educators need to reexamine prevailing beliefs about parents, their capabilities and interests;

- Interest in parent participation is going beyond the early elementary grades, up through middle and high school.

Moles suggested some key factors in effective parent involvement programs, including teachers and parents working together in the design and development of the program; staff training and development; personal contact between family and school; and commitment on the part of teachers, schools and school systems.

Rhoda McShane Becher discusses the factors determining effective parent practices and programs in her 1984 report, *Parent Involvement: A Review of Research and Principles of Successful Practice*, published by the National Institute of Education. She looks at the ways parents can be trained to improve their children's academic achievement, and identifies several key family "process variables," which refer to parental behavior that is clearly related to student achievement. These include such things as high expectations, frequent interaction, reinforcement of subject matter learned at school, improved communication between parent and child, and the parents serving as models of learning and achievement.

University of Illinois researcher Herbert Walberg reviewed 29 controlled studies on school-parent programs, as reported in his article "Improving the Productivity of America's School," *Educational Leadership*, Vol. 41, 1984, and found that family participation in education was twice as predictive of academic learning as family socioeconomic status. Walberg also discovered that some parent involvement programs had effects 10 times as large as socioeconomic status and provided additional benefits to both older and younger students in the family. He concludes that school-parent partnership programs to improve academic conditions in the home have an outstanding record of success in promoting achievement.

BENEFITS OF PARENT INVOLVEMENT

Student Achievement

In *The Evidence Continues to Grow: Parent Involvement Improves Student Achievement*, Anne Henderson summarizes 49 research studies which document the major hypothesis of this annotated bibliography: that when parents are involved, children do better in school, and they go to better schools. In her introduction, Henderson sums up her findings:

> Programs designed with strong parent involvement produce students who perform better than otherwise identical programs that do not involve parents as thoroughly, or that do not involve them at all. Schools that relate well to their communities have student bodies that outperform other schools. Children whose parents help them at home and stay in touch with the school score higher than children of similar aptitude and family background whose parents are *not* involved. Schools where children are failing improve dramatically when parents are called in to help. . . .

Some of the major benefits identified are higher grades and test scores, long-term academic achievement, positive attitudes and behavior, more successful programs, and more effective schools.

Janine Bempechat has written on "The Role of Parent Involvement in Children's Academic Achievement," in an article in the Fall/Winter 1992 issue of *The School Community Journal*. She notes that there is widespread agreement that parents' behaviors with their children influence the children's cognitive and social development, but little consensus on which specific behaviors are likely to maximize children's achievement. In this article, Bempechat explores cognitive and academic socialization patterns that foster high achievement and describes the structure and effectiveness of parent involvement programs. She suggests that middle class parents appear to have both the material and social resources to implement appropriate practices, and that parents of educationally disadvantaged children can provide comparable support, especially if they are assisted by parent education programs. Bempechat concludes that when teachers and educational administrators are strongly committed to drawing parents into their children's education, the academic outcomes for children can be very positive.

Teachers' Work Satisfaction

Annette Lareau looks at the effect of parent involvement on teachers' work satisfaction in her article "Family-School Relationships: A View from the Classroom," published in *Education Policy*, September 1989. She identifies three factors related to parent involvement which result in greater teacher satisfaction: (1) children come to school prepared to learn, (2) parents can provide help to the teachers in the classroom, and (3) parents give children support at home by working with them on activities such as homework and reading. However, Lareau also points out that there still may be some conflict between teachers and parents, because teachers may not want partnerships with parents, but prefer instead to establish the parameters of parent involvement themselves and to count on parents to support them.

School Climate

In an article in the *Journal of School Psychology*, Vol. 27, 1989, Norris M. Haynes, James P. Comer, and Muriel Hamilton-Lee report on "School Climate Enhancement Through Parental

Involvement." They examine the implementation of the Parent Program developed by Comer's School Development Program. The program was to be introduced into 14 schools in two phases; the seven schools starting the first year served as experimental schools, while the other seven were control schools. The perception of school climate by teachers, students, and parents was surveyed. Positive and significant changes were found in the seven experimental schools, while the perceptions of school climate in the control schools showed no change for teachers, and students and parents rated the schools significantly lower in school climate.

Suzanne Ziegler in her October 1987 report, *The Effects of Parent Involvement on Children's Achievement: The Significance of Home/School Links*, presents a comprehensive review of the literature on parent involvement. She discusses how parental participation in educational activities at home can affect children's academic performance, and concludes that "The influence of the home on children's success at school is profound." She further suggests that parents involved in the schools can be equally powerful.

Ziegler hypothesizes that the effectiveness of parent involvement "may be explained by the message children receive when they see their teachers and parents in direct, personal contact centered on the children's learning and progress." She continues that "the more direct, first-hand, frequent and personal the parent-teacher contact, and the more visible that contact is to the child, the greater is its potential."

BROADENING THE DISCUSSION TO LOW-INCOME, MINORITY PARENTS

Both James Comer and Moncrieff Cochran implemented their programs with low-income, minority populations. Their research demonstrates that parents with little education, on welfare, or with low-paying jobs are effective in contributing to their children's success in school. Joyce Epstein, in her study of parents helping out at home with their children's school work, found that all parents, even those who may not have completed many years of formal education, could help their children with homework, especially if the teacher was dedicated to designing ways in which parents could help their children.

Frank Nardine suggests that it was not until the 1960s that educational policymakers began to question the deficit model which had pervaded the field. Urie Bronfenbrenner and Moncrieff Cochran took exception to the deficit model attributed to low-income, disadvantaged parents. They believed that all families have strengths, and their Family Matters program, research, and writings contributed to the emergence of the concept of empowerment.

During the past 10 years, many other researchers have joined the discussion about the benefits from the involvement of all parents, those with little education themselves, those who speak another language, and those brought up in another culture. The survey, conducted by the Southwest Educational Development Laboratory in the early 1980s, included 1,188 Black and Hispanic parents in the sample. In a chapter on "Minority Parents and the Elementary School," in *Families and Schools in a Pluralistic Society*, Nancy Feyl Chavkin and David Williams report on the results. Almost all of those responding (95%) said they want to be more involved with their children's education, help with homework, and also have more influence in their child's school.

The Metropolitan Life Survey of The American Teacher 1987, "Strengthening Links Between Home and School," revealed that parents in inner-city school districts report less contact with teachers than do parents in suburban area schools. Parents who have lower income and education levels and single parents are less satisfied with their opportunities for parent involvement than are parents with college training and higher incomes.

Reginald Clark, in his study on 10 poor, black families and their high school aged children (reported in *Family Life and School Achievement: Why Poor Black Children Succeed and Fail*, 1983) concluded that the educational success of the children was determined by the family practices and home living patterns, rather than by the parents' education, income level, or family structure. In the high achievers' homes, there was much interaction and communication between parent(s) and child, strong parent encouragement of academic pursuits, consistent monitoring of how time was used, and clear and consistent limits. By contrast, the lives of those students who were failing at school were characterized by "unsponsored independence," minimum parental supervision, negative expectations for success, and no reinforcing pattern of school-home encouragement.

Milbrey McLaughlin and Patrick Shields discuss the efforts to involve low-income parents since the mid 1960s, in their December 1986 paper on "Involving Parents in the Schools: Lessons for Policy." They note that federal legislation (*e.g.*, Head Start, Chapter 1, Education of All Handicapped Children Act, and the Bilingual Education Act) includes parent involvement mandates, intended to empower parents and to improve the educational outcomes for poor and under-achieving students. McLaughlin and Shields discuss the two types of parent involvement: (1) advisory councils (PACs) whose purpose is to include parents in decision making efforts related to the program, and (2) home-school partnerships, which include school-based and home-based activities.

They emphasize that all of the evidence demonstrates that low-income and less educated parents want to help in their children's education. A lack of knowledge about how to assist their children does not represent a lack of interest. Lacking are strategies and structures appropriate to the involvement of these parents who have often been excluded from the schools.

Another reason for focusing attention on the issue of parent involvement derives from demographic data. Only 7% of today's school-age children come from families that were typical in 1965—two parent, single-wage earner families. Changes in the differential birth rate between minority and majority populations, family patterns, immigration trends, and divorce rates, are resulting in an increase in the number of children from low-income families, single-parent families, and homes where the primary language is not English. McLaughlin and Shields conclude:

> It is evident that the success of the schools in serving these student groups can be enhanced significantly by reaching out and engaging their parents. Experience suggests that school success is as much an act of social construction undertaken by families and schools as school failure has been shown to be.

Annette Lareau develops the concept of cultural capital to explain some of the reasons why middle class parents are often more involved in their children's education and appear to be more effective in their activities. Middle class children and their parents possess the attitudes, perspectives, and demeanor which are more compatible and congruent with the policies and practices of the typical public school. Because they lack the background and experiences valued by many school personnel, low income parents may be viewed as deficient in their attitudes and expectations for their children's educational accomplishments.

In her 1990 report, *Parent Involvement and Success for All Children: What We Know Now*, Susan McAllister Swap suggests that effective schooling requires a continuity between home and school environments. In the case of families with diverse cultural, economic, and linguistics backgrounds, significant discontinuities between home and school exist. She proposes a parent-school partnership model, based on mutual respect, shared power, and the empowerment of parents.

In an article on "Family Programs for Academic Learning," published in the Spring/Summer 1992 issue of *The School Community Journal*, Herbert J. Walberg and Trudy Wallace discuss parent-partnership program models to involve low-income parents both at home and in the classroom. They introduce the "Matthew effect," (based on *Matthew* XXV:29) as one of the rationales for the importance of parent involvement. The Matthew effect refers to the fact that those who are disadvantaged at the beginning of school fall even further behind as they "progress," while those who start ahead often gain at a faster rate.

The programs reviewed in this article include:

- Preschool programs, such as home-oriented preschool education, HIPPY, and the Parental Empowerment Program in New York; and

- Elementary school programs, such as Parents in Action in Alice, Texas, which trains parents in reading and math, Parents as Tutors (Home & School Institute), and APPLE (Arkansas Parents: Partners in Learning Experiences) sponsored by the Arkansas State Department of Education.

The last effort discussed is the Alliance for Achievement, sponsored by the Academic Development Institute (ADI), to organize the parents in 15 Chicago schools to work with the teachers and administrators on school reform. They conclude that:

> . . . while ongoing local evaluation and further research are in order, there seems little reason to hesitate in implementing more widely and systematically programs featuring home visiting, parent reading, parent tutoring, and other partnership programs. . . .

RESEARCH STUDIES ON SPECIFIC PARENT INVOLVEMENT PROGRAMS

Dr. James Comer initiated one of the first comprehensive school improvement projects at the elementary school level, emphasizing substantial parent involvement as one of the factors to improve the quality of education in two inner-city schools in New Haven, CT. He reports on his experiences in the 1980 book, *School Power*, as well as in many subsequent magazine and journal articles. Parents were members of three committees established to provide policy guidance and direction to the school. Parents were hired to become teacher aides, and were encouraged to serve as volunteers in all aspects of the school program.

Both schools using the Comer Process attained the best attendance records in the city, recorded greatly reduced student behavior problems, experienced minimal parent-staff conflict, and achieved near grade-level academic performance. At one of the schools, the students moved from 20th in reading and 31st in math to 10th place in both among all New Haven schools.

Family Matters is an early childhood intervention program featuring home visits and neighborhood-based parent support groups. It was designed and implemented by Urie Bronfenbrenner and Moncrieff Cochran, at Cornell University. The program was offered to 160 families, each with a 3-year old child, in 10 different neighborhoods in Syracuse, NY. Education aides were trained to give the parents information about child rearing; to demonstrate examples of parent-child learning activities in a series of home visits designed to reinforce the parents' feelings of importance and effectiveness; and to pass on ideas and practices of other parents. Though there were some variations in results depending on race, income, and family structure, the evaluation provided some evidence that children who had participated in the program attained better academic performance when they entered public school.

Joyce Epstein, a researcher at Johns Hopkins University, conducted a study on the effects of teachers' practices of parent involvement, based on longitudinal data from test scores of 293 third and fifth grade students in the fall and spring of 1980–1981. The students were in the classrooms of 14 teachers who varied in their emphasis on parental involvement. Analysis of test scores showed that teacher leadership in promoting parent involvement in learning activities at home positively and significantly influenced improvement in reading achievement. Epstein concludes that "There is consistent evidence that parents' encouragement, activities, interest at home and their participation at school affect their children's achievement, even after the students' ability and family socioeconomic status is taken into account."

Another piece of research which has been very influential in the field of parent involvement is based on a survey undertaken by the Southwest Educational Development Laboratory in six states (Arkansas, Mississippi, Louisiana, New Mexico, Oklahoma, and Texas). Parents, teachers, principals, and school associated professionals were surveyed on five different aspects of parent involvement in the elementary grades: attitudes, decisions, roles, activities, and teacher training. Results show that parent involvement is acceptable to all groups surveyed, but parents and educators have distinctly diverse views about the desirable roles for parents in the schools. Both parents and school personnel indicated strong support of home activities related to education; parents also expressed a high degree of interest in being involved in school governance activities. Thus, parent involvement interests extend beyond those areas designated as appropriate by the schools. In order for parent involvement to become more acceptable, viable and effective, a clear definition is necessary — one on which all can agree.

DIRECTORIES DESCRIBING EFFECTIVE OR SUCCESSFUL PROGRAMS

One of the earliest descriptive reports on parent involvement programs in the schools was by Don Davies, *Schools Where Parents Make a Difference*, 1976, published by the Institute of Responsive Education. This is a collection of stories, written by education writers and journalists, about schools in all parts of the country. In each of the 10 schools described in the book are concerned, involved parents who support, help operate, and shape their schools to meet the special needs of their own communities and children.

The Institute of Responsive Education in Boston published another report a few years later (1982) by Carter Collins, Oliver Moles, and Mary Cross describing *The Home-School Connection: Selected Partnership Programs in Large Cities*. This report includes information about 28 programs in grades 4–12 initiated by school systems in large cities. School systems were asked to provide material on programs that might help parents become active in educational capacities, such as home tutors, monitors of homework and attendance, or guides for their children in the use of community educational resources. The program profiles include program objectives, major activities, staffing, target populations, funding, evaluations, materials available, and the name of a contact person.

P.A. Griswold evaluates parent involvement components in 116 Chapter 1 projects, in the 1986 publication *Parent Involvement in Unusually Successful Compensatory Education*. A wide range of participation was reported, including serving on school advisory committees, parent-teacher interaction, home reinforcement of school learning, and parent training. Griswold concluded that many of the effective Chapter 1 programs placed only minor emphasis on home reinforcement of school learning, though in his view this parental involvement role shows great potential for improving student achievement.

Working with Families: Promising Programs to Help Parents Support Young Children's Learning, by Barbara Dillon Goodson, et al., published in February 1991 by Abt Associates, Cambridge, MA, reports on 17 programs located throughout the country. The information collected focuses on famiiy education programs that work with parents with the primary goal of enhancing children's cognitive development and school-related achievement.

The 17 programs represent a variety of approaches to family education, utilizing multiple strategies to work effectively with families. Only one of them describes a program at a single, local school, the Kuban School in Phoenix, AZ. The other 16 represent multiple locations and diverse sponsorship, including state sponsored, school district programs, national models, private, nonprofit organizations, colleges and universities.

Three of the programs described in this book are also included in *Working with Families*: the McAllen Parent Involvement Program, HIPPY, and TIPS. The HIPPY program described in *Working with Families* is located in Miami, FL, with a very different population from that in Warrensville Heights, OH. The TIPS program targets families with students in K-8 and applies to the mathematics curriculum. The TIPS program in the current volume is located at two middle schools in Baltimore, MD, where the TIPS activities are designed for Language Arts and Science/Health courses.

Norm Fruchter, Anne Galletta, and J. Lynne White, with the Academy for Educational Development, wrote and published a study in 1992 which identifies and analyzes 18 programs of reforms stressing parental involvement. The authors organize the report around four broad categories of new parent involvement efforts:

- Programs for parents of preschool-age children;

- Efforts to help parents support their children's school learning;

- Parents' roles in major school improvement or restructuring efforts; and

- Involvement of parents in recent governance reforms.

The programs in the first three categories have been designed and developed by educators, private nonprofit educational organizations, researchers with colleges and universities. The study describes the models, providing information on target population, origins and development, scope, goals, components, resources, funding, and evaluation. This is a valuable resource for schools who wish to learn more about a number of diverse approaches to the role of parent involvement, particularly in schools serving low-income and disadvantaged students.

One of the programs described in the Fruchter, Galletta, and White report is the League of Schools Reaching Out, developed by Don Davies and his colleagues at the Institute for Responsive Education at Boston University. In 1990, 40 urban public schools became members of the League of Schools Reaching Out; in 1991, 70 public and private schools joined, including some in rural areas and some clusters of urban schools. Rather than introducing a single design or model on individual schools, the League of Schools Reaching Out seeks out schools which are committed to the goals and principles of the organization. They have developed into a collection of individual schools implementing their own plans for increasing student success through family-community-school interaction.

In their February 1992 publication, Don Davies, Patricia Burch, and Vivian R. Johnson present *A Portrait of Schools Reaching Out: Report of a Survey of Practices and Policies of Family-Community-School Collaboration*, published by the Center on Families, Communities, Schools & Children's Learning. In this study, the authors sought answers to the following questions: (1) What strategies and practices are used to achieve school-community-family collaborations? and (2) How do formal and informal policies influence these strategies and practices?

Many conclusions can be drawn from this survey, including the following:

- The field is at an early stage of development;

- Policies are plentiful, fragmented, and confusing;

- Without exception, the schools are carrying out their reaching out strategies without a clear policy system or framework which fosters and supports a comprehensive effort;

- There is a clear need for more systematic, focused study and evaluation, of the components implemented to increase parent involvement and what their effects are on children's and families' learning.

The survey revealed that many schools are redefining themselves as community institutions by serving families and other community residents in a variety of ways, and by exchanging resources with other community institutions. The level and variety of reaching out activity reported and observed is high and impressive. All the schools use multiple strategies to communicate with families, but traditional strategies continue to be predominant. Parent volunteering and advisory councils are examples of the conventional activities in most schools.

At-Risk Families & Schools: Becoming Partners, by Lynn Balster Liontos, 1992, from the ERIC Clearinghouse on Educational Management, Eugene, OR, is an impressive compilation of policies, practices, programs, strategies, methods, and barriers, organized into a readable and useful document. As Don Davies writes in the "Introduction:"

> This book makes a major contribution in filling this gap (between general theory and specific technology) by providing good descriptions of how educators, family members, and community people are actually collaborating and by offering many practical, how-to-do-it suggestions. Although the book falls short of being a complete "tool-kit," it makes a good beginning.

In addition to the factual information and practical suggestions, each chapter contains sidebars with brief program descriptions which are carefully placed to relate to the content of the chapter. Many of them have appeared in several of the other directories mentioned above, but their inclusion here is especially helpful because they are integrated into the theoretical framework.

REFERENCES

Barth, Richard. "Home-Based Reinforcement of School Behavior: A Review and Analysis," *Review of Educational Research*, Summer 1979 (Vol. 49, No. 3), pp. 436–58. EJ 215 250.

Becher, Rhoda McShane. *Parent Involvement: A Review of Research and Principles of Successful Practice*, 1984, National Institute of Education, Washington, DC. ED 247 032.

Bempechat, Janine. "The Role of Parent Involvement in Children's Academic Achievement," *The School Community Journal*, Fall/Winter 1992.

Bronfenbrenner, Urie. *A Report on Longitudinal Evaluations of Preschool Programs, Vol. II: Is Early Intervention Effective?*, Office of Child Development, U.S. Department of Health, Education, and Welfare, 1974. ED 093 501.

Chavkin, Nancy Feyl and David L. Williams, Jr. "Minority Parents and the Elementary School: Attitudes and Practices," in *Families and Schools in a Pluralistic Society*, edited by Nancy Feyl Chavkin, 1993, State University of New York Press, Albany, NY, pp. 73–84.

Clark, Reginald M. *Family Life and School Achievement: Why Poor Black Children Succeed or Fail*, 1983, University of Chicago Press.

Cochran, Moncrieff. *Empowering Families*, 1988, Family Matters Project, Cornell University, Ithaca, NY.

Cochran, Moncrieff. "The Parental Empowerment Process: Building on Family Strengths," *Equity and Choice*, Vol. 4, No. 1, pp. 9–23.

Coleman, James S. *Parental Involvement in Education*, June 1991. Policy Perspectives, Office of Educational Research and Improvement, U.S. Department of Education, Washington, DC.

Collins, C.H., O. Moles and M. Cross. *The Home-School Connection: Selected Partnership Programs in Large Cities*, 1982, Institute for Responsive Education, Boston, MA.

Comer, James P. "Educating Poor Minority Children," *Scientific American*, 1988, Vol. 259, No. 5, pp. 42–48.

Comer, James P. *School Power*, 1980, MacMillan, The Free Press, New York, NY.

Davies, Don, Patricia Burch and Vivian R. Johnson. *A Portrait of Schools Reaching Out: Report of a Survey of Practices and Policies of Family-Community-School Collaboration*, Report No. 1, February 1992, Center on Families, Communities, Schools & Children's Learning, Boston, MA.

Davies, Don. *Schools Where Parents Make a Difference*, 1976, Institute for Responsive Education, Boston, MA.

Epstein, Joyce L. "Effects on Student Achievement of Teachers'

Practices of Parents Involvement," in *Advances in Reading/ Language Research*, Volume 5, 1991, pp. 261–76. JAI Press, Inc., Greenwich, CT.

Fruchter, Norm, Anne Galletta and J. Lynne White. *New Directions in Parent Involvement*, 1992. Academy for Educational Development, New York, NY.

Goodson, B., J.P. Swartz, and M.A. Milsap. *Working with Families: Promising Programs to Help Parents Support Young Children's Learning*, 1991, Abt Associates, Inc., Cambridge, MA.

Gordon, Ira. "What Does Research Say About the Effects of Parent Involvement on Schooling?," Paper for Annual Meeting of the Association for Supervision and Curriculum Development, 1978.

Griswold, P.A. *Parent Involvement in Unusually Successful Compensatory Education*, 1986, Northwest Regional Educational Laboratory, Portland, OR. ED 279 428.

Haynes, N.M., J.P. Comer, and M. Hamilton-Lee. "School Climate Enhancement through Parental Involvement," *Journal of School Psychology*, 1989, 27:87–90.

Henderson, Anne T. *The Evidence Continues to Grow: Parent Involvement Improves Student Achievement*, 1987, National Committee for Citizens in Education, Washington, DC.

Henderson, Anne T. *The Evidence Grows*, 1981. National Committee for Citizens in Education, Washington, DC.

Lareau, Annette. "Family-School Relationships: A View from the Classroom," *Education Policy*, No. 3, September 1989.

Lareau, Annette. "Social Class Differences in Family-School Relationships: The Importance of Cultural Capital," *Sociology of Education*, Vol. 60, No. 2, April 1987, pp. 73–85.

Liontos, Lynn Balster. *At-Risk Families & Schools: Becoming Partners*, 1992, ERIC Clearinghouse on Educational Management, Eugene, OR.

McLaughlin, Milbrey and Patrick Shields. *Involving Parents in the Schools: Lessons for Policy*, 1986, Designs for Compensatory Education, Conference Proceedings and Papers, Washington, DC. ED 293 290.

Metropolitan Life Insurance Company. *The Metropolitan Life Survey of the American Teacher: Strengthening Links Between Home and School*, 1987, New York, NY.

Moles, Oliver C. "Collaboration between Schools and Disadvantaged Parents: Obstacles and Openings," in *Families and Schools in a Pluralistic Society*, edited by Nancy Feyl Chavkin, 1993, State University of New York Press, Albany, NY, pp. 21–49.

Moles, Oliver C. "Synthesis of Recent Research on Parent Participation in Children's Education," *Educational Leadership*, November 1982, pp. 44–47.

Nardine, Frank E. "The Changing Role of Low-Income Minority Parents in their Children's Schooling," *New Directions for Adult and Continuing Education*, No. 48, Winter 1990, pp. 67–80.

Scott-Jones, Diane. "Family Influences on Cognitive Development and School Achievement," Chapter 7 in *Review of Research in Education*, edited by Edmund W. Gordon, 1984, American Educational Research Association, Washington, DC.

Swap, Susan McAllister. *Parent Involvement and Success for All Children: What We Know Now*, 1990, Institute for Responsive Education, Boston, MA.

Walberg, Herbert J. "Improving the Productivity of America's Schools," *Educational Leadership*, Vol. 41, 1984, pp. 19–27.

Walberg, Herbert J. and Trudy Wallace. "Family Programs for Academic Learning," *The School Community Journal*, Vol. 2, No. 1, Spring/Summer 1992.

Ziegler, Suzanne. *The Effects of Parent Involvement on Children's Achievement: The Significance of Home/School Links*, 1987, Toronto Board of Education, Toronto, Ontario, Canada. ED 304 234.

Appendix A

Alphabetical List of Programs

Vaughn Street School, San Fernando, California—Vaughn Family Center *(p. 140)*

Wapato Primary School, Wapato, Washington—FOCUS (Focusing our Community and Uniting for Success) *(p. 147)*

Warrensville Heights City School District, Warrensville Hts., Ohio—Warrensville HIPPY (Home Instruction Program for Preschool Youngsters) *(p. 49)*

Appendix B

References about Parent Involvement Programs

Ascher, Carol. *Changing Schools for Urban Students: The School Development Program, Accelerated Schools, and Success for All*. February 1993, 41 pages. ERIC Clearinghouse on Urban Education, Box 40, Teachers College, Columbia University, New York, NY 10027.

Banerian, James. *Parent Involvement and the Asian/Pacific Population: Strengthening Home-School Partnerships with Asian/Pacific Families*. 1991. Asian/Pacific Education Council and the Community Relations and Integration Services Division, San Diego City Schools, San Diego, CA.

Cale, Lettie B. *Planning for Parental Involvement: A Handbook for Administrators, Teachers and Parents*, 1991. Phoenix, AZ.

Chavkin, Nancy Feyl, editor. *Families and Schools in a Pluralistic Society*, 1993, State University of New York Press, Albany, NY.

Chrispeels, Janet. *Communicating with Parents*, 1988. San Diego County Office of Education, San Diego, CA.

Comer, James. "Educating Poor Minority Children," *Scientific American*, 1988, Vol. 259, No. 5, pp. 42–48.

Comer, James. "Parent Participation in the Schools," *Phi Delta Kappan*, Vol. 67, 1986, pp. 442–46.

Epstein, Joyce L. "School and Family Partnerships." Report No. 6, March 1992. Center on Families, Communities, Schools and Children's Learning, Boston, MA.

Epstein, Joyce L. and Susan L. Dauber. "Parents' Attitudes and Practices in Involvement in Inner-City Elementary and Middle Schools," in *Families and Schools in Pluralistic Society*, 1993, edited by Nancy Chavkin. State University of New York Press, Albany, NY.

Families and Education: An Educator's Resource for Family Involvement, 1991. Wisconsin Department of Public Instruction, Milwaukee, WI.

Fearn, Gloria Wilber, *Building the Good School: Participating Parents at Charquin*, 1993. Ohlone Press, Hayward, CA.

Garlington, Jocelyn A. *Helping Dreams Survive: The Story of a Project Involving African-American Families in the Education of their Children*, 1991. National Committee for Citizens in Education, Washington, DC.

Greenberg, Polly. "Parents as Partners in Young Children's Development and Education: A New American Fad? Why Does It Matter?" *Young Children*, May, 1989, pp. 61–75.

Guide to Parent Involvement Resources, 1992. Council of Chief State School Officers and National Coalition for Parent Involvement in Education, Washington, DC.

Henderson, Anne T., Carl L. Marburger, and Theodora Ooms. *Beyond the Bake Sale: An Educator's Guide to Working with Parents*, 1986. National Committee for Citizens in Education, Washington, DC.

McLaughlin, Milbrey, and Patrick Shields. "Involving Low-Income Parents in the Schools: A Role for Policy?," *Phi Delta Kappan*, Vol. 69, No. 2, October 1987, pp. 156–60. EJ 359 353.

Nicolau, Siobhan and Carmen Lydia Ramos. *Together is Better: Building Strong Partnerships Between Schools and Hispanic Parents*, 1990. Hispanic Policy Development Project, New York, NY.

Parent Involvement Programs in California Public Schools: Families, Schools, and Communities Working Together, 1991. California Department of Education, Sacramento, CA.

Partners for Student Success: Home and School. A Handbook for Principals and Staff, 1990, 55 pages. San Diego City Schools, San Diego, CA.

Rich, Dorothy. *MegaSkills: How Families Help Children Succeed in Schools & Beyond*, 1993. Houghton Mifflin, New York, NY.

Salerno, Anne and Mary Fink. *Promising Practices for Home/School Partnerships*, 1992. BOCES Geneseo Migrant Center, Geneseo, NY.

Schorr, Lisbeth. *Within Our Reach: Breaking the Cycle of Disadvantage*, 1989. Anchor Press/Doubleday, New York, NY.

Southwest Educational Development Laboratory. *1992–93 Directory of Partnership Programs and Councils Connecting the Home, School, and Community*. Austin, TX.

Swap, Susan McAllister. *Developing Home-School Partnerships: From Concepts to Practice*, 1993, 212 pages. Teachers College Press, New York, NY.

Swick, Kevin J. *Teacher-Parent Partnerships to Enhance School Success in Early Childhood Education*, 1991. A Joint Publication of National Education Association and Southern Association on Children Under Six, Washington, DC.

Wikelund, Karen Reed. *Schools and Communities Together: A Guide to Parent Involvement*, September 1990. Northwest Regional Educational Laboratory, Portland, OR.

Williams, Michael R. *Neighborhood Organizing for Urban School Reform*, 1989. Teachers College Press, New York, NY.

Appendix C

Parent Involvement Organizations

Accelerated School Project
CERAS Building
Stanford University
Stanford, CA 94305
(415) 723-0840
Contact: Henry M. Levin

Aspira Association
1112 16th Street, N.W.
Suite 340
Washington, DC 20036
(202) 835-3600
Contact: Elena Pell

Appalachian Educational
  Laboratory
P.O. Box 1348
Charleston, WV 25325
(304) 347-0400
Contact: Becky Burns

Center for Collaborative
  Education
1573 Madison, NY 10029
(212) 348-7821
Contact: Heather Lewis

Center on Families,
  Communities, Schools and
  Children's Learning
Johns Hopkins University
3505 North Charles Street
Baltimore, MD 21218
(410) 516-0370
Contact: Joyce Epstein

Children's Defense Fund
122 C Street, N.W., Suite 400
Washington, DC 20001
(202) 628-8787
Contact: Delia Pompa

Citizens Education Center
  Parent Leadership Training
  Project
105 South Main Street
Seattle, WA 98104
(206) 624-9955
Contact: Judy McBroom

Coalition for Essential
  Schools
Brown University
Box 1969
Providence, RI 02912
(401) 863-3384
Contact: Theodore Sizer

HIPPY USA
National Council of Jewish
  Women
53 West 23rd Street
New York, NY 10010
(212) 645-4048
Contact: Catherine
Greenberg

Hispanic Policy Development
  Project
250 Park Ave. South,
  Suite 5000A
New York, NY 10003
(212) 529-3923
Contact: Carmen Ramos
1001 Conn. Ave., NW,
  Suite 310
Washington, DC 20036
(202) 822-8414
Contact: Mildred Garcia

Home and School Institute
  (HSI)
1201 16th Street, N.W.
Washington, DC 20036
(202) 466-3633
Contact: Dorothy Rich

Institute for Responsive
  Education
605 Commonwealth Avenue
Boston, MA 02215
(617) 353-3309
Contact: Don Davies

League of Schools Reaching
Out
Institute for Responsive
Education
605 Commonwealth Avenue
Boston, MA 02251
(617) 353-3309
Contact: Etta Green Johnson

MegaSkills Education Center
The Home and School
Institute
1201 16th Street, N.W.
Washington, DC 20036
(202) 466-3633
Contact: Harriett Stonehill

National Association of
Partners in Education
(NAPE)
209 Madison Street, Suite 401
Alexandria, Virginia 22314
(703) 836-4880
Contact: Janet Cox

National Coalition for Parent
Involvement in Education
Box 39
1201 16th Street, N.W.
Washington, DC 20036
Contact: Elena Pell

National Coalition of Title I
Chapter 1 Parents
National Parent Center
Edmonds School Building
9th and D Streets, N.E., #201
Washington, DC 20002
(202) 547-9286

National Committee for
Citizens in Education
(NCCE)
900 Second Street, N.E.,
Suite 8
Washington, DC 20002
(202) 408-0447; (800) 638-9675
Contact: Anne Henderson

National Education
Association (NEA)
1201 16th Street, N.W.
Washington, DC 20036
(202) 822-7015
Contact: Warlene Gary

National Parent and Teacher
Association (PTA)
700 North Rush Street
Chicago, IL 60611
(312) 787-0977
Contact: Tari Marshall

Parent Institute of Quality
Education
6306 1/2 Riverdale
San Diego, CA 92120
(619) 285-9904
Contact: Vahac Mardirosian

Parent Involvement Center
Chapter 1 Technical
Assistance Center
RMC Research Corporation
400 Lafayette Rd.
Hampton, NH 03842
(603) 926-8888
Contact: Diane A. D'Angelo

Parents as Teachers National
Center
9374 Olive Blvd.
St. Louis, MO 63132
(314) 432-4330
Contact: Mildred Winter

School Developoment
Program
Yale University
Child Study Center
230 South Frontage Road
P.O. Box 3333
New Haven, CT 06510
(203) 785-2548
Contact: James P. Comer

Stanford Center for the
Study of Families, Children
and Youth
Building 460, Room 150
Stanford University
Stanford, CA 94305
(415) 723-1706
Contact: Sanford M.
Dornbusch

Quality Education Project
690 Market Street, Suite 1100
San Francisco, CA 94115
(415) 398-9224
Contact: Judith Johnson

Southwest Educational
Development Laboratory
211 East 7th Street
Austin, TX 78701
(512) 476-6861
Contact: David Williams

Appendix D

Programs Contacted but not Included in Book

The following programs were considered for inclusion in this book. They are all strong programs, but were excluded because of space limitations.

Charles Barrett
97th Street School
419 W. 98th St.
Los Angeles, CA 90003
(213) 756-1419

Mrs. Pilar Jimenez
Buffalo P. S. Parent Center
15 E. Genesee St.
Buffalo, NY 14203
(716) 851-3747

Clemmie Collins
Birmingham School District
Chapter 1 Parent Education
125 63rd St., NO.
Birmingham, AL 35212
(205) 583-4878

Ruby Houston
Charlotte-Mecklinburg S.D.
Ch. 1 Parent Resource Center
Plaza Road School
1000 Anderson
Charlotte, NC 28205
(704) 343-5822

Gloria Fearn
Charquin School
P.O. Box 779
Hayward, CA 94543
(510) 537-3439

Kate Martin
Cyrus School
100 N. Nelson
Cyrus, MN 56323
(612) 795-2216

Dr. Carolyn Spurlock
Fairfield Court Elementary
2510 Phaup St.
Richmond, VA 23223
(804) 780-4639

Robert Auchenpaugh
Hershel Jones Middle School
100 Stadium Dr.
Dallas, CA 30132
(404) 443-8024

Phyliss Johnson
Lincoln Elementary School
1667 E. 118th St.
Los Angeles, CA 90059
(310) 898-6450

Maria Ortega
Longfellow School
3610 Eucalyptus
Riverside, CA 92507
(714) 788-7335

Diane Johnson
Shoctaw Tribal School
P.O. Box 6008
Community School Ed. Ctr.
Philadelphia, MS 39350
(601) 656-5251

Sr. Christine Stephens
Roosevelt High School
3300 W. Mockingbird
Ste. 732
Dallas, TX 75235
(214) 351-6595

Jane Marlow
Fond du Lac Ojibway School
105 University Rd.
Cloquet, MN 55720
(218) 879-0241

Sylvia Long
La Familia Unida
Phoenix Union H.S. Dist.
1900 W. Thomas Rd.
Phoenix, AZ 85015
(602) 271-3277

Martha Young
Little Havanna Institute
Cuban American Natl.
   Council
7400 S.W. 104th St.
Miami, FL 33156
(305) 642-3484

Lisa Matthews
Miles Park Elementary
   School
4090 East 93rd
Dleveland, OH 44105
(216) 341-1585

Bill Cox
Oakwood Elementary School
3230 85th St., South
Tacoma, WA 98409
(206) 589-7800

Tim Lavery
Seymour Middle School
920 N. O'Brien
Seymour, IN 47274
(812) 522-5453

Deborae Harris
Wells High School
P.O. Box 579
Wells, ME 04090
(207) 646-7011

Jackie Lazarewicz
Parent Partnerships
Clemens Crossing Elem.
  School
10320 Quarterstaff Rd.
Columbia, MD 21044
(410) 313-6866

Ezekiel Bloyce
Shugart Middle School
2000 Callaway
Temple Hill, MD 20748
(301) 894-2425

Index